ΜΥΣΤΙΚΟΣ ΠΟΛΕΜΟΣ

SECRET WAR

Rigas Rigopoulos

GREECE – MIDDLE EAST, 1940-1945

THE EVENTS SURROUNDING THE STORY OF SERVICE 5-16-5

TURNER PUBLISHING COMPANY

SECRET WAR
Rigas Rigopoulos

Award of the Academy of Athens
as an amalgam of history and literature

Original Greek text published in Athens, 1973

English edition by Jesse M. Heines

in collaboration with Rigas Rigopoulos and Dionysis Rigopoulos
from a draft translation by Eleni Dedoglou

The cover is a woodcut offered for this book by Greek painter Spiros Vasiliou.
It was created during the German Occupation for a handwritten book
(in 100 copies with woodcuts) to accompany poems for liberty and resistance
by Angelos Sikelianos.

TURNER PUBLISHING COMPANY
Publishers of America's History

www.turnerpublishing.com

Editor: Randy Baumgardner
Designer: Peter Zuniga

Library of Congress Catalog No.
2003104153
ISBN: 978-1-68162-354-2
LIMITED EDITION

TABLE OF CONTENTS

PART TWO

Chapter D: THE CONSPIRACY

Chapter E: THE FINAL RECKONING

APPENDICES

Στους	To
Αλεξανδρο Καϊρη	Alexander Kairis
Νικο Παλιατσεα	Nicos Paliatseas
Πετρο Δρακοπουλο	Petros Drakopoulos
Νικο Μενεγατο	Nicos Menegatos
Σταματη Τρατρα	Stamatis Tratras
Σωκρατη Τσελεντη	Socratis Tselentis

who gave their lives for all of us,
I dedicate this book with gratitude.

R.R.

FOREWORD

The Second World War dauntingly continues to fascinate and intrigue both historians and the general public alike. Indeed, the end of the global conflict in 1945 also served as a catalyst for inspiring hundreds and thousands of books, memoirs, biographies, and, of course, film and television. Perhaps, movies and television programs, more than any other medium, have served to keep the war alive by providing a visual reminder of the horrors as well as the extraordinary achievements of the men and women who struggled to overcome totalitarian rule. This is particularly true of those individuals who fought in the shadowy world of espionage. They risked torture and the threat of death for the Allies to win the intelligence war against the Axis powers.

Espionage has been aptly labeled as the "second oldest profession." During the Second World War, the role of secret intelligence was critical in the defeat of Nazi Germany and Imperial Japan. The ability of the British to break and read Germany's codes enabled the Allies to win several decisive battles. The victory of the war in the Atlantic and even the success of D-Day on June 6, 1944, owed a great deal to the code breakers toiling at Bletchley Park.

However, the most dramatic use of secret intelligence in the Western Theater resulted from covert operations against the Nazis in the cities of occupied Europe, which were implemented, to a great extent, by young men and women. For the most part, their stories remained shrouded in secrecy. Only in the late 1970s, with the opening of British and American archives, did the exploits of these remarkable people see the light of day. Until then, a plethora of books and articles testified to the gallantry and significant contributions of the resistance forces in occupied Europe, but little was written about the clandestine war in the urban centers. Readers were carried away reading the brave feats of the partisans in the mountains, deserts, and jungles, while the strategic role of the spies and saboteurs in the cities remained almost anonymous.

There are several factors that contributed to the slender bibliography of the intelligence war in the post-war period. Espionage, dealing with wartime intelligence, remained a subject for mystery novels and fiction rather than for serious works of history. The few studies that emerged following the end of the Second World War were confined to carefully vetted memoirs and official accounts of major intelligence operations. Memoirs by actual participants of the intelligence war were further limited by the official secrets acts of Great Britain and the United States and by the fact that most of these covert warriors were either killed during the course of the occupation or continued as professional intelligence officers after 1945. Furthermore, with the exception of British, American, German, and, to a lesser degree, French archives, most of the countries that participated in the Second World War refused to allow access to their archives. Consequently, most English language studies of the occupation period in Europe focus on Anglo-British operations against the Axis. Under these circumstances, the limited publications that do concentrate on the history of espionage and other covert operations in occupied Europe are still viewed through a British or American prism.

In the case of Greece, accounts of the occupation period (1941-44) concentrate on the history of the guerrilla fighters in the mountains and the British liaison officers who tried, in vain, to coordinate the Greek partisan bands. As was the situation in

Europe and North America, the story of the guerrilla war eclipsed the equally significant and harrowing history of the spies and saboteurs. For many decades after the Second World War, the publication of memoirs and autobiographies of Greek and British participants with the resistance dominated the history of the Axis occupation of Greece. Many historians as well as other specialists were intrigued by the creation of mass resistance movements such as EAM (the National Liberation Front) and its military wing ELAS (National Liberation Army). The fascination was fueled by the crisis between the left and right forces that dominated the development of the resistance in occupied Greece and obscured the covert war waged in the cities and towns.

The history of intelligence operations, sabotage, and espionage in occupied Greece is inextricably tied to the story of Britain's wartime Special Operations Executive (SOE), which was set up to implement guerrilla warfare, subversion, and sabotage in occupied Europe and Asia. The SOE was created during the dark days of July 1940 after the fall of France, when Britain stood alone against what appeared to be the irresistible onslaught of Nazi Germany. Winston Churchill issued the new organization a simple directive – "Set Europe Ablaze" – which aimed at sparking and sustaining mass resistance against the German occupation forces.

This mandate entailed organizing guerrilla groups and preparing sabotage and intelligence networks regardless of political affiliations and post-war agendas. Indeed, during the first phase of the Second World War (1939-1942), little thought was given to the political fallout from such activity in countries such as Greece. Greek resistance groups were dominated by left-wing and anti-monarchist leaders whose plans for the post-war period did not include the establishment of the pre-war political status quo – the restoration of the Greek king and his supporters. Ultimately, SOE's foray into guerrilla warfare in the Greek mountains ran against the left-wing and republican ideology of the Greek resistance, which led to the first round of civil war in 1943, to the December Uprising against the British in liberated Greece in 1944, and to a much longer and more destructive civil war during 1946-1949.

However, the SOE's relationship with clandestine groups in Athens and other Greek cities and towns yielded impressive results without the political complications of the resistance organizations and guerrilla forces in the mountains. It is against this backdrop that Rigas Rigopoulos presents his account of "The Secret War: Greece – Middle East, 1940-1945, The Events Surrounding the Story of Service 5-16-5." Rigopoulos offers a rare insight into the world of espionage and sabotage and the daily terror that characterized covert operations in Athens and Piraeus. Rigopoulos was one of many young Greeks appalled by the Axis occupation, but one of the few who was prepared to undertake the hazardous role of spy and saboteur.

Almost from the arrival of the first German and Italian troops in Athens, Rigopoulos entered the murky world of urban warfare. In the context of the 1940s, this meant leading a clandestine existence of safe-houses, secret communications, fake identities, and – above all – living with fear. The life of the spy holds different horrors than that of the guerrilla fighter. The latter is subject to short periods of intense firefights, while the spy is forced to accept the reality of constant fear. For the spy, in occupied Greece, a wrong move – a single mistake – led to capture, torture, and death.

Rigopoulos's memoir offers a rare, first-person insight into the clandestine world of covert operations and exposes an intriguing aspect of the resistance that took place in occupied Athens. For the historian, the occasional anachronisms of language and unfashionable patriotic sentiment are useful in understanding the motivation of men such as Rigopoulos and why they chose the covert war in the cities rather than joining the partisans in the mountains. Rigopoulos represents a significant element of young Greeks who were less concerned with ideology and more with fighting the Axis. In this respect, the "Secret War" is a testament to the unsung heroes of the resistance and a unique perspective on the role of covert operations in the Second World War.

Professor André Gerolymatos
Chair, Hellenic Studies
Simon Fraser University

Introductory Thoughts

More than half a century has passed since we lived that great adventure...

Right after the Liberation, when we old close comrades met again, we felt that we'd rather keep our story to ourselves.

A purely emotional need drove us to this struggle, whose unforgettable moments offered us complete satisfaction. Any commotion about these experiences, full of passion and exaltation and linked to the memory of lost comrades, would disturb our contentment and peace of mind.

Even when the newspaper *Ethnos* (Nation) started publishing a series of articles on the activities of our "Service," I requested in a letter published on March 3, 1945, that they condense and complete the story as soon as possible. The series stopped after the fifth installment.

We only allowed ourselves to honor the memory of our dead with a public ceremony in an Athens conference hall. This created a wider sensation for a few days, but shortly the commotion abated.

In the years elapsed since then, many references to "Service 5-16-5" and its members — always honorable, but not always accurate — appeared in Greek and foreign books, newspapers, and magazines. No one could control or restrict them.

With the passage of time the dust has settled, and today I have ceased viewing the struggle of that epoch through my personal feelings. Historical data do not belong to individuals. Likewise, the fascination, the agony, and the creations of an era do not belong to any single person.

Living through the intense conditions and the multifarious reactions of the occupation, and also from the standpoint of the head of an intelligence organization, I witnessed the tragic drama and grandeur of an unequal struggle, decisive and effective, with incredible political and social repercussions.

I saw in the darkness of slavery the bright glow of intellectual and spiritual flashes. I saw heroic deeds filled with grandiose simplicity, and simple daily deeds filled with heroic grandeur. I met individuals who lived and died in silence, but who deserve a place in the memory and hearts of the people. I also witnessed painful errors and shameful actions by both Greeks and foreigners who did harm.

Starting with the story of some young men who constituted "Service 5-16-5," I describe in this book these momentous situations and emotions, as I lived through them moment by moment in Athens and in the Middle East, trying to be as objective as possible.

Many pages are filled with love and admiration, others are marked by pain. Every word is written with complete sincerity, without prejudice but also without fear. They tell the clear and often bitter truth, a truth needed by our unsettled times and, most of all, by the restless and justifiably rebellious young generation.

"Events" lose none of their importance when they cease being "action" and become "history." There is always some hope that if people turn their eyes toward a clearly certified account of the past and unscramble its magnificent as well as its terrible lessons, they may be able to better experience the present and to more wisely shape the future.

R.R.

PART ONE

THE RETREAT

(Instead of Prologue)

INTENSE MOMENTS IN HISTORICAL HOURS

After so many years I can see even myself from a distance: A lad of 26 years who had seen our victories in Albania from behind the lines. A lad who lived the wonderful exaltation of that epoch without contributing to its creation.

When the bells of war sounded in Athens on October 28, 1940, I rushed to enlist, but all my enthusiasm was drowned in a railway battalion storehouse in a small station in the village Amfiklia, near Mt. Parnassos.

There came the news from the front. There came the thrills of courage and the palpitations of daring and sacrifice. Echoes from far away. There I was named an officer: Second Lieutenant of Administration…

I would rush to the station to see the Italian prisoners in the trains. Our soldiers would offer them cigarettes to renounce Mussolini.

"Mussolini, critsi critsi," they said while moving a hand across the throat, and taking the cigarettes. This was my contact with the enemy.

I asked to go to the front and faced the rage of my superiors. "What would happen if we all went ahead… Everyone has his role…"

In Amfiklia, I filled my idle hours by studying, as an amateur, a bolt-action mechanism that could be fitted occasionally into a "Mannlicher" rifle to allow it to shoot full automatic fire. Thus I was passing my time with a rather war-like occupation. This study was examined by the Technical Service of Artillery and was found to be theoretically correct. I was called to Athens and they decided to post me to the base in Volos, near the factory that would try to manufacture it.

There I had my baptism of fire. The baptism of bombardments near non-combatant civilians.

We gawked at the Italian planes flying high among the anti-aircraft fireworks, and we sometimes heard their bombs without seeing them.

In April we were surprised by the new enemy, the Germans, who darted low over the roofs, embroidering the earth around us with their machine gun fire. I jumped blindly into a trench and fell face down into the mud that had gathered there. I hurriedly took off the wet overcoat of my uniform, feeling full of humiliation and anger.

Now the news from the front was bad. The Germans had thrown all their weight against us to save the defeated Italians. The last tenacious resistance at the Macedonia fortifications seemed to be able to stop them. The enemies spoke with admiration for the defenders of our fortifications. But they attacked through Yugoslavia and easily passed onto Greek soil. Their heavy motorized divisions were coming down towards Larissa. General Tsolakoglou would sign the capitulation. Our victorious army was breaking up.

Holy Friday, April 18, 1941, our commander called an officers' meeting. "In a few hours perhaps," he said, "the Germans will enter Volos. We must receive them with self-control, keep order, and avoid needless bravery."

My blood rushed to my head. Others had defended the honor of our country, freezing in the snow for months and months, and had won and brought glory to Greece. The frontier and the mountains of Albania were littered with the bodies of those who had resisted. There in the north history was written by a few distinguished men who disregarded the number and means of the invaders, who went to die and succeeded in winning, chasing the Italian legions to the sea.

Now I, out of the war and having lived in comfort, would be among those who would bow their heads to the conqueror. With self-control. With order and with dignity. Every fiber of my being revolted.

Other young officers in the meeting must have felt the same way. Spontaneously we formed a small pocket of opposition.

"No, we're not going to stay here to receive the enemy. We won't be able to control ourselves…"

"You may go if you wish, gentlemen," said the commander, "but I don't see where you'll be able to go."

"Wherever there's a free rock," we answered.

I heard that as we were leaving he had damned us to hell.

Using a truck we found, we headed south. I drove frantically on the wretched roads, stopping now and again to hide when we saw airplanes. Along the way, we picked up wretched soldiers who were going on foot.

Saturday evening we arrived in Kifissohori, a village at the foot of Mt. Parnassos. Tired and hungry, we slept in the railway station.

Early Easter morning, we were awakened by an aerial bombardment. We burst out of the collapsing building and fell into ditches, each of us wherever he could. In a few moments, the little station became a hell of fire. A stationary train full of ammunition burned at our side, and the bullets exploded and zipped around us.

For more than two and a half hours, the barrage kept us immobilized at the focal point of the bombardment. The airplanes were following the rails and passed in continuous waves, so we didn't have time to get out of the target area.

I lay side-by-side with a young lieutenant — I still remember his name: George Kontoulis — and around us everything was dug up and ruined.

Only our position seemed to be intact, and we waited from moment to moment for our turn, screaming at the airplanes and blowing off our nervous excitement with jokes and pleasantries. We bent our heads every now and then when we saw bombs coming towards us, to avoid being blinded by the stones and the dust that blasted out and covered us.

In such a moment, an incredible incident saved our lives.

As we lay with our eyes closed, we felt our ditch shift and displace us. Just like that, without any noise, without the sound of a nearby explosion, a movement of mystery in the general turbulence. Kontoulis raised his head.

"Are we dead?" he asked me.

"How do I know? I've never died before…"

We looked around us. One meter from our position a bomb had stuck in the earth without exploding. We jumped up, disregarding everything. Other bombs were coming from above. We had hardly fallen behind a ruined wall when the earth trembled under our feet and our temples thumped from a dreadful explosion, much louder than all the other horrible explosions. The whole place where we had been before was now a shapeless pit chocked with smoke and dust. Our time had come, but we were not there. We had been driven away by the bomb that hadn't exploded.

From our new position, the retreat was easier. Jumping every now and then and stumbling among dispersed bodies and blood, we pushed on. We met with another two or three colleagues — we never saw the others — and went up the mountain.

Night overtook us in the village of Agoriani. The old villagers saw us as deserters who had abandoned the front. "Why did you dump your arms and run away?" they asked. "Show us your marching orders." We didn't have any.

We hurried down the other side of the mountain towards the sea and found ourselves in the little town of Itea. The German *stukas* — their infamous dive bombers — were attacking the ships in the harbor. We came upon a small caïque — a boat with both motor and sails — that was just lifting anchor, and we embarked for Aigion.

We finally arrived by train at Nafplion. We had heard that from there we could cross over to Crete and help keep this island free.

Greek and British units — soldiers and officers — were concentrated in Nafplion to escape captivity and slavery.

There was a complete lack of organization. Food and medicine were minimal. The hospitals were full.

A big ship full of ammunition was burning in the harbor, in danger of exploding and blowing up the whole town. Other ships, already burnt, were sunk in the shallows. The German *stukas* were bombing continuously. Regarding departure, not a word. Only the British remained self-controlled and cool-headed. They maintained radio contact with their ships, waiting for them to come pick them up.

In this deplorable atmosphere, the only exception was the heroism of a young lieutenant. To save others, he towed the burning ship out of the harbor with a small vessel, risking to be blown up any minute. I regret I never learned his name.

Without anything to do, without any mission, and doubting whether our departure would ever take place, we hung around our headquarters hoping to hear some good news...

But all we heard were the air raid sirens, the enemy's bombs, and the curses of the general standing in his wide open window, screaming as we rushed to the shelters.

"Can you really be Greek officers, hiding in holes like rabbits? Get out of there, immediately! You should be ashamed!"

In the meantime, I found myself something to do: with two soldiers and a lorry I gathered as many wounded as I could. Most of them were horribly mutilated and died along the way. We gathered Greek and British indiscriminately — something surprising to the British — and I left them in the hospital corridors with very little hope that they would receive medical attention.

Doctors and nurses seemed to have passed the limits of their endurance. I struggled not to be seized by desperation.

I soon realized that if I didn't take care of myself, I risked falling prey in Nafplion to what I had avoided in Volos. The Germans were approaching. An organized departure of Greek units was totally out of the question. Under the continuous pounding, the town was being deserted little by little.

I went to the British. Their commander received me with great pleasure. He needed an English-speaking officer to deal with the Greek fishing-caïque captains who would ferry his troops to their warships outside the harbor. "I think I can take you with us," he said. "I'll let you know soon."

I reported to my commanding officer, Lieutenant Colonel Kyriakos Valassidis, who undertook to cover my absence. He was a kind and understanding man. "I congratulate you," he said. "I would like to follow you, but there are reasons which oblige me to stay. Good luck!"

The British sent word to me that same night. The ships were waiting for us in the open sea. That whole night we helped the British troops embark.

We filled the caïques with soldiers and watched them vanish in the dark waters, out of the harbor, and return to us empty. It was as if the sea was swallowing their human cargo.

Standing still and silent in rows of four, the British waited patiently and embarked in strict order. Only the sound of their feet, as every unit passed towards its caïque, broke the monotony in the thick darkness.

I had continuous work, as I was the only one who could communicate with the British and with the Greeks of the caïques. I was coming and going from the commander to the caïques and from the caïques to the units. Little by little, as the hours passed with this monotonous and silent night endeavor, fatigue and weariness overtook me. The fatigue and weariness that were dropped on me by God's hand, to save me once more from death...

We few officers and the last soldiers remained on the shore, no more than a single shipload of men. All the caïques went away full of soldiers, and I had arranged for the last one that would return to take us. My work had finished.

I collapsed into a corner and leaned my head back to have a short rest while we waited. I instantly fell asleep. A sleep heavy as lead. An irresistible bodily need.

Suddenly, the sun struck my eyes. I jumped up in confusion. The coast was deserted. Only an old fisherman from last night was sitting near. He looked at me as if I were a ghost.

"How come you didn't embark with them?" he asked me.

"I fell asleep and they left me behind."

"The Englishman was looking for you. It was God's will that you be saved."

"Saved? What happened?"

"The last caïque hit a mine in the open sea. We didn't find anybody."

First the bomb which did not explode. And now the caïque which was blown up without me. Badly shocked from the loss of so many men and from the cold grip of death which I had narrowly escaped, I began to view these accidental events as purposeful exceptions granted to me for some unknown reason by my destiny.

I will not die without fighting, I thought.

❉   ❉   ❉

Nafplion now seemed completely empty. It was a dead town. Every now and then the *stukas* bombed the ruined houses, the burnt ships, and the vehicles which the British had rendered useless.

Going by the British barracks I saw a rough inscription. "Go to Monemvasia." I met two of our soldiers who ran up to me asking me questions.

"We have to go to Monemvasia," I said. "About 200 km. Let's find a car."

Among the many lorries in a big field, which were more or less put out of commission by the British, I found one with little damage. Only its distributor cap had been broken. We searched the other vehicles and found another cap in good condition, which I tried to fit into our lorry.

For a long time I methodically rearranged the position of the wires in the six sockets, hoping to find the correct combination. In the meantime, airplanes forced us to hide now and again in a semi-ruined shelter made from propped-up sand bags. The ground quaked with every bomb. The dust blinded us. We risked losing the lorry before we had time to repair it.

Finally, the engine caught right when they were bombing. I couldn't leave it now for them to destroy. I accelerated among the explosions and hid the lorry under the trees.

Driving out of Nafplion we found some British soldiers walking. We took them with us and they told us that British troops would embark from Tolo, just a few kilometers away. And Monemvasia? This might have been written purposely to mislead enemy spies.

In Tolo that evening we found the British waiting at the seashore. They promised to take me with them.

A very dark British naval officer, a man of strange racial features, suggested that we go to the open sea with the only fishing boat available. He wanted me to get on with the boatman. He was the liaison with the ships of the fleet, and he had to give agreed signals with his flashlight so that the ships would approach and take us. I followed him, and we went out into the dark sea.

He gave signals in all directions.

During the night we sailed out of the gulf four times, giving signals without getting an answer. The last time the naval officer gripped the tiller and, instead of turning towards land, he headed to the open sea.

"Look here," he said. "The ships aren't going to come. Ask the boatman if he has enough fuel and if he would agree to sail the three of us to Crete."

I thought of the people on the shore, expecting their salvation from this officer and from the fishing boat.

"That's completely unacceptable," I answered. "We can't abandon so many people waiting for the ships, taking the only caïque that could serve them…"

The foreign officer interrupted me in a fury. In a tremendous rage, he screamed that if we didn't leave immediately, we would be condemned with the others. It was impossible for me to change his mind.

I explained to the fisherman what we were discussing, with the hope that he would not accept the British officer's proposal, but he agreed. If I insisted on reacting now, I would have two men against me. I feared that they would take me with them against my will. I had to gain time.

"Listen," I said to the stranger. "The trip is long. The passage won't be easy. There are also the enemy planes, which don't miss a thing. Let's wait at least until tomorrow night. Maybe the ships will appear by then."

I argued in this vein for some time, and finally I convinced him.

"Tomorrow night," he said, "without fail."

We returned to the shore. I was cold and terribly hungry. The previous day I had eaten only a lemon, which I ate with its skin. I lay down in a corner to sleep. In the morning I tried to see the British officer. He had disappeared. The fishing boat was also nowhere to be seen.

The fault was mine. I should have prevented this disgrace more forcefully.

Seventeen hundred British, seven hundred of them unarmed, were waiting in Tolo. I also met three hundred Greek soldiers, originating from Crete, without arms. They had come from Athens to embark for Crete. They all gathered around me. I was the only Greek officer in Tolo.

I accommodated them in a school and tried to improvise a mess for them. Four gendarmes and as many customs guards eagerly offered me their assistance. I also met a local industrialist, Elias Papantoniou, who helped as much as he could. As we were making these arrangements, we heard machine gun fire behind the hills.

"Don't move from here," I said to the Cretans. "I'll go see what's happening."

Somewhere behind the hills, German paratroopers had been dropped. I climbed to see their position. I lay beside some British and we saw them advance with small bounds towards a hill opposite us. From there, they could fire directly into the village. The British estimated their number at about 450.

I rushed down as quickly as I could and told the gendarmes and customs guards to evacuate a large part of the village that might be hit by enemy shells. The inhabitants would have to move to the part of the village near the mountain, which was safe from enemy fire.

The people made the officers' job very difficult. They didn't want to leave their homes. "It is an order of the … 'garrison commander'," the officers said, and they sent them along against their will.

In the meantime, the Cretans were furious about being kept inactive and made quite a fuss. "Find us knives to eliminate them!"

I would have liked to have been able to arm them. With great difficulty, I kept them inside the school and left again for the hills.

The German shells were soon exploding in the evacuated part of the village. No one was hurt.

The British held their positions steadily throughout the day. They fought with coolness and accuracy.

All I had with me was my useless revolver as I lay beside a British officer who was firing a machine gun. I was trained as a machine gunner as a recruit, and I craved it childishly. I finally took it in my hands when he left it to eat prickly pears, which were growing close by. Those pears were our only food that day. He tried them after he saw that I, who had been eating them for some time, had not died.

We kept our position until late in the evening, taking turns firing the machine gun while the German bullets whistled over us. At that point, we were informed that we had surrendered.

I thought I misunderstood what the motorcyclist who screeched up to us had said. I couldn't comprehend how 1,700 British could surrender to 450 Germans who had not advanced a single step.

I went down the hill and asked for an explanation from the Colonel in command of the British.

"I have nothing to answer," he replied, looking in a very British way at the one little pip on my uniform.

"Sir," I said while standing at attention, "I have 300 unarmed Greek soldiers under my command, which your decision obliges me to surrender to the enemy. I am the only Greek officer in this area. I think you owe me the explanation I am asking for."

He turned and stared directly into my eyes.

"The Germans captured 20 of my men," he answered. "They sent word that they would execute them if we don't surrender in half an hour."

"Hand me over 300 rifles, sir," I said. "We can attack by bayonet while you are surrendering. The Germans will have no time to react."

He looked at me condescendingly.

"In an open field of 500 meters, no one ever attacks with bayonets. They will mow you down. Besides... I promised to surrender with my arms. There is nothing to be done."

Meanwhile, the British began boarding their trucks with shocking composure. I had to admire their self-control. They went to give up as if they were starting a parade.

I rushed to the Cretans.

"It was in our destiny to be enslaved," I said. "Scatter away. In fives at the most, not to be obvious. Get into the mountains to avoid being taken prisoner."

I turned to go to the mountain, but the local people wouldn't let me. "We will give you civilian clothes and hide you in our houses," they said.

I was terribly excited.

"I will not take off my uniform," I screamed. "I am not going to hide. I will go away..."

They led me to a little house up the dark mountain.

"Wait here," they said, "and let's see what happens. There is time for you to leave for higher up."

From up there we saw the headlights of the German vehicles as they entered Tolo. After such a long blackout, this bold illumination of our conquerors seemed to me strangely tragic. I was choked by pain and rage: pain without hope, rage without vent. Whatever I had tried to this point was now finished. Everything was now under enemy control.

Soon someone came up from the village and said that the Germans spoke to the people through an interpreter. The Germans had said that they liked the Greeks and were coming as friends. Only the British would be treated as prisoners of war, and it was strictly forbidden for the Greeks to hide them. The Greeks should go on about their work as before. The Greek officers and soldiers were free to circulate in uniform. Nobody would touch them. The Occupation authorities would give them any assistance needed to return home.

"Come on," they said to me. "See? There was no need to run to the mountains. Come down, now, just as you are."

"Bring me civilian clothes," I said, "to go down..."

They thought that I had misunderstood the Germans' concessions. When I insisted, they looked at me, wondering.

"You are a strange man," they said. "When we offered you civilian clothes to hide you, you didn't want them. Now that they let you circulate in uniform, you want to take it off…"

Finally, they sent word to the industrialist Papantoniou, and he brought me one of his suits. He also took me to his house. After such a long stint in the military, it was strange to find myself in a family home with his wife, their baby, and an elderly lady.

We were all quite upset. We were living amid circumstances unknown to us. I sympathized with the agony of a man with a family, worried by problems without solutions. I thought of my family in Athens. How would things be there? …

Heavy knocks surprised us, hammering the door. Papantoniou rushed and opened it himself. I heard the Germans speaking to him. I saw Papantoniou turn, terrified.

"I don't know, but I think that they want the house… Speak to them, please. You know their language. Tell them we have a newborn baby. Please, please…"

I went into the corridor and spoke to the German officer. I pleaded with him. He had already posted the requisition notice on the door. He glanced, he saw the baby and smiled at me genially. He also praised my good German.

"Very well, sir," he said. "The house will not be requisitioned. Heil Hitler!"

I bent my head slightly to return his salute. As I shut the door in front of me, I opened the kitchen door and shut myself in. A cry came to my throat and I couldn't stop it. Between my heavy, uncontrollable sobs, Papantoniou tried to calm me.

"Oh, no, my lieutenant… They are not worth it… Not you, our brave one… No…"

The humiliation and dishonor I felt were unbearable. I was broken by the thought that a Greek officer, camouflaged in civilian clothes, had pleaded for — and accepted — the favor of an enemy who had come into his country as a conqueror.

❊   ❊   ❊

In two or three days I left for Nafplion, still in civilian clothes, with Elias Papantoniou and a few others. My 300 Cretans had returned to Tolo and I wanted to report to my superiors and get orders for what to do about them.

As we passed our headquarters, I saw the General sitting in the garden. He was the "tremendous" one who had cursed us when we hid during the bombardments. Some officers stood around him. I asked my friends to wait outside the low fence. I entered the garden and reported myself officially.

"Second Lieutenant Rigopoulos Rigas, I have the honor…"

"What's this?" he interrupted me. "Is this the appearance of an officer? You have thrown away your uniform as soon as you found the occasion?"

Outside the fence Papantoniou interrupted aggressively.

"My general," he said, "you can't speak that way to the lieutenant. He was the only one who fought till the last moment in Tolo."

"Did you fight in Tolo?" the General interrupted again.

"Yes, my General," I answered with a hidden satisfaction.

"Who told you to fight?" he roared. "You expose us with such initiatives! Did you have such an order?"

With lips trembling from restrained rage, I answered him: "No, my General, I had no order. I only kept the officers' oath: 'To defend our arms and the flag till the last drop of my blood.' "

He looked at me in confusion. For a while he didn't say a word. Afterwards, with a low voice, he apologized: "Lieutenant, the Germans are keeping me here under restraint. You are free to return home. I don't know if I will see my family again. I am too upset. I take back what I said before. Please tell me what you have to report."

"Nothing, my General. Allow me to be dismissed."

I saluted, standing at attention, and went out of the headquarters garden.

The next day I wore my uniform so that the Occupation authorities would allow me to leave for Athens. I presented myself and arranged the necessary documents. Going toward the railway station, I saw the British behind wire fences. Something was steaming in a huge cooking pot that the Germans had brought to them, and they rushed to meet the pot with obvious impatience. Who knows how long they had been without food. But then I saw them overturn the pot and dump it out in a rage. It contained only plain tea.

I went on my way feeling terrible revulsion about gaining my freedom through submissiveness, wearing my uniform which secured the protection of my enemies, acting polite during my obligatory contact with them, and having in my pocket the German permit and the ticket for Athens. An irresistible need for reaction grew in me with increasing intensity, and I felt unbearably suffocated by the anguish of my inability to do anything about it. Rage and shame boiled within me.

Thus, I departed with a troubled conscience. In two days I was in Athens.

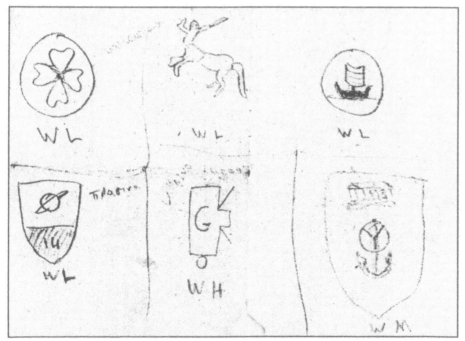

Sketches of symbols on German vehicles
(the writing indicates their colors)

PREPARATIONS

AN UNUSUAL ATHENS

There are many who believe the Germans entered Athens like beasts. But beasts they were proven later.

In the beginning, their tactics and general attitude toward us were disciplined, in a deliberate program of good relations. One could see their obvious intention to befriend the Greeks, or at least to soften our first reactions.

I have spoken before about their initial friendly manifestations, where I saw them, and about their treatment of our military personnel in Tolo and in Nafplion. In my own contacts with the German authorities I met eager assistance and impeccable behavior. German sentries formally saluted Greek officers, and the German officers expressed their admiration for Greek bravery at every opportunity.

"Our Führer," they would say, "honors and respects the Greek people. You fought as was dictated by your duty."

This appreciation of our fighting virtues by warlike people like the Germans seemed to be sincere, in spite of the fact that this behavior stemmed from orders intended to facilitate the domination.

In Athens, the Germans' attitude was similar.

The Occupation authorities used the Greek puppet government, which was immediately formed by the generals who had capitulated, as their mouthpiece. They promised safety and prosperity to the Greeks. It would be essential, with such promises, to put to rest the fighting spirit they knew they would face.

At the same time, they accused the Greek government, which had escaped abroad with the King, of both abandoning the Greek people and betraying them. These were easy accusations intended to divide the Greeks, a people inclined to internal strife.

German officers had orders to rise when receiving Greeks in their offices and to salute when they entered public places. We loved watching them, when they entered central pastry shops, stand by the entrance, stretch their arm, and stomp their foot in a Nazi salute. Of course, nobody responded. When the Italians took over the command not long thereafter, kids amused themselves by passing in front of the sentries again and again, saluting, and thereby making them snap to attention and tap their guns on the pavement.

Soon the Occupation authorities realized how unnecessary these ceremonious courtesies were and abolished them.

At any rate, Athenians showed from the beginning that they had no desire for friendly relations of any kind. Nor did they desire any kind of contact, no matter how necessary. They were certainly terrified by the idea that a foreign conqueror had stepped onto their land and was ruling as an absolute master. But they hid their fear with dignity, which they soon counterbalanced with a persistent animosity. They did not hesitate to show their aversion openly whenever the conquerors tried a friendly approach.

Reaction was something that emerged from the beginning, simply and spontaneously.

Just a glimpse of the Nazi flag with its swastika flying on the Acropolis was enough to upset us. Furthermore, the enemy uniforms that filled Athens, the black boots and the heavy, rhythmic stomping that echoed loudly in the night silence, the shouts and orders heard in a foreign language — all these, from one day to another, created a suffocating atmosphere under the Athenian sky, chilling us and keeping us in a continuous state of tension. Even the Germans' marching songs, with their pleasing harmonic structure and characteristic staccato rhythm, were incompatible with our temperament. They displeased and infuriated us.

The first orders of the German *Commandatur,* without being unreasonable, revealed the hard tactics that would follow:

> *It is forbidden to be in the streets after 10 p.m. Patrols will shoot if necessary.*
>
> *It is forbidden to possess arms. All types of firearms must be turned in within 24 hours.*
>
> *The tuning of all radios must be fixed to the Athens station and sealed. It is forbidden to listen to foreign stations.*
>
> *It is forbidden to give shelter to the British.*

Violators risked the penalty of death.

We had no intention of obeying. We hid firearms. We hid radios to listen to London and later to Cairo. We even circulated stealthily by night, satisfying our impulse for defiance.

In the beginning, the patrols were tolerant. They detained people now and then, but released them in the morning.

One night, we used an excuse to an Italian patrol that we were admiring the beautiful moonlight!

"*La luna e molto bella...*"

"*Pasienza* (patience)," answered the benevolent sergeant. "So is the war. Go home now. *A la casa, a la casa...*"

We eagerly waited each evening near the radio. Between the noise of the interference produced by the enemy to neutralize the Allies' broadcasts, we distinguished with difficulty the beloved signal, "Pam pam pam paaammm...," three dots and a dash. The letter V. The sign for Victory.

"Greeks. Our thoughts are near you. You are the heroes who said the big 'No' to a strong enemy. You are the ones who offered the first victory to the Allies. We admire you and we are grateful. The time is approaching when your country will again be free and glorious. Our struggle continues until the final victory..."

The news followed. News, filling us with hope. We were armed with patience and courage. We dreamed of a Greece that was free and strong and glorious.

The next day the news passed from mouth to mouth, from stranger to stranger. The forbidden broadcasts were the common secret of all Greeks. The risks of disobedience filled us with satisfaction. The radio broke our isolation, animated our spirit of national pride, and reinforced our souls' resistance.

Little by little our reaction started to show through acts that indicated not only courageous initiatives, but also coordinated actions.

Walls of buildings started to fill with slogans written in the dark nights, mainly the *OXI* ("*Ochi,*" No) and the English *V* (for Victory).

The Germans and Italians erased them and doubled their night patrols. They erased one and the next day they found ten. They went around at night with the patrol wagons and filled them with anyone they caught after the curfew hour. But the slogans on the walls kept multiplying.

Typed news of the war and verses for freedom started to circulate from hand to hand. Clothes and food started to be collected for the British in hiding.

People from all parts of Athens gathered in the evenings at the Tomb of the Unknown Soldier in Constitution Square to salute our flag as it was lowered. A crowd of men, women and children stood at attention, deeply moved, in absolute silence. That moment, the beatings of our hearts answered the sound of the Greek bugle.

Worried again, the Occupation authorities forbade both the lowering of the flag and the assembly.

And one day, we saw, with tears in our eyes, the German war flag with the swastika missing from the Acropolis. It had been lowered by Greek hands.

Thus, the Germans and Italians found themselves among a people who revealed their hostility by all means. A people who scorned them, mocked them, and something more: who fought them.

The conquerors' counterattack was immediate. Their initial kindness was replaced by real rage: searches of houses, arrests on the streets, beatings for no reason. The prisons started to fill. In the interrogations, torture began.

In addition, the cruelty of individuals competed with the organized cruelty of the authorities. German and Italian officers and soldiers tried to display and impose their dominance in any way they could. A tremendous inferiority complex drove them to angry explosions.

One day on Panepistimiou Avenue I saw an Italian officer repeatedly slap a little boy who was selling bathing suits. We who were near protested, and the *carabinieri* started hitting people with their rifle butts. They thought the child was making fun of them because he was moving his hands as if swimming, trying to explain what he was selling. Perhaps they had one day been chased by our soldiers in Albania, with the shout, "To the sea, to the sea."

A German officer hit a friend of mine who happened to take off his hat and the German was deceived and saluted him in return.

"I will not stand to be mocked," the German roared. Keeping our self-control, we explained that we had not even noticed him. He was surprised to hear German, and went off cursing.

One morning, as I was getting on the tram, I stepped on a German soldier's foot. He screamed to raise hell and grabbed my hands. He wanted to take me to the *commandatur.* I did my best to apologize, and my command of the German language saved me again.

Another morning, I took an overloaded tram to work. Five or six of us were hanging outside on the step. A German truck that was following suddenly darted to overtake us and, passing too close, swept us with the cargo bay. Some of us were badly hurt. I had the back of my jacket torn to shreds. The truck's driver guffawed at his achievement.

Such were the small, daily episodes that made our life insufferable. In the wake of the official authorities' new program for systematic violence, vicious acts of individuals were driving us to despair.

In addition to violence, another horrible weapon of the conquerors was deprivation. Little by little, everything we needed was missing. No electricity, no petroleum, no coal. In a short time we had no means of transport. Worn-out people were carrying wood with pushcarts, cutting the pine trees of Attica in a circle of many kilometers. Those who had no additional clothes were threatened with nudity.

But worst of all, hunger started tormenting us to an unbelievable degree. We ate vegetables without oil and bread made from lupine. Cabbage leaves and groats were a variety. Locust-bean honey was a luxury.

Later on, we came to the point where we saw people dropping in the street, unconscious or dead. Little children, like ghosts, with skin stuck to their bones, with eyes bulging out of their sockets, with hands and feet swollen, eagerly searched the trash at street corners to find something to eat.

Sicknesses decimated the population. The Germans started killing. A little child stole a loaf of bread from a German car. The German broke the child's hand and the child died of a hemorrhage. This kind of event, retold from mouth to mouth, stirred us.

Like the steam in a sealed vessel that builds up pressure until it breaks its container, the resistance boiled and expanded and grew more powerful in reaction to the stifling oppression that crushed us.

The conquerors' initial plan to keep us quiet with displays of generosity had failed. They opposed our first generalized reaction with terrorism, frenetic acts, programmed hunger, and wretchedness. The result was the opposite of what they were expecting.

In this atmosphere, the secret struggle of the enslaved ripened quickly and became a necessity.

HOME AND FRIENDS

My paternal home stood on 3rd September Street, not far from the Archaeological Museum. It was a four-story house in the old Athenian style.

In only a few months, our life had changed completely.

My father had aged suddenly in his seventy-seventh year. Until then I remembered him with his grand stature, lively step, and imposing spirit, charming friends and strangers alike. He spent most of his time at his desk, writing scholarly works on the mathematics of economics, which he was the first to introduce and teach in Greece. Now his brilliant mind had begun to dim. He was consumed by the hidden illness that was to take him from us under tragic conditions two years later.

My mother was always by his side when she wasn't at the hospital assisting those injured in the war. She was a volunteer head nurse, and she held her position there, where they needed her, for a short while.

Of my three sisters, two were married and lived separately with their families. I remained in the house along with my unmarried sister Popi, of whom I was very fond. We would return in the afternoon, she from the hospital where she helped the war casualties settle their family and personal matters, and I from the Bank of Greece, where my many dreams as a young scientist were drowned in routine. But it wasn't the time, during occupation, for me to pursue new careers.

Popi and I tried to somehow escape the depression caused by the frightening changes in life both inside and outside our home. We tried to create around us — and around our sick father — a tolerable atmosphere that could in some way remind us of the good old times. We read a great deal and debated many things. The intellectual output of the occupation era had already begun. Day by day it became ever more inspired and ever more daring. There we found refuge and spiritual warmth.

My study at home was a separate kingdom. There I had absolute seclusion when I studied or worked. None of my family would ever disturb me there.

In this study my friends and I would isolate ourselves and discuss everything. That little room then took on different dimensions. It expanded to contain all sorts of problems and visions. In there we did not seek escape. On the contrary, in there we tried to face the frightful reality. We tried to foresee the course of events and to evaluate our potential for any kind of reaction.

Amongst these friends, a selection process came about, little by little. Those who had something to offer stood out. They were the ones whose invincible love of freedom made them emotionally prepared for dangers and hardships.

Two of these were my closest friends. Michael Hors was an architect. He was the son of Admiral George Hors, who would later be invaluable to me when I was pursued by the Germans.

A sensitive and restless spirit, Michael was suffocating under the atmosphere of occupation and was even bothered by his name, which was of Bavarian origin and had a German sound (the original spelling in German was "Horsch"). He was planning to leave for the Middle East at the first chance, like his brother, a naval officer, who had left with our fleet.

My other friend, Mitsos Rediadis, was a lawyer and the son of a lawyer. He and his father and brother were an old established firm and maintained their office in Piraeus.

The Rediadises had special relations with the naval world and with the port authorities. Deucalion Rediadis, the father, was formerly Minister of Mercantile Marine, and the firm's shipping affairs kept the family in constant contact with the maritime circles. Using his contacts, Mitsos was later able to develop our organization's Harbor Division.

With the germ of politics in his blood, Mitsos Rediadis was an orator, but also a skeptic. In our debates, he was always the most analytical.

Mitsos was of medium height and somewhat plump, but had nervous gestures and sharp features. He planned his every step carefully, but when he decided to advance he was dashing and courageous.

We would lock ourselves in my study for many hours and analyze the matters of the time as methodically and as thoroughly as we could.

What was the state of the war and what was the situation in Athens? What could each of us offer, and what path would each have to follow?

The news from all sides was disheartening. We saw around us an omnipotent enemy who dominated all of continental Europe. On June 22, 1941, Hitler had launched his violent attack on Russia, with his troops advancing on Russian soil despite the Russians' brave resistance.

The German troops of Africa were advancing from Libya, pressuring the British toward Egypt. Great Britain, despite the incredible psychological strength of her people and the decisiveness of her leadership, didn't seem to be in a position to face the German steamroller.

We saw enemy armored vehicles — frightful monsters — passing through Athens to be loaded up for Africa. Every type of enemy unit — infantry, artillery, tanks, and mechanized vehicles of all types, with their abundant, brand new materiel — was in constant motion.

Luftwaffe planes tore the air just above our houses, making the windows shake. German and Italian troops rapidly fortified our shores. They built pillboxes, planted mines, and camouflaged anti-aircraft guns. Ships left daily in different directions, loaded with troops and war materiel.

We were watching a well organized military machine in intense activity. All of this, which we witnessed firsthand — and equally the many things we heard from others — would no doubt constitute valuable information for the Allies. But how could we get it to them?

Thousands of plans about how to contact the outside world crossed our minds.

Had our military established communication with the Allies? Many of our officer friends had gone abroad. Other officers were unknown to us. Those we approached knew no more than we did. We hesitated to turn to the political world. Each of us had his own political views and his own personal political friendships. But an attempt at an underground movement should neither be split between various groups nor monopolized by a single political party with the risk of reactions. In view of the supreme national danger, we shuddered at the Greek political haggling. Through various contacts we had already confirmed that many obstacles could be created by positions of individuals in different political parties and by the differences of their feelings toward the King. The struggle for independence had to remain clean and be kept clear of such complications.

We discussed such basic subjects one by one until we came to an agreement.

Every now and then one of us would protest that by incessantly screening our ideas, we risked remaining inactive and isolated. Then we'd start the discussion over again...

Little by little, we began to think that we had to get organized and act by ourselves. We searched for someone superior and more experienced than ourselves to follow, but we couldn't find anyone. On the contrary, plenty of young people we knew were ready to move with us.

Somehow, we had to clear a path and move ahead with our limited resources. The drama we were experiencing erased our hesitations and gave us self-confidence disproportionate to our potential. We recognized, however, that great caution and systematic preparation were needed.

Another serious concern was that the Greek people had to maintain their drive, dignity, and the spirit of independence. By no means should people be left inactive, as that would inevitably lead to disappointment and moral degradation.

We had already taken note of the first cases of collaboration with the enemy, not only by simple people, but also by those of upper social classes whose cultural development more heavily stigmatized their treachery. The food shortages we faced and, more generally, the shortages of all kinds of necessities, led to the appearance of black marketeers and trade with the Germans and Italians. Prostitutes earned their bread from them, and some feather-brained Athenian women gave way to their sexual propositions. Some lowlifes started selling their services to the enemy or, much worse, started trading on treason.

Although the number of these cases was small within our total population, they scared us. They revealed sick cells in our otherwise strong, healthy body. They constituted danger. They had to be considered enemy targets.

At the same time, we saw people around us eager for action. It was impossible for them all to have the opportunity to act. Yet, it was necessary for as many individuals as possible to participate at least emotionally in the struggle. They had to learn all of the international and domestic news. They had to maintain their fighting spirit. They had to be trained for the struggle and direct themselves toward the right objectives. They had to be protected from detrimental influences and deceit. They had to be armed with faith and enthusiasm.

A lot of productive work could be done in this direction. We thought about how useful it would be if we succeeded in printing an underground newspaper. Perhaps this first step would create new possibilities for us to come into contact with our allies and the Greeks who had succeeded in escaping.

We began searching for a suitable typographer and spoke to friends within trusted circles to set up a broader information network. Many around us responded to this proposal. Others told us they had already undertaken related efforts.

The matter of the printing press was the most difficult. We searched in many different directions without success. Little by little, our efforts waned and our initial attempt remained fruitless.

Every now and then, one of the friends we had contacted would come to find me with some information on organizations that had started to show up, on political movements, on brutalities of the conquerors, and on good or sordid deeds of our own people. "What's happening with the newspaper?" they'd ask, and they'd leave disappointed.

✳ ✳ ✳

Athens was full of small circles of friends similar to ours.

Michael Hors and I often spent time with the brothers Dinos and Spiros Vovolini, old friends who were in constant motion, always preparing something with the ingenious Ricos Piniatoglou and John Milios.

Mitsos Rediadis and I frequently saw George Vichos and John Zacharakis, who, along with Nicos Grigoriadis as the moving spirit and a few others, were drawing up their own plans.

At my work in the Bank of Greece, I often had discussions with Trifon Triantafilakos, who worked at an adjoining desk. He was also trying to get something going within his own circle of friends, with his characteristic bustle and a wealth of plans.

In the Bank, I was also close with the particularly calm and methodical Alkis Delmouzos. He and I often discussed problems that would arise from an organized resistance.

These were some of our friends who, like us, were preparing for resistance and eventually reached the desired results, some sooner and some later. The Vovolinis circle produced the best-printed secret newspaper of the occupation, *Ellinikon Aima* (Greek Blood), and other publications. The Grigoriadis-Vichos-Zacharakis circle formed the organization *Ethniko Komitato* (National Revolutionary Committee), printed the secret newspaper *Eleftheri Skepsi* (Free Thought) and other material, and offered many noteworthy services throughout the occupation. Triantafilakos, George Drosos, and others, with Panagiotis Sifnaios as their leader, created the organization *Ethniki Drasis* (National Action), printed the newspaper *Machi* (Combat) and other newspapers and leaflets, and, in general, instigated various national actions. Alkis Delmouzos, who worked with his brother Panagis and many others, eventually became leader of the organization *Apollo*, which took up sabotage and other related activities.

At the Bank, I heard about the huge organization that had begun to form at that time, *Ethniko Apeleftherotiko Metopo* (National Liberation Front), known by its initials, EAM. Some proposed that I take part in this movement which, from the beginning, seemed to have solid foundations and many resources. Various friends of mine were already members of the EAM. Everyone talked of its "politically neutral character" and its "purely national orientation" with almost the same words.

This absolutely identical line, given to EAM members and reminiscent of familiar methods, along with the fact that many who spoke to me about EAM were known leftists, made me suspicious.

Our group, which to some extent had started to form during our attempt to print a newspaper, along with other groups of our friends, systematically kept an eye on EAM's early actions.

Certain EAM actions were impressively patriotic. EAM youths, we learned, had pulled down the German flag from the Acropolis. They were heroic fellows struggling for freedom.

On the walls of houses, next to the *OXI* (No) and *V* (victory) signs, *EAM* appeared more and more. Occasionally, and with less daring, the hammer and sickle appeared, the symbols of communism. Later, we also saw *ELAS* spelled with one L.

At first we didn't know what this strange misspelling meant. (In Greek, *ELLAS*, with two Ls, means Greece.) They were the initials for *Ellinikos Laikos Apeleftherotikos Stratos* (Hellenic People's Liberation Army), the armed wing of the EAM which was beginning to form.

Various EAM publications began to circulate which, despite their purely national slogans, convinced the careful observer of their origin just as much by their ill-sounding, clumsy and extremist, colloquial language as by their style and content.

Our various groups exchanged observations and immediately concluded that EAM was a communist organization. However, a great number of people unfamiliar with communist methods believed the opposite. This was exactly what worried us. Communism would never create a truly patriotic organization, because that would contradict its systems and global ideology. EAM was using national camouflage in an attempt to sway patriots to its side.

An example of the Communist Party's politics, and their ability to switch policies quickly when situations changed, had recently occurred on the Albanian front. During the victorious advance of our army, the first communist declarations characterized it as a "fascist conquering war of Metaxas" (the Greek Prime Minister and dictator at that time). In letters dated November 22, 1940 and January 15, 1941, Nikos Zachariadis, Secretary General of the Greek Communist Party at the time, urged the Greek people and army to welcome the Italians and install a "popular anti-fascist government." But then the better conceived preaching that followed took on a purely patriotic character to reflect the strong general and popular spirit of the times.

Now the communists appeared again with a nationalistic mask. This sort of maneuver couldn't but hide dangerous plans. We were frightened by the idea that a split in the national struggle, which we were trying to avoid, could originate from there. The EAM matter required careful observation.

❊   ❊   ❊

One day, on Patission Street, I met with Starvos Vrachnos, a cousin of Admiral Hors. At that time he was a Lecturer in Chemical Engineering at the National Technical University of Athens.

Stavros, who later became the leader of the General Information Division in our organization, wasn't one of my old friends. However, he was one of those people who immediately gain one's trust. He had a thin and active face with a vivid yet somewhat piercing glance behind the thick lenses of his glasses. Stavros had a positive, down-to-earth mind with a strong dose of ideological zeal. He was, from family tradition and personal temperament, a fanatic royalist.

A short while before, he had spoken to me enthusiastically about the EAM. He had suggested that I become a member, and he had emphatically disagreed when I revealed to him what was hiding under their national camouflage.

Now he confessed that he had confirmed the truth for himself and was convinced that the EAM was communist at its core. However, with his characteristic energy, he had decided to go ahead with a daring plan. "We will stay in EAM," he said. "We're a whole group, and we'll try to provoke internal strife and turn the organization in a national direction. Working from the inside, we'll be able to neutralize its communist core more readily and take the organization into our own hands."

Without hiding my reservations for his plans, I wished him good luck, adding that if he were ever to change his mind, I'd be waiting for him to work with us. In the meantime, I asked him to keep me informed about anything he found interesting. "You know my house," I said. "I'm sure we'll talk soon."

At that time, when I spoke about our group to friends whom I considered useful, I tried to keep them "on call." I hoped that I'd soon achieve some kind of progress toward our goals, and that I'd then be able to engage their collaboration immediately.

Time was pressing. It was already October 1941, and we were still struggling to realize even one of those goals.

Then Michael Hors found a way to flee to the Middle East. That's where his heart drew him, and since we hadn't yet achieved anything substantial in Athens, it would have been unreasonable to try to hold him back.

Besides, this trip gave us a first-class opportunity. We agreed that Michael would try to contact the responsible Allied services and tell them that there are people in Greece willing to undertake any kind of mission they'd deem useful. He was also to give my address for any direct contact. For a long time I waited for some kind of liaison to appear and I fretted over his delay. Later, I learned that Michael had been greatly delayed on his way to Egypt. For about a year he suffered hardships in Nigdi, in Turkey, deep in the highlands of the Taurus mountain. That's where our "friends," the Turks, confined Greeks who tried to escape to freedom.

By now I was enthralled by the idea of the secret war which engulfed and excited me. I wrote articles and poems which circulated anonymously from hand-to-hand. Close friends came to my house in the evenings, always expecting to hear something new. Within the atmosphere we created inside these closed quarters, we felt liberated.

A breath of grandeur elevated us above the sufferings of those harsh times. In my home and in the homes of my friends I experienced moments full of exaltation which became motives for creation.

Day by day, Greek intellectuals showed a more intense presence. Craftsmen of the pen and the paintbrush worked with exceptional spiritual intensity.

I remember Spiros Vassiliou in his studio, drawing, carving, printing, tireless and incessant. Small, lively, and full of internal flame, you might say he was a bomb ready to explode at any moment. Always cheerful, jovial, and serene, he worked feverently on Greek subjects. He revived moments of beauty and glory from distant and nearby times. He talked as he worked. Simple and pure concepts, like his work, would communicate to you something of his courage and optimism.

I remember two of our eminent poets, the infuriated Sikelianos and the immovable Kazantzakis, figures and images that wouldn't fade with time. The one with a broad, clever forehead, long white hair and piercing blue eyes. The other dark-skinned, with bushy eyebrows and an evocative, ascetic profile. Both of them tall and majestic.

I'd sit silently and watch them chat, molding their words and deepening their meanings. They'd stop occasionally at a word to laugh heartily, unrestrained, Homerically, like ancient, feasting gods.

Kazantzakis, whose ethical conflict between his indisputable Greekness and his internationalist philosophy kept him inactive during that productive time, left one day for the island of Aegina and we didn't hear anything about him until after the Liberation. His panhuman concerns trapped his spirit. They subjugated and suffocated this lord of thought and phrases, keeping him mute and expressionless before the drama that was being acted out in front of him with such pathos.

But I often met with my old friend Angelos Sikelianos in my home or his. His being throbbed with the indomitable pulse of his enslaved land. We'd listen to his new verses and were lifted step-by-step into the sanctuary of his thought, finding exaltation and freedom beyond the weaknesses and evils of mankind.

THE FIRST EFFORTS

It was the end of October 1941 when I finally found the printer we had sought for so long. It was Elias Filipakopoulos, who had a small printing press on Kapodistriou Street, next to the First Aid Station, and typesetters he could trust. He accepted the task enthusiastically.

I immediately contacted Mitsos Rediadis and we eagerly began producing our own newspaper. The title would be *O Apeleftherotis* (The Liberator). I painted a nice composition of the letters with India ink to make a zinc plate. However, finally we preferred to typeset the title so that the plate wouldn't stay permanently in the printing press or expose us to the zincographer.

Mitsos and I mobilized our friends to gather information and we edited the material for our first issue: the inaugural column calling on all Greeks to push aside domestic quarrels about politics and the monarchy and to cooperate in a common struggle against the conqueror until Liberation; radio summary with all external news of the last two weeks; domestic news; articles on the food supply problem, the conquerors' brutalities, heroic deeds of Greeks, quislings (enemy collaborators); a patriotic poem. It would be an interesting issue.

We stayed up two or three nights in a row to save time. We found the paper we needed and organized a plan for distribution. Satisfied with our setup, we handed the materials over to the printer.

Two or three days passed. Filipakopoulos was running late. We were impatient. I went to his print shop and yelled at him. He took out the typesetting plates and showed them to me. They were almost ready.

"I've got to protect myself as best as I can," he said. "The Italians keep coming into the shop to check. I've got to find a time to print. Imagine if they found the plates on the press. I'd better wait until they come in, and then start up the machine as soon as they leave."

I answered sharply. "The job must proceed without delay. The paper will be bi-weekly. If we wait for the Italians every time, the news would be stale by the time it's circulated. We either do a job and face its dangers, or we give up and leave it to someone more suitable."

Filipakopoulos was ignited. "Tomorrow night the paper will be ready," he said. "If anything happens, so be it."

The next night, I found a note from him on my door which I still have in my records. He was furious with his workers at the print shop.

Dear Rigas, I am not dealing with real men. Therefore, I am unfortunately forced to resign from this task with sorrow.
With respect, Elias Filipakopoulos.

I ran to find him the next day. "Yesterday afternoon the Italians entered the print shop," he told me. "We were ready to put the plates on the press. As soon as the typesetters saw them, they flipped the plates over and destroyed them. They were terrified. They said, 'If you continue, we will leave.' Nothing can be done..."

I realized it would be pointless to insist. I was seething with frustration and swallowed the words I didn't want to come out. Quite simply, we were capable of nothing. We had failed. That was all.

Frightfully embittered, Mitsos Rediadis and I suspended our fruitless collaboration, even with each other.

We were getting into December 1941. The Germans were advancing on every front. Our domestic situation was hopeless. We suffered terribly from cold and starvation. The Occupation Authorities hardened their tactics. They had started shooting patriots a month ago.

From our side, our goals greatly surpassed our accomplishments. I saw other groups around us moving at the same slow pace. It seemed that anyone starting at that time without means, without preparation, without experience, and without specific commission from the Allies, which would mean valuable support, faced the same difficulties. But with our entire being dedicated to the idea of the struggle and the effort to speed liberation, it was only natural to be impatient and to blame ourselves and our companions for delays that stemmed from genuine difficulties beyond our control.

The restlessness of my soul was given a small outlet when a family friend, Manos Karzis, President of the Medical Association, proposed that I assist with the "Shelters for Urgent Medical Care." I had never been involved with hospitals or philanthropic organizations. However, I accepted Karzis's proposal thinking that I might be able to use the shelters to lodge resistance cells, to cover secret gatherings, to serve as an excuse to be in the streets by night, and, generally, to form centers for the struggle.

We established a related association and printed identification cards to facilitate the circulation of members. I also started to place my own volunteers at different shelters. In the end, the small network that developed was limited to providing information of an internal nature. Only Popi Sakelaridis, one of the basic members in our subsequent organization, got her teeth into the mission at that time. At the Kipseli district shelter in which I placed her, she formed a nucleus of youths who wanted to take part in the national resistance. At the same time, she gathered information on the movements of EAM, which was also attempting to use the shelters.

But even this preparatory action failed to give us immediate satisfaction.

Around me were impatient people. Stavros Vrachnos came to see me. He had given up on his plan to get a majority of people truly devoted to Greece into EAM. "There is no way for us to change the situation in there. They don't even give us a chance to offer services for the struggle. Their system is to accept patriots of all political hues into their organization. They then either proselytize or immobilize them so that they can continue their communist plans undisturbed. They are very well organized and guided by the Russians. But the worst part is that they are extensively financed by the British. At any rate, we decided to leave EAM and to work with you."

I didn't want to disappoint Stavros and lose him. I counted on the hope that Michael Hors would have by now contacted the Allied services in Egypt and that one of their delegates would appear at any time.

"I hope that something will soon come up for your team to do. I'll contact you," I told him.

I saw him frequently from then on, at my house or in the chemistry lab at the Technical University. Members of his group were asking him for action. After their disappointment with EAM, he had spoken to them about an organization that would meet their expectations.

It is an organizational postulate that people offering to help pursue a goal should not be left inactive. Only practical activity can maintain one's enthusiasm and energy.

Stavros and I discussed the possibility of his group working on an intriguing operation during this transition time.

The Germans had obliged many central shops to display Hitler's picture in their windows. It was a pompous and provocative demonstration that enraged Greeks. If all over Athens every window with the hated despot's picture would break at the same moment, every heart would fill with satisfaction and new strength against the depression of slavery.

Stavros and his fellow chemical engineers would have to design and build small explosive devices with elastic suction cups that would break the shop window glass thirty seconds after adherence without causing harm to passers-by. Experiments went on for several days at the Technical University's Chemistry Lab, but unfortunately they did not produce the desired results. The suction cups came off with the explosion without breaking the four to five millimeter thick glass used in shop windows. With a greater amount of explosive, we risked hurting people.

We had failed once again. I felt terrible. Nothing was going right. I blamed myself. I was slowly attracting more and more people around me and I couldn't find a way to use their services. I lived through the Albanian War in the rear, and I was behind in the internal resistance. Perhaps others, at that very time, working hard and positively somewhere near us in Athens, were breaking the chains of slavery link by link.

I spent days filled with bitterness and disappointment and then I rebounded. It would be shameful if the first difficulties scared and immobilized us. No one had experience in the secret struggle, and it was going to be a difficult beginning for everyone. However, the war was continuing, and we would have to hold on until final victory, the victory for which we would work tirelessly and unceasingly, and which we would surely, one day, celebrate, at least those of us still alive.

I started to write again and to circulate articles and poems full of faith and enthusiasm. I also often saw Angelos Sikelianos, who urged me to continue and gave me courage. He was like a high priest to me, the new little initiate.

"Do write, Rigas. I love your poems. The written word is food for our people, especially today when no other food exists!"

He smiled that luminous smile of his.

＊　＊　＊

It was then that one of my poems gave me the opportunity to meet Kostas Perrikos, the aviator who later blew up the building of a pro-German organization and was executed by the Germans.

One of the youths helping me hand out my poems told me about Perrikos. He showed me an article Perrikos had written about October 28.[1] It was the first com-

---

[1]October 28, 1940, is the day Italy attacked and brought World War II to neutral Greece. A counterattack forced the enemy to retreat through Albania. Battles over the next six months saw continuous victories for Greece until the Germans came to the Italians' aid and prevailed. October 28 is now celebrated as a national holiday.

bative publication I had seen. The youth told me how Perrikos, full of ardent patriotism, became enthused as he read the poem and that he wanted to meet me. He wanted me to collaborate on the newspaper that his secret organization, *Stratia Sklavomenon Nikiton* (Army of Enslaved Victors), was about to produce.

My heart fluttered at the thought of a printed newspaper and an organized struggle, but I wanted to be sure about what I had heard.

"I prefer that you set up a meeting for me at his house," I told him.

The following evening I met with Perrikos at his house on Michael Voda Street. He opened the door himself when I knocked and I remember his clever, suggestive look as he cordially stretched out both hands to shake mine.

Kostas Perrikos was a dreamer full of faith and vigor. He was the type who won you over from the first moment you met him. We stayed up late, discussing all the issues of the time, domestic issues, the situation at the fronts, and the political and diplomatic activity abroad.

He told me about the brutalities in Macedonia and Thrace that were committed by the Bulgarians, who had been appointed by the Germans to rule these areas. They were disgusting. They were unbelievable. In Drama, the Bulgarians had blown up the Church of the Holy Trinity with 600 women and children inside. They executed another 300 with machine guns. In Serres, they took away all the men between the ages of 19 and 50 and no one ever saw them again.

All of the inhabitants of Agisti, Komistra, and Doxato — men, women and children — were executed with machine guns. In Prototsani, a German employee of the local tobacco company told Perrikos that the Bulgarians massacred 3,500 people.

We talked about the dreadful hunger we suffered in Athens, about the reign of terror, and about the executions that increased day by day. Aid had to be organized to save the population from complete destruction.

We spoke about Greek traitors and collaborators who benefited financially, and whom Perrikos believed should be lynched by the Greek people so that treasonous deeds would be struck at the root.

The situation at the fronts was always critical. The pressure of the German troops on the Russian front was suffocating, and General Erwin Rommel, the leader of the Africa Corps, was threatening Egypt. But there were some consoling points of success: the immobilization of the Germans in Leningrad and the Crimea, the localized Russian victories at Donets and Rostov, the considerable decrease in Allied ships lost in the Atlantic, where the British prevailed more and more, and the hope that movements of the two rival forces in Libya allowed us to maintain.

By now we considered it certain that America would come into the war. Aside from the generally decisive attitude of the Americans, we were also persuaded by the fact that they had recently revised the law regarding neutrality.

Now, more than ever, we needed intense internal action, both outright combat and espionage. We also needed visible resistance and publications that would stir the Greek people to harass and distract the enemy forces in Greece in a myriad of ways.

"In a few days, our newspaper *Megali Ellas* (Great Greece) will be circulated," Kostas Perrikos told me. "I would like to have your poem, *The Time Will Come*, in the first issue. This struggle needs the inspiration conveyed by poetry. But I'd also like your general cooperation. At this time, three of us manage the "Army of Enslaved Victors." This is the title we've chosen for our organization. Come, let us be four. You will meet the others as well, and you will be delighted. We need you."

I answered him with all of the warmth his personality awoke in me. I said that his personal charm and openness had won me over. I told him about my failed attempts, about my hopes to establish contact with the services abroad to transmit information, and about the opportunity he was giving me to act immediately and give work to my people. I was certain that our collaboration would be fruitful.

Before I left, he stopped me, squeezing my hand.

"One more detail, that I already know you will agree with. You are a person with a liberal and independent spirit. This is why I think that I can anticipate your answer." He stopped a bit, still holding my hand. "If, after Liberation, they want to impose the King on us, we shall keep him away, even with machine guns if necessary."

After all the patriotic initiation that had preceded, this sudden jolt pained me deeply. This pain had nothing to do with the King. After all, I had been raised in a democratic family and my father was a friend of Eleftherios Venizelos (a famous democratic politician who became Prime Minister of Greece in the early 20th century). It is irrelevant that after liberation I would align myself with those favoring King George's return because I considered it a national necessity. At any rate, I wasn't inclined to royalism, so Perrikos's position did not distress me.

I was pained, however, because I could see the struggle for liberation in jeopardy from divisive slogans. I was pained because I had before me one of the most passionate patriots I had ever met, and I saw him keen to contribute to this divisiveness. For me, there was one and only one idea that I allowed to rule my thoughts: the unification of all Greeks in a coordinated effort to shake off the yoke of slavery. Any other idea not aligned with this was unacceptable to me, regardless of whether I was for or against that idea.

I did everything I could to explain these thoughts to Kostas Perrikos and the imperative need that dictated them. I could not persuade him. He saw the two matters as a single inseparable patriotic duty to secure true freedom. In addition, he believed that addressing an issue in preparation for post-Liberation couldn't possibly affect the current struggle.

I disagreed fundamentally and considered the danger both immediate and significant. My beautiful dream of collaboration with Kostas Perrikos stopped right there.

Very late that night I returned home, pensive and embittered, through the frozen, deserted streets where circulation was forbidden. What would be the fate of my homeland? Would our efforts result in a beautiful historic struggle? Or were we Greeks in danger of some day fighting against each other rather than fighting the enemy and causing yet another accursed era of national division?

In the next few days, I received the first issue of the newspaper *Great Greece* dated December 1941. On those two small pages, Perrikos and his companions spread the national palpitations of their hearts. Much of what we discussed the evening we met was printed there: the Bulgarian atrocities, the need to punish Greek traitors, and information about current war events.

As a foreshadowing of the death that awaited Kostas Perrikos, his five close companions, and the three others executed with him, the main article ended with this verse by Mistral:

> *And if we are to die for Greece,*
> *Oh, divine laurel! One dies only once.*

My poem, which had brought us together, was on the second page.

THE TIME WILL COME
To the Greek warrior

Amid the storm,
be manly and boldly empty
slavery's cup.
Choke the pain. For a festive joy
to fill your soul,
the time will come.

Don't be worried.
Earth's people know who deserves
the laurel of gold.
Wait for it firmly. To wear it with glory
in an unconquered country,
the time will come.

Don't be frantic.
Don't shed your heart's tear
on your spirit, on your pulse.
It's not worth it. For your strong arm
to strike with force,
the time will come.

From that time on, Perrikos sent me the newspaper regularly.

In the third issue, published in January 1942, the war news allowed a bit of optimism. America, after the sudden devastation of her fleet by the Japanese at Pearl Harbor, had come into the war. Following the meeting between Churchill and Roosevelt, twenty-six nations had signed the anti-Axis pact, declaring their resolve to struggle with all their forces until the final triumph of liberty and justice throughout the world. The British and Russians had undertaken several initiatives on the African and European fronts and had noteworthy localized successes. The Chinese, under Chiang Kai-Shek, had defeated 100,000 Japanese in the region of Chiang Sha.

The full-page main article throbbed with faith in a final victory. With a retrospective of war events and of the contributions of the British, Greeks, and Russians in the historic evolution of the war, the article demonstrated that these three would be the basic contributors to Victory. It was an article full of pride, historical faithfulness, and confidence.

The article concluded with a call for unity along with a hint of the internal differences which would require settling in the future:

This is why we, who express the free will of our people from within the darkness of slavery, declare that we shall equally contribute to the creation of tomorrow's world. Brothers, the people of Earth expect more deeds from us. Let us unite. And when the time comes, let us also settle our family differences.

Another of my poems, entitled *Look at Me* and addressed "To the Conqueror," was also published in this issue.

My emotional ties with Kostas Perrikos, despite our initial disagreement on the subject of internal dangers, grew closer day by day.

HELLENIC PATRIOTIC SOCIETY OR SERVICE 5-16-5

The year 1942 saw a picture of Athens that was both tragic and glorious. The cold that January was unbearable. Perhaps we felt it more because our bodies, exhausted from hunger, could no longer offer resistance and allowed it to pierce to the bone. In that frightful cold, you also felt the hunger more intensely, hunger that had reached its peak.

At night, the cold became stronger. Outside on the streets, tattered, shuddering shadows moved slowly, without strength, to reach the shelter that would give them some protection. And then you'd hear that frightful voice of death that emanated from an empty stomach like an animal's howl: "I'm huuunnngrrryyy…"

At dawn, a cart passed by and gathered the stiff corpses — men, women, small children — scraggy remnants of bodies now extinguished, having used up all their reserves of their flesh, denying Death the privilege of gradual erosion.

During the day, people went to their jobs. They formed lines wherever anything edible was sold, and you were lucky if someone introduced you to a black-marketeer who could bring you a little flour or olive oil or, very rarely, a piece of meat at exorbitant prices or in exchange for things from home, because the value of money crumbled from one day to the next.

That's how we came to lose our piano, some gold family jewelry, a big sewing machine, and all our copper kitchen cookware just to get some foodstuffs to help us celebrate Christmas and take courage for the New Year. With great effort, I found some very expensive lamb, after so many months without tasting even a bite of meat. I was even happier thinking of the joy it would bring to my sick father, who had become permanently bedridden. However, I couldn't resist feeling the lamb inside the package. By the time I got home, I had managed to tear off a little piece with my fingers. And I felt sheer delight as I chewed the raw flesh in the street.

Often you'd see some person next to you suddenly collapse unconscious on the pavement. White lips, turned-in eyes, shivering throughout the whole body. People would gather around for a short while. Someone might get a couple of vile pieces of candy from the nearest confectionery shop — inedible things made from lupine and carob bean — to fill his hungry mouth. When little by little the person began to chew, the people would begin to disperse again. The conquerors went by indifferently. Even if there was someone amongst them who would sympathize, he knew that the people would not accept his help.

I saw two little boys outside the German canteen on Panepistimiou Avenue looking through the large shop window at the food, famished. Their big eyes sparkled with desire from their scraggy sockets. A German popped out and offered them some sweets, smiling. The little boys ran off. I chased after them, deeply moved. When I caught up to them I said, "Stay at the corner. I have something for you." They were soon greedily eating some terrible sesame candy that I found and bought for them. "Why didn't you take the German's sweets?" I asked. The smaller one, with his mouth full, just shook his fist threateningly…

Through the hunger, the cold, and the death of that Athens winter of 1942, human dignity prevailed with all of its grandeur.

In this phenomenal atmosphere, full of excitement and contrasts, where life in Athens ranged from physical exhaustion to emotional exaltation, under the intense pressure of the conqueror and his maniacal threats, one could find some barely perceptible but positive signs that the secret struggle had begun to boil clandestinely, but intensely.

Friends and acquaintances disappeared from one day to the next and you'd hear strange excuses from their families to cover up who knows what mission inside the country or out. Concealed British prepared for departure and one day we lost them suddenly in a mysterious way. Cryptic messages were heard on broadcasts from London and Cairo: "A clear sky doesn't fear lightning…" "Mountains are used to snow…" "May God protect you from injustice…" Who knows to which secret agents they were giving instructions. Printed leaflets with combative content would be found on doors or in offices, or they would be passed from hand to hand, without anyone knowing from where they had sprung.

Many times, people who saw each other every day worked in separate teams toward common goals without suspecting anything of each other.

In the Bank of Greece, I met every day with my fellow student and colleague, Takis Poumpouras. Only after the Italians arrested him, along with his sister Alexandra, did we learn that they were working with the Allies' British envoy John Atkinson, to help British soldiers escape. Atkinson was captured in Antiparos Island and executed on February 24 with four Greeks.

The Archbishop Damaskinos demonstrated open resistance, battling with the Occupation authorities to defend basic rights of the enslaved, to spare part of the olive oil crop from plunder, or to save a person's life from the executioners. The brave Prelate risked his life to save all those who needed him, without distinguishing between Christians and Jews, right-wingers and leftists, or devout church-goers and atheists.

The weight of his Grace's daily struggles was borne by his young friend and legal advisor, Professor John Georgakis, who spoke perfect German and provided the legal support needed for all efforts of the Leader of the Greek Church. We got to know Georgakis's personality more closely later on, when he tried to save the life of one of the most important members of our "Service" by undertaking his defense in the German court-martial.

Another risky business was protection of the families of the executed. This wasn't at all easy, because the Germans had warned that "whoever helped the families of those executed would be considered accomplices in the condemned's original crime."

Nevertheless, a lively movement to assist them began in Athens with the initiative of Lili Theotokas and the support of the Red Cross. Later, in April 1943, the Archbishop adopted this movement, creating a specific service in the Archdiocese despite the intense German reaction. Joanna Tsatsou, who had organized soup kitchens for children since the end of 1941 and was doing everything humanly possible to save them from annihilation, was put in charge of this service.

Men, women, and even little children handed out secretly printed materials and wrote slogans on the walls. They made their fighting presence known in every way, secretly or openly, defensively or offensively, always facing a myriad of dangers and defying the wrath and revenge of the conquerors.

From day to day, we felt the resistance around us spreading and swelling: underground publications, spying, formation of partisan groups, sheltering of British soldiers, protection of Greek patriots, caring for starved Greek children, organizing escapes.

The Germans and Italians sensed the danger and reacted accordingly. With any hint of suspicion they threw people in jail and subjected them to torture. Their vexation was reflected in their behavior toward the Greeks, their strict forewarning orders, and their increasingly oppressive measures. Their vigilance heightened to the extreme.

In the first days of April we were upset by grievous news. The Germans had arrested Michael Akilas, an Air Force officer, poet, and writer, as he attempted to escape to the Middle East. Along with him they also arrested the harbor officers Kazakos and Kotoulas and other officers and civilians.

About this time, the Germans began using people under arrest as hostages. The German Commanding Officer of Southern Greece published a warning in the newspapers. "In the event of sabotage against the German army, the hostages will be executed. All who are or will be arrested under suspicion of acts against the German Army will be considered as such. Similar measures will be taken against the families of those who depart abroad to fight against Germany and Italy."

Akilas, Kazakos, Kotoulas, and three members of the escape caïque's crew were executed two months later on June 5, 1942.

In the beginning of April, Kostas Perrikos came to see me. "I felt the need to see you and to speak with you," he said.

The conversation turned to the escapes of Greeks for abroad and to the recent arrests. Perrikos was enraged. "These beasts will kill them," he said, "and they will kill many others. What will they accomplish? Can they kill all the Greeks? No. There will always be Greeks to fight them.

"The day before yesterday, Panayiotis Kanelopoulos[1] left for Egypt," Perrikos continued. "I hope he gets there alright and that he helps our country. Kanelopoulos is a national asset. He is our most pure and honest politician. He thinks as you do, putting aside political oppositions for the sake of the national struggle.

"Parallel to *Stratia Sklavomenon Nikiton* (Army of Enslaved Victors) we have established PEAN, *Panellinios Enosis Agonizomenon Neon* (PanHellenic Union of Fighting Youths).

"I have been very preoccupied with your thoughts since the first time I saw you. The Army of Enslaved Victors will continue the liberation struggle and spread the spirit of cohesion and cooperation. In PEAN, most of us are friends of Kanelopoulos. The organization will also carry on patriotically. We'll spy on the enemy, form combat teams, and carry out sabotage. One day I'd like you to meet some of our friends. I know that you'll get along. What do you think?"

I was sincerely pleased by Perrikos's orientation. I shook his hand and wished him success in his new ventures.

"I've met Kanelopoulos," I told him. "He is a person of rare moral character. As a student I attended his lectures on sociology and admired him. I have also studied his scholarly writings. He will surely offer a lot to this country if his political deeds balance out the damage done to the University by his departure. In time we will talk about all these things and perhaps there will be a chance for us to coordinate our efforts. For the time being, you know my unswerving conviction: struggle and only

---

[1]Panayiotis Kanelopoulos was a well-known Professor of Sociology, author, and politician, who later became Prime Minister of Greece for a short time.

struggle. On this issue, I am a bit rigid. But tell me, do you have any way for me to leave for abroad?"

Perrikos was taken aback. "Why would you leave?"

"With the intention to return," I responded. "I've wasted enough time already. I must get in touch with the Allied services at any cost and bring back a wireless set."

Some time ago, when we began talking about the increasing escapes, the idea of a trip started working in me. A trip might instantly procure for us the communication we had sought for so long. Now, within a few moments, I felt this idea transforming into an immediate and imperative need. Perrikos, having close ties with Kanelopoulos and being a colleague of Akilas, had to know a way to escape.

He extended his hands and held me by the shoulders, peering, as he used to do, straight into my eyes. A lively spark played in his gaze. "Let it be as you wish, my friend," he said. "Since you want to go, you will. But not immediately. Let us allow some critical days to pass. Things have gotten tighter with the latest arrests. I will contact you at the first chance. Until then, just stand by.

"In the meantime, I can offer you something else," he continued. "It won't give you complete satisfaction, but in some way it may be of service to you. Every so often, I see an informant of ours from the partisans. He brings me various items for the newspaper. They have a wireless set up there and they look for information. Give me whatever you have and I will send it to them. This way isn't ideal, of course, but I believe that at some point the information will get where it needs to."

❋   ❋   ❋

The next day I went to see Mitsos Rediadis, who lived at 9a Rethymnou Street, not far from my house. After our latest disappointments, we saw each other only occasionally and without our original zeal. Now I had decided to stir him up for good. I announced my intention to leave and the possibility of an indirect communication with abroad until I could obtain a wireless set of our own.

"We have little time to prepare," I told him. "The moment has come for us to mobilize all those around us. I need as much information as possible so I don't show up before the Allies empty-handed. They have to be convinced that our contribution will be useful so they will supply us with the means needed for communication. If we do things right, we can set up a basic organization in just a few days and provide precious information. While I'm away, information will be sent to the mountains. By the time I return, our collaborators will somehow have systematized their jobs so that we can move as energetically as possible on my return. If everything goes well, we will very soon have everything we need at our disposal."

Mitsos debated a bit the idea of the trip, the dangers, and the potential delays. He also weighed the pros and cons of our sending information to the mountains. He had his objections and his doubts. He faced my arguments with great skepticism.

"It would be good for us to avoid this," he said finally. "But, as things stand, the trip seems to be a necessity. Let's examine all of the basic assumptions to be as certain as we can that it will succeed. And may God help us." With this discussion, Mitsos had caught fire and finally recovered all of his old enthusiasm and energy.

"We start again," he said, "and this time you'll see what I'm able to achieve. The information we'll give to the Allies will have to be at least worth the dangers of the trip."

The port of Piraeus, as I have mentioned earlier, was Mitsos's specialty. We decided that he should immediately mobilize the harbor staff along the general lines of the plan we had discussed long ago. We arranged to meet at my house the next day to give some sort of structure to the management of our work, at least for a start.

We also decided to immediately mobilize Stavros Vrachnos's team. The Germans were fortifying the coast of the Saronic Gulf with each passing day, and Stavros's technicians could prepare topographic drawings of these fortifications with as much detail as possible.

Various other friends who collaborated with Mitsos, like Commander George Hatzigeorgiou, the harbor officer who introduced Mitsos to many other harbor people, and senior police officer Aristeidis Papadopoulos, would give us information on enemy units arriving in or leaving Athens: their arms, their equipment, their camps in the outskirts, and their numerical strength, or any other information they thought would be useful.

From Mitsos's I went straight to the Technical University. I found Stavros in the chemistry lab, with his white lab coat among the smoke and fumes, giving the students examinations. He looked at the papers one by one as he received them, and we talked while he graded them. I presented him with the task without saying anything about my trip. I only told him that he had to gather his team for their first trial mission and roughly explained what we were expecting from them.

"Gradually, I will transmit more instructions," I told him. "For now it is important that no more than two work together, and, if possible, that no more than three know each other by name." I added that Stavros would have to stop meeting as a group with the six or seven close friends who had been discussing matters with him since the beginning and now followed him.

At that time Stavros didn't know our extent or our abilities or who our leadership was. He relied on me without asking anything more and maintained the same secrecy with his friends. They didn't know anyone but him.

His excitement on finally receiving an order for action was boundless. Who knows how many he flunked or passed with his grading that day without realizing it? "What is our organization called?" he asked.

Mitsos and I had thought about different names long before, but without settling on one conclusively. In that moment I chose the name I had suggested one day and which, in the meantime, had ripened inside of me and had displaced all others. It was a name which accentuated our "Hellenic" nature and our "Patriotic" goals and recalled, in a way, the tradition created by the first secret liberation organization, *Filiki Etaireia* (Society of Friends).[2]

"Hellenic Patriotic Society (*Elliniki Patriotiki Eteria*)," I said to him. "Today it is still in an embryonic state, but it has valuable members. You, too, should do as much as you can so we can move rapidly ahead."

The next night, Mitsos Rediadis came to my house. We shut ourselves in my office and went over every minute detail of this first assault.

Of all the harbor staff with whom he had contact, Mitsos was to meet only with Manolis Koutsoudakis, a captain of the Merchant Marines and chief pilot in charge of the Port of Piraeus Anchoring Office. Mitsos had already reached an agreement

---

[2]*Filiki Etaireia* was a secret society whose goal was to organize the Greek struggle for liberation from Turkish domination.

with him, and we had even entrusted some of Koutsoudakis's information to friends of ours to pass to the Allied services with persons leaving for the Middle East or via other means at their disposal, so that it would not get lost.

Koutsoudakis was to be the leader of the Piraeus Harbor Division. He would undertake the task of following the central administration's orders and transmitting them to the members of his team. Mitsos would give him the same initial instructions I gave to Stavros Vrachnos: to avoid meetings of members and all group activities, and to burn every needless note or plan connected to our work.

Information was to be written on small sheets of thin paper so that they could be made to disappear easily or even be swallowed in case of danger. Names of organization members were never to be mentioned in messages.

For the time being, information would have to be such that it would be useful even if it reached its destination after some delay. To be fair, we would also emphasize to Koutsoudakis that this mobilization would be experimental.

We appointed George Zentelis as a liaison between Mitsos and Koutsoudakis. George was a young and serious law student, full of courage and enthusiasm. Mitsos and Koutsoudakis would only communicate directly when absolutely necessary.

On the other hand, I would continue to see Stavros Vrachnos directly to organize his team's ventures, but only at night when he was always alone in the chemistry laboratory of the Technical University.

In general, all notes would be gathered at my house. I would put them in a good hiding place, an opening behind a wooden drop shutter that closed one side of my desk, until I learned them by heart. I would even try to memorize the sketches they brought me, so that, if possible, I wouldn't have anything written with me on my journey. Before I left, I would destroy everything…

Only the most urgent information would leave for the mountains in the meantime. The idea of sending our messages into the unknown didn't please us. So we would only send information that would have been useless if it was delayed.

Later, we verified that the information we sent through Kostas Perrikos arrived at its destination promptly.

As our discussions progressed, we saw the dreams we'd had for so long become, from one moment to the next, living and breathing realities. From the beginning, prudence kept pace with exaltation, and rationality kept pace with frantic emotionalism.

That's what that time was like, and such were our reactions. If they hadn't been so, we would never have started, without means and without experience, to chase a hope that the thousands of dangers we'd face right from the beginning made almost impossible.

But to our eyes, this hope was already accomplished. Here are our own people and here is our "Hellenic Patriotic Society." Here is our information and here is my journey to Egypt. Here are our wireless sets and submarines at our disposal. Here is my return to the enslaved Athens and here is a thoroughly planned and well-oiled spy machine, which, coupled with the parallel, more general effort, would untiringly undermine the enemy. We were already seeing in front of us and celebrating that greatly desired day of freedom.

Our exaltation was unlimited. We talked a lot more about the struggle and its daily expansion, the suffering and the proud backlash of our people, the psychological and material damage to the enemy, and the spiritual uplifting that had already granted a superb deliverance to the embattled Greeks, struggling under the weight of their yoke.

It was very late when Mitsos and I shook hands and separated. Each of us would take care of his sector, and we would only see each other again if matters arose that required new decisions and instructions. Otherwise, I would see him with the first messages from the port.

That night, I lay sleepless in my bed for hours, envisioning our future operations and filled with the beauty of our secret struggle and the joy of our certain victory.

✳ ✳ ✳

The next day, at the bank, I couldn't get anything done. My mind was preoccupied with preparation for my journey. I was anxious to get the first information in my hands. I was worried that the information from those days wouldn't be significant enough. Perhaps I would have to secure other sources of information as well.

A few days before, a new underground newspaper entitled *Machi* (Combat) had been published by the organization *Ethniki Drasis* (National Action). Early that morning, Trifon Triantafilakos gave it to me at the bank, glowing with joy. The paper's publication was an important landmark achievement in the initial efforts of Trifon and the team to which he belonged.

Perhaps I'd be able to get some supplementary information from *National Action*. I decided to sound out Trifon and started discussing with him the latest war events that we'd heard about from the hidden radios.

Although the general situation on the different fronts was still exceptionally critical, the first sunny days of April had warmed our optimism with some victories of local importance.

The Russian troops had begun a general counterattack on the Eastern front and had retaken quite a few important locations like Rostov, Kerch, Tula, Tikhvin, and others. On the Libyan front, Rommel's troops were checked by the British west of Tobruk, on the Gazala-Birhakim line. American carrier-borne aircraft were bombing Tokyo.

In our own country, despite the increasing pressure of the Occupation Authorities in proportion to their increasing rage caused by the war news, people had begun to feel somewhat better. The blessed summer months were approaching, providing at least a sensation of comfort.

Triantafilakos believed that his organization would soon be in a position to produce a "Radio Bulletin" to more easily keep people informed about events.

Concerning the subject that preoccupied my mind, I didn't reveal my plans. I only told him that someone I trusted completely would soon be leaving for Egypt. I knew that their team hadn't established contact with the outside, and I asked that they gather all the information they deemed useful to be conveyed within a few days.

Finally, the information we had from *National Action* was minimal. However, I always followed their various demonstrations and considered them to be an extremely serious organization, as I later mentioned in my report to the Prime Minister of Greece in Cairo, which is included in an Appendix to this book.

✳ ✳ ✳

That afternoon, as I was returning home with my mind continuously on my upcoming actions, I came across Dinos Vovolinis on September 3rd Street. "I need you," I told him. "Someone very close to me is leaving in a few days and it's an opportunity for us to send information to the Middle East. If you have anything interesting, give it to me so it can be sent."

"What are you doing with your team?" he asked me.

"We're moving slowly."

"We're progressing full speed. Soon, we will circulate our newspaper. It's perfect in every way, on a big four-page format. Its title is *Ellinikon Aima* (Greek Blood). Our slogan is 'Liberation and the King'…"

Once again, I felt my blood boil. "Our slogan is 'Liberation' and only that," I answered intensely.

Dinos was surprised. Certainly, he must have thought that I knew him far less well than I should have.

"But liberation is the basic presumption. I never imagined I'd have to clarify that to you. The King constitutes our security against the evils that might follow. Against communism and anarchy."

I myself believed in what Dinos Vovolinis supported: the assurance that the King's presence would provide after Liberation. I also believed that the legitimate Greek government which would one day return to Greece would have to return with its legitimate supreme ruler. If the need then arose, just one plebiscite could ensure expression of the popular desire and determine the form of government for the future.

But at that moment with Vovolinis I felt as I did at my first meeting with Perrikos, despite the fact that they held completely opposite views. In fact, I was hurt more, precisely because I was seeing two ardent patriots with opposite views on a matter that could lead them to confrontation before Liberation at the expense of our common struggle.

I briefly expressed my thoughts and fears, but Vovolinis, like Perrikos before him, was unyielding. "We are not going to liberate Greece just to throw her into the hands of the communists," he answered.

In the middle of the street, at midday, there was no way for us to say more. We separated, and as I walked I pondered how two different views can both have many correct points, and how considerable caution was needed if one tried to weigh the good and bad points to determine how the scale would tip.

Vovolinis throbbed with the desire to offer real services to our country. Perhaps his view — or Perrikos's in the opposite direction — was right. Perhaps, along with shaking off the yoke, an internal cleaning-up would be needed to build a better national future.

But my companions and I couldn't open up about such reflections. We only felt that we were being drowned by slavery and our only concern was to be free as soon as possible. We couldn't settle for anything else. This was our emotional state and we would struggle accordingly. We would, by all means, remain steadfast in the direction we had chosen.

At this point, I must say that *Greek Blood*, as we will see, never followed a path of regimental opposition. It struggled for liberation and liberation only, declaring the need for us to fight united. For Vovolinis, as it was for Perrikos, the need of freedom was stronger than any particular ideology.

❊   ❊   ❊

An additional source of information could be created with Popi Sakelaridis and the youngsters she had recruited in the Shelters for Urgent Medical Care from the time I had placed her there as a volunteer, back when I worked with the Medical Association to organize them. That very night, at her house, I gave her some instructions for her little group.

It wouldn't be difficult for them to observe the railroads for a few days and to list every type of unit that arrived at Larisa Station in Athens and the Piraeus terminus of SEK (*Sidirodromoi Ellinikou Kratous*, Railways of the Greek State), the motorized means (armored vehicles and tanks) that were being transported on freight trains, and the distinctive symbols on each of them.

For Popi, this offer was a vitalizing injection after such a long time in which I hadn't mentioned anything about internal struggle or resistance.

She had just gotten over being bedridden for many months with typhus and related complications which had made her a shadow of her old self. She was naturally slim, rather tall, with long slender legs and a graceful instability in her walk. I used to call her, smiling, "the unbalanced one." Now she attempted, with great will, to strengthen her body and to regain her old self.

Something bonded Popi and me that I might call a tender friendship. Maybe something more. She was a pleasant girl, with imagination and good judgment, who knew how to chose the books she read and hold interesting conversations without getting lost in theory and withdrawing from reality.

Under the system I followed, Popi of course knew absolutely nothing about our general actions or the other companions involved in our efforts. Even now, I didn't tell her anything about my intentions or about the trip I was planning. She only thought that I was in contact with some national organization.

Now she was glad with all her heart for the opportunity I was giving her and for its certification that she was once again healthy and useful. We discussed all of the relevant details.

"I also have a potential new partner who offered himself spontaneously," she told me. "But I didn't want to tell him anything about our group before I asked you. The matter is delicate from many aspects. The other day, Alexander Kairis came to see me. I don't know if you've learned that he is working in a German service, and, as a matter of fact, in a position of considerable trust."

I knew that. And at that instant I uncovered inside me a strange contradiction between my categorical convictions and violent reactions against all enemy collaborators, and the fact that I never opened a discussion about Alexander Kairis with the intention to condemn him. If I happened to discuss the matter, I don't think I would have differentiated him from any of the others who worked with the conqueror. Maybe I would have just voiced my wonder. How could it be that Alexander Kairis, whom I had always believed a pure idealist with rich and developed substance, had gone astray and tumbled down this wretched slope?

But I'm only thinking about all these things now. Back then, perhaps I developed a subconscious evasion of this subject precisely because I had respected Alexander from childhood, and the thought of his national treachery clashed with my confidence in the loyalty of his character.

Naturally, I was most excitedly interested in his offer.

"Alexander is a fervent patriot," Popi continued. "Here at my house he unloads all of his wrath against the conquerors when we talk and I give him the underground press to read. The other night, we were discussing German culture of past eras and I listened to Alexander attacking Hitlerism which, as he said, 'has transformed the new German generation into hard and inexorable gears of a war mechanism that, if it prevailed, would eliminate spirit and beauty from the earth for a great many years.' And then Kairis suddenly asked me: 'Do you perhaps happen to know of any organization that could convey war information abroad? A lot of valuable information passes through my hands. I could give it to you so you could transmit it to wherever it is needed.' And he added bitterly, 'You are one of the very few people who, I hope, trusts me.' "

Alexander knew my ties with Popi. "Ask Rigas, too," he had told her. "He, particularly, must know something."

The matter was truly delicate. It was very possible that Kairis, as a Greek in a German service, might be under surveillance by the German counterespionage. In using him, I would create an immediate danger for him, and a significant increase in danger for all of us who would have contact with him.

On the other hand, the services he could provide from the strategic position in which he worked would certainly be valuable. With Kairis, perhaps we could enter the sector of strategic secrets. So it was definitely worth the risk.

However, our communication with the outside wasn't yet assured. Weighing all the factors, I decided to use him only once I'd established regular and immediate information transmission to the Allied services.

If Kairis wasn't a childhood friend, I would also be concerned that maybe his overtures to the resistance were made at the instigation of the Germans. This possibility I completely excluded. As I've said earlier, I rejected the thought that Kairis could be their collaborator. I would revolt against the idea that he could be an informer. Moreover, the notion that he would now try to find out whether his old friends had ties with the resistance so that he could betray us was something that both my logic and my heart rejected without question.

I didn't yet know why Kairis had started to work with the Germans in the first place. However, I was certain that his work with us would be beneficial to our country and to the Allied struggle. In any case, it required great caution.

"Keep him on standby," I finally answered. "Tell him that you'll look into it and that you'll contact him as soon as you succeed in finding something. In the meantime, he should be careful and win the trust and friendship of his superiors as best he can."

※　※　※

In a few days, information started to pour in like rain, all kinds of information about unit movements, loadings of war materiel, defensive constructions, fuel stores, movements of merchant and war ships.

Even I was surprised by the speed with which the machine we had put in motion was gaining momentum. I never expected that our first temporary mobilization, born with the hope that we'd get a few good pieces of information, would grow into a true frenzy practically overnight.

I feared that I had started a ball rolling that was automatically gaining speed, and that if I tried to put a barrier in its path I might destroy it once and for all. Instead I should now try, in every way, to at least direct it as best I could.

I classified the messages and rewrote them, deleting all the superfluous points, and unifying those that were repeated from different sources.

There was so much information, and it sometimes contained such incredible detail, that I started to grow uneasy about their authenticity and objectivity. I asked for some verifications and sent a message to Koutsoudakis and Stavros Vrachnos to emphasize to their members how important it was to only transmit completely verified information towards the center. If there was the slightest doubt about the precision of any information, this doubt should be mentioned in the message.

I also thought that to apply some control, or to at least make the informants take some responsibility for the information they sent, every message must be signed with a code indicating who had sent it. So I established four divisions in the order of their creation, and I labeled them with distinguishing letters:

A. Administrative Division
B. Harbor Division
C. Liaison Division
D. General Information Division

I then instructed that messages should be signed with the letter of their division and the initials of the informant, mixed, however, with two meaningless random letters in the following sequence:

1. Division letter
2. Random letter
3. Initial of informant's surname
4. Random letter
5. Initial of informant's first name

This way, the messages were "signed" and therefore made more responsible, but without the possibility of deducing the signer's identity from his initials, which would have put our members in danger. As we will see, this initial system was later improved so that we would be able to identify the informant immediately, regardless of how far away he may have been from the center.

I was finally persuaded that I had to command an organization which, with the first signal, had mobilized far beyond the range I expected. The enormous responsibility to make these results useful as fast as I could weighed heavily on me.

But what if something went wrong? What if, for some reason, I failed? What if I fell into the hands of the Germans before reaching my destination? Well, so much the worse. I was risking everything and flipping a coin for my life with this venture. My companions would have to risk theirs with me. But I knew I would not fail. I would do everything I could to leave as soon as possible, and the information I would transport would be precious to Allied Staff.

The following week, I received two pieces of news that filled me with joy and fortified my confidence that the job I had started was headed in the right direction.

Answering the latest organizational instructions, Koutsoudakis informed us that, as agreed, he would be the leader of his division so that he could communicate with us and organize the network according to instructions from the center. However, the true leader of the team would be the Piraeus harbormaster and Commander, Antonis Bachas, who had joined our organization together with the second-in-command of Piraeus harbor, Lieutenant Commander Dimitris Samantzopoulos.

Information would be inspected by Bachas before being sent to us, so we could be certain that it was completely definite and verified. In any case, the messages would be signed according to our instructions.

Participation of the Piraeus harbor leadership in the "Hellenic Patriotic Society" was more than I could have hoped for. It was our guarantee that work in this sector had the ability to achieve maximum results. Later, when I met Antonis Bachas personally, I saw up close not only the abilities that made his participation in our organization so valuable, but also his genuine sacrifice when he continued his patriotic work with an exceptional calmness despite being scorned by friends and acquaintances who believed him to be a trusted friend of the Germans. And he often proceeded to serve our cause with such boldness that we were forced to hold him back so that his boldness wouldn't end up causing us irreparable harm.

The participation of Bachas and Samantzopoulos in our organization was one of the two pieces of pleasing news that I received from Piraeus. The other, somewhat related to the first, was that we could arrange a departure from Piraeus for abroad within fifteen days at most.

So, if the journey was delayed from Kostas Perrikos's side, I could leave by our own means and, as a matter of fact, with fewer hardships, straight through the harbor with the blessings of the Germans.

Following Koutsoudakis's recommendations, I would have to get four pictures taken which they would use to make me a false sailor's identity card. This was a detail I disliked, despite the fact that I would be sure to change my appearance as best I could before being photographed and traveling, so that at least I wouldn't be recognized by people who didn't know me well and so that I could pass for a sailor if the Germans made any inspections before my departure.

A few more days passed, full of fervor over the first moves of our service and the preparations for the journey.

Mitsos and I discussed my idea to give the Allies a code number instead of the name "Hellenic Patriotic Society." With the initiation of new members by our older ones according to the system of triads we had put into practice, our name, unchanged or with its Greek initials EPE (*Elliniki Patriotiki Eteria*), would be known by a large number of people.

I was afraid of people's frivolousness and of a misfortune that might bring our name to the German's ears.

If they heard of the EPE here in Greece, maybe they wouldn't even give it much attention. After all, organizations had begun to sprout in Athens like mushrooms, and only those which revealed themselves through dangerous activities would interest the Germans and the Italians. If, however, it happened that enemy espionage in the Middle East revealed that the EPE is in contact with the Allied services and is transmitting information to them, they would start using all means to follow its members in Greece and neutralize it. We could avoid this danger by communicating with the Allies using only a code number.

This is why we decided that our name should be represented by the numbers that correspond to its initials in the Greek alphabet. EPE corresponds to the numbers 5, 16, 5. Thus our name to the Allied services would be "Service 5-16-5," and this name would be known only to our inner circle.

We worked, full of certainty and with an unlikely elation that one can only feel at exceptional moments.

I communicated with the divisions on a great many details. I sorted and sent to Kostas Perrikos any information that would lose its importance if its transmittance was delayed. I studied and memorized all the other information until I was sure that nothing would escape me when I would recount it in Egypt. And in the meantime, I found time to give outlet to my emotional turbulence by writing verses.

> *... I will struggle*
> *With my hands, with my spirit*
> *I will struggle to cross through*
> *the rapid torrent's current...*

When Mitsos would come to discuss various organizational issues, before everything else he'd ask, "Did you write anything new?" And we'd open, with the beating of our hearts, the road of rational processing.

That's how things were when we learned that a group of friends of mine who collaborated with the British on Mt. Taÿgetos, were caught one after the other by the Italians. They were Leonidas Limberopoulos and his mother, and Yiouris and Nicos Kalogeropoulos. They were brought to Athens and locked up in the Averof prisons with their leader, the British Captain MacNabb, who was the last to be caught here in Athens.

This fact radically changed the way we finally communicated with the Allied services.

We would soon have a wireless set and two caïques at our disposal.

How We Acquired the Wireless Set. Radio Message from the Allied Service.

The trial of the Limberopouloses and the Kalogeropouloses made quite a stir in Athens. Both were well-known Athenian families, most of whom had lately been living abroad. As soon as war was declared, they returned to Greece to offer themselves to the homeland. They continued their struggle in a British service during the occupation.

They were all sentenced to death. When the court-martial was ready to pronounce judgment, Leonidas Limberopoulos turned to his mother, guessing her anguish, and said simply, "Well, I don't think we're going to lose face..."

The mother gave her son a smile. That smile continued to illuminate her slender features even while their death sentence was being read.

The Kalogeropouloses, grandchildren of Colonel Kalogeropoulos, the well-known, heroic figure of the old Athens, faced their court-martial with the same composure.

The Italians locked them in the Averof prisons without mistreating them. In a few days, their leader, the British Captain MacNabb, sent word to the Italians that he was willing to surrender himself if they spared the lives of the condemned. However, the Italians managed to catch him where he was hiding.

In the end, no one from this group was executed. The end of the war found them in German work camps.

The prisoners were all acquaintances and friends of mine. I heard the news of their sentences from Leonidas's sister, Eleni Limberopoulos, who often visited them in prison. She told me about all the events surrounding the adventurous capture of her mother and brother, along with various details concerning their organization and the operation of their British-Greek service.

From all I learned, I came to the conclusion that this service must certainly have had a wireless telegraph. However, no wireless set operator had been mentioned in the trial, nor had anything been said about the discovery or destruction of a wireless set.

Thus, this wireless set should be somewhere along with its operator, who most likely had secluded himself in hiding. Could one of the prisoners perhaps find a way for me to approach this wireless set operator?

Not wanting to involve Eleni in a situation that was dangerous enough, I decided to risk a visit to the Averof prisons. I only asked her to notify her brother that I was coming and that I would try to talk to him secretly, apart from the Italian guard whom I knew observed and tried to listen in on all conversations.

"As I'm sure you understand, there is a serious reason for my visit," I told her.

As I suspected, the Italians didn't view the prisoners' visitors with suspicion. Even the little package of food that I brought with me was barely examined.

The visiting room was divided in two by tall iron bars. Behind these bars Leonidas Limberopoulos soon appeared. He was a truly handsome young fellow, tall and dark.

Next to us, through the same bars, another prisoner was talking to his folks. The Italian guard, a jovial person who spoke Greek quite well, walked up and down the room. Things were going well so far.

At an appropriate moment, amid other conversations in hushed voices and without changing tone, I said, "I need a wireless set for our organization." Leonidas indifferently continued our initial conversation.

Now that the active role of my mission had ended, I felt my heart pounding. Why doesn't he answer, this devil? A simple "yes" or "no" would have ended my anxiety.

At one point, the Italian told us to finish up. "Good bye," Leonidas said. "I'll tell Eleni to take care of you."

The Italian smiled at both of us and we separated.

❋   ❋   ❋

At this time, only two sisters of Leonidas lived at the Limberopoulos's house at No. 9 Sorovich Street. They were brave girls who, despite their young age, endured the drama of their family and their loneliness with an incredible stoicism and dignity, and without ceasing their work for the resistance. That is where we arranged my first meeting with the wireless set operator, Nicos Paliatseas.

Before the meeting I chose a pseudonym which included the second of my two first names, unknown to most of my friends, and an army rank appropriate for my age. Thus Eleni introduced me as "the Captain Nicos," and then she left us alone.

Nicos Paliatseas was a tall, stout young man of 22. He had a naïve, child-like face and an enthusiasm typical of his years. He had been a wireless set operator in the Greek Air Force, where he had served as a flight sergeant. He didn't know who I was or what I wanted of him. He had only been told that he was to meet with a trustworthy person.

Paliatseas answered all my questions without reservation. My first question, of course, was whether the wireless set still exists and if he still maintains communication with abroad.

"Of course, it exists," Paliatseas replied, his eyes glowing. "Every Wednesday and Saturday evening I have a regular contact at 8 o'clock. They give me a signal and I answer them: 'Nothing new. Until next time. Over.' That's it. We don't say much, so the radio detectors can't catch us. And of course we use a cryptographic code."

I realized that he was anxious to learn the objective of our meeting, but I had to be careful. There were two serious matters that had to be resolved at the outset.

First, how did Paliatseas avoid arrest with his wireless set? Did the enemy perhaps leave him free on purpose so that they could follow his movements?

Second, was the wireless set still communicating with the Allies or did they now consider it out of action? Had the enemy perhaps discovered the code and would we actually be transmitting directly to the enemy?

To answer these questions I continued interrogating Paliatseas systematically. I learned the whole history of the wireless set. In Athens, there was a whole echelon of wireless set operators maintained by the British Secret Services. Aside from the MacNabb group which the Italians had captured, the Germans had recently captured various wireless set operators from the echelon without connecting them to the previous case. Paliatseas, who hadn't been persecuted, suddenly found himself alone with a wireless set that risked falling into German hands. He grabbed it and moved it to Nea Smirni, to the home of an elderly couple who had a nephew, Nicos Menegatos, who was an agent for the same British service. That's where he, too, finally settled. However, he had lost all of his contacts and had been completely inactive ever since.

Paliatseas was careful. No one had ever followed him. He hid well, very seldom went out, and systematically took notice of those around him. He was specifically trained to take these types of precautions. It was impossible that his new refuge had been located.

"The wireless set communicates regularly with the same people it has always communicated with," he emphasized. "I am completely certain of this. We use the same schedule we always have. Every so often we change the days, times, and wavelength of communication. The operator at the Allied station is the same. I know his expressions and sometimes his jokes... Besides, the service regularly sends me money to support myself."

Paliatseas told me all this and much more in explicit detail.

"Come on Wednesday," he said, "at the communication's scheduled time and you can ask them whatever you want and use the code to decipher their answers yourself. What else can I tell you? This wireless set has to start working regularly. It is unbearable to have this waste continue."

It was now time to talk to him about our work. The investigation I had done up till now had secured most of the basic guarantees. Paliatseas was our man.

"Our organization is called Service 5-16-5," I told him. "You can pass this along to the Allies, but don't mention it to anyone else. We have set up information networks and have a lot of continuous information that has to be transmitted."

Paliatseas didn't hide his enthusiasm. "I imagined this," he said. "Give me the information immediately. Tonight I have supplementary listening time in which we don't speak if we don't have anything to say. In one hour, I can transmit whatever you give me." The zeal of this young man, who so enjoyed his dangerous work, was touching.

"Let's not rush," I said. "Before we start sending information we need a positive proof that whatever we transmit will be received by the Allied services. We must be completely certain that we are communicating with them. Can you ask them to send us a message during the regular broadcast of the Cairo radio station?"

The request was beyond the regular scope of his work. He was hesitant. He tried to dissuade me. Finally, when I told him that only with this condition could we start working together, he said he'd ask them that very day and hoped to succeed.

"What kind of message do you want them to send us?"

I thought of something simple yet, at the same time, incomprehensible to the enemy counterespionage.

"Hello, Attika, five sixteen five," I answered.

※   ※   ※

The next days went by without any new developments. Paliatseas had requested them many times to send us the message, and we listened to all the Cairo broadcasts without hearing any sort of response.

I scheduled frequent meetings with Paliatseas in different parts of Athens. Many times I let him walk ahead so that I could convince myself he wasn't being followed, and then I would present myself before him. Most of the time, he detected my presence before I showed myself, and with a certain pride he'd tell me at what point he had noticed me.

He was anxious about the delay of the message. "Each time they assure me they will send it," he'd say. "I can't understand the delay."

One night, when the anxiety had choked me, too, I gave Paliatseas some information to pique the interest of those at the other end. He took the messages from my hands with obvious satisfaction and quickly put them in his pocket.

"What time will you transmit them?" I asked.

"If I hurry, I can make it for the extra communication at 9 o'clock."

"I'm coming with you," I said.

In half an hour we had gotten off the bus at a square in Nea Smirni. I observed Paliatseas from afar. He changed direction often, taking remote dirt roads. I tried not to lose him in the dark, looking behind me every now and then. Rarely did we see anybody in these parts, and it would have been difficult for anyone to follow us without being noticed.

Finally, Paliatseas stopped in front of a wrought iron door, made sure that I was coming, and, going up a few steps, disappeared inside a house. To this day, that old two story house with a small garden still exists at 23 Sebastias Street.

Climbing the inside stairs we went up to the second floor, to Paliatseas's room. I felt genuinely touched as I watched the young operator remove the wireless set from a valise, encode the messages, and, with the headphones on his ears and his finger on the key, give repeated, even signals.

Shortly, we heard similar faint tones in response. Communication had been established. In the small wireless room, I felt the air of freedom coming from the dark space, flooding us.

When the information was transmitted, we asked that our "message" be broadcast "as an indispensable requirement for the continuance of our transmissions." They merely answered that "our signals had been received normally" and that was the end of communication for that night.

We listened to the Cairo broadcast for a few more evenings, but we still didn't hear our message. My anxiety had reached its peak. In addition, Mitsos was bombarding me daily with suppositions and suspicions. The fact was that we had the telegraph ready, waiting for us, the information was flooding in every day, and yet we were staying inactive with our hands tied. However, the more I thought about the delay of our message, the more firmly I held to the conviction that we must not start systematic transmissions without the verification I sought.

Finally, one night, Paliatseas told me that the liaison, Nicos Menegatos, had arrived from abroad with orders to meet me. "This guy can also take care of the message. If you agree, you can meet him tomorrow night at the grove in Nea Smirni, as soon as you go in from the road, on the right." I agreed to meet Menegatos the next night at 9 o'clock.

"I have described your appearance to him," Paliatseas continued. "Menegatos is of medium height, rather fat, around 45. When you see him, ask if he has matches for your cigarette. He will answer, 'I don't have matches, but I have a lighter.' Then put the cigarette in your pocket without lighting it. These will be the signals of recognition."

When I told Rediadis about my rendezvous with Menegatos, he offered to come with me to watch the grove before and during our meeting. "You never know what can happen sometimes," he said. "It's better to be careful."

That night, we set out together. At 8:45, Mitsos left me and went towards the grove. At exactly 9 o'clock, he returned.

"Everything's in order," he said. "I saw someone waiting. There isn't another soul around the grove."

Within two minutes Menegatos and I had recognized each other and gone to a bench. Meanwhile, Mitsos patrolled and was to notify us if anything suspicious appeared.

This time, it was the newcomer who started the interrogation: How does our organization work? Does it have any relationship with the British? Approximately how many members are there? What kind of information can we give? And so on.

"Listen," I told him. "You don't know me and I don't know you. We both depend on Paliatseas, a young 22-year-old fellow whom I, at least, have only known for a few days. Since you have a responsible position in this work, you will understand and respect my precautions. Of all you ask me, I can only tell you this. At this moment I represent Service 5-16-5, which was organized in Athens by Greek initiative. We have not yet had any type of contact with the Allies. We need a wireless set at the exclusive disposal of our service because there is a lot of valuable information that has to be transmitted as quickly as possible. Information will be sent constantly because we are well-organized for this purpose. We are asking you for the 'message' because we want to make sure that our information is reaching the responsible hands of Allied services and isn't being sent in vain or being transmitted to the enemy. Every day we risk our lives in this organization to offer services to the struggle. We aren't looking for anything in return. The only thing we want is to be sure that our goal is being fulfilled."

Menegatos was a simple, practical person. He immediately understood the situation and made his decision.

"In two days you will get your message on the Cairo broadcast," he told me. "Today is Wednesday. You will hear it Friday night."

Then, from the pocket of his gabardine coat, he took out a little package and set it next to me on the bench. "These are for your expenses," he said.

I didn't understand what he meant. "What are these?" I asked.

"Pounds. Gold pounds. As soon as you begin to send information they will set the sum you will receive regularly for your organization. For now I am giving you these so we can get started."

Later, I learned that Menegatos went back and forth to Turkey with various missions and frequently spent his nights in Athens out on the town. He was extremely generous, and when he was in good spirits he'd throw pounds onto the table, leaving large tips for the music and the check.

Menegatos was a truly daring man. He was positive and fast in his work, smart and well-intentioned. However, I later had to warn him that if he didn't stop such boisterous displays, which attracted attention and aroused suspicion, I would have to report him to his superiors via telegraph.

That evening, I was only somewhat surprised by his offer. "We have no intention to take money," I said to him, "either now or in the future. We deal with the minor expenses for our activities by ourselves, and we don't pay any of our collaborators. Everyone offers his services voluntarily."

"But you will need to buy information from somewhere, rent a house, make a bribe, free a prisoner. All organizations take money."

"For the time being, we don't need anything. If a situation arises, we will ask."

Menegatos put the little package back in his pocket. Then he started telling me about his trips to Turkey.

"Espionage is huge there," he said. "The German consulate in Smyrni [Turkish Ismir] is close to the British and American consulates. Both sides spy on each other with the help of the Turks. But we also spy amongst ourselves. There are different Allied organizations there, and the one tries to put out the eyes of the other."

I was surprised by what I heard.

"We hide our information from the others," Menegatos continued, "and we take care that they don't snatch it from us. If you ever want to send anything written abroad, give it to me. We have two caïques at our disposal, which will also be at your disposal. Don't ever send anything with one of your own people. If you ever need to go to Turkey, make sure you go to Constantinople and ask for a British major with the pseudonym 'Hatzis.' He's the head of our service. Don't trust anyone else, neither Greek nor British."

All that Menegatos was telling me seemed exceptionally strange. But just in case, I made a mental note of the name "Major Hatzis" and didn't pay much attention to the rest. As a matter of fact, Menegatos seemed to me a bit superficial and garrulous. How was I to know that I would one day verify for myself some of what I had heard that night, and that I would live through the consequences of the rivalry that existed among the opposing and mutually sabotaging British services?

I was very pleased to hear that we would be able to use the caïques. We already had some engineering drawings and diagrams that had to be sent and we would have many more in the future.

The caïques, I later found out, were the *Chrisanthi* and the *Santa Teresa*. The second one must have come from the Italian-occupied Dodecanese. Ostensibly, the caïques transported fruits and vegetables between the different islands and Piraeus. The Germans and Italians frequently chartered them. When they went to Chios, they'd cross over at night to the Turkish coast, near Tsesme. By dawn, they would be back on their known route. They had places to hide things and skillfully made double floors.

Once, when Menegatos brought a wireless set from Turkey, the Germans had perhaps sensed an unjustifiable gap in the *Santa Teresa's* itinerary. They searched her intensely from bow to stern without finding the hidden compartments. But even if they had found them, the wireless set wasn't there. Menegatos had hung it in a water-tight box under the boat that was swaying next to the caïque.

After the search, Menegatos took the Germans aboard this boat and brought them across to land. He unloaded some packages the Germans had searched and left some others to be taken on a second trip. He said good-bye to the Germans with a hand-shake and departed. Later, he returned to unloaded the remaining packages. He calmly pulled the wireless set from the water and passed it, carefree, right in front of the German sentry box.

I told Menegatos that one of our liaisons would meet regularly with Paliatseas to give him information. Through this liaison they should send word to me about the caïque departure, some days beforehand if possible, so that we could prepare whatever had to be sent. We would give him the relevant package, which would be as small as possible, at the last minute.

We said good-bye and I quickly lost him in the darkness. It was the first and last time I saw him. From then on, I would only communicate with him through third parties until the day the Germans caught and shot him. He was executed on the same day as our wireless set operator, Nicos Paliatseas.

Two nights later, Mitsos and I listened to the radio broadcast from Cairo at my house. It was the first time that the news of the war went by practically unnoticed.

With the volume low as always, and among the terrible rumbling of the interference that the enemy put out to block the broadcasts, we tried to make out the words. We feared that we would miss the phrase that absorbed all our attention. The broadcast that night was one of the worst. The speaker was barely audible.

Suddenly, we were granted a miracle. The broadcast cleared up. And we heard, with our entire nervous system in a state of extreme tension, the lively voice of the speaker say, "And now we will broadcast a special message: Hello Attica, five, sixteen, five."

Full of excitement, we jumped up from the radio, shouting. Nothing else mattered.

We had been assured of the regular communication of our wireless set and something more: we had actual proof that the Allies considered our offer useful. And we were ready to prove that our contribution to the common struggle would have a noteworthy effect. We had already tried the enthusiasm and capabilities of our members. From now on, Service 5-16-5 could mobilize with all means at its disposal.

Communication with the Allied services was finally a fact.

God be with us.

IN ACTION

THE ASSAULT. ESPIONAGE IN THE GERMAN HEADQUARTERS OF SOUTHERN GREECE.

From this point on, we drove our organization at full speed. The excitement caused by recent events quickly gave way to careful and methodical labor.

The first information was ready and classified. We just needed to divide it into two types: messages to be transmitted immediately via the wireless set and drawings to be sent via the caïques at the first opportunity.

Mitsos Rediadis and I were busy with various organizational details and devised an entire process for getting information from its source to its destination. Zentelis would continue to bring the Piraeus information from Koutsoudakis to Mitsos. Mitsos, Stavros and Popi would give their notes and drawings directly to me. The processing of all this information and its transcription into wireless set messages or reports with drawings would be done at my house.

Mitsos would give the messages ready for wireless set transmission back to Zentelis, who was by now well-experienced as a liaison for this type of transfer. Zentelis would meet Paliatseas at a certain time just after dark, in a different place each time according to a prearranged schedule. There he would hand over the telegraph messages.

Following the plan we had already put into place, Zentelis would advance and Paliatseas would follow him at a distance. When Paliatseas saw that the road was completely deserted, he would overtake Zentelis, taking the messages from him. If Paliatseas had anything to give us from the Allied services, he would hand over his messages at the same time. In accordance with our overall system of security, Zentelis wouldn't know that Paliatseas was our wireless set operator.

Any conversation between the two would be strictly forbidden, except if Paliatseas had a serious reason to meet with me. In that case he would simply say, "Let the captain come." I would then go to the next meeting instead of Zentelis.

With each transfer we would only give Paliatseas as many messages as could be transmitted in a single broadcast. Immediately after their transmission, he was to burn all of the notes.

With this process in place, we immediately informed all of our divisions that information would now reach its destination within a few hours. This meant that they could begin giving us information with a limited useful life.

The first night after the message from Cairo, I met Nicos Paliatseas on a side street near Metaxourgiou Square. I gave him new instructions and signals of recognition for his first contact with the liason, which was to take place nearby in a short while. I also told him the time and agenda for their next meetings.

Paliatseas was in heaven. "Finally!" he said to me. "It's about time! I was beginning to be disappointed."

Nicos Paliatseas
wireless set operator

I observed the meeting between our wireless set operator and the liaison from afar. The liaison didn't know me. Everything went according to plan. Our first regular information left for the wireless set.

For the next few days, I maintained regular contact with Paliatseas. I would see him a little before he was to meet Zentelis to learn news of the transmissions. I wanted to make sure things got off on the right foot.

Paliatseas had asked for additional hours and transmitted almost daily. Contacts were brief to avoid detection by the enemy's counterespionage services. Based on their duration, we planned our messages so that none would be left for the next day.

When I asked Paliatseas how he burned the notes, he answered, "Don't worry. I always have a brazier next to me with a small spirit stove on top of it to make my coffee. As soon as I finish, I throw all the papers into the stove and they burn right up. The ash falls apart in the brazier. In addition, I have even secured our broadcasts," he said with a certain pride.

He explained that the Germans had mobile radio detectors. The moment they hit upon a broadcast, they could determine the direction it was coming from. If another radio detector, in another location, simultaneously found the same broadcast, they could locate the position of the wireless set on a map of Athens at the point where the two directions crossed.

This danger, Paliatseas believed, was substantially reduced for us because his wireless set was at the conjunction of broadcasts from two strong foreign stations. He scheduled his transmissions during their broadcasts, which confused and misled the radio detectors. The detectors would have to be very close to detect his broadcast and thus be able to locate him.

It seemed that our first information had impressed its receivers. "Every night they congratulate me heartily," Paliatseas told me enthusiastically.

It is a fact that our information, although we hadn't yet organized ourselves well, was relatively complete. We transmitted information on all ship departures from Piraeus, including the times of their departures and the cargo that each transported, plenty of details on the movements of military units by land and sea, and descriptions of motor vehicles and cannons that the railroads unloaded in Piraeus. We also had engineering drawings of some beach minefields, mines laid in the harbor entrances, and installations of anti-aircraft artillery at several points around Athens and Piraeus. These we kept for the first caïque departure.

Soon we had our first request from the Allied services. They asked us to send them sketches of the symbols stamped on German vehicles. It seems that from these symbols, they could tell which enemy units were in Greece.

The technicians of Stavros Vrachnos's General Information Division were the most appropriate ones for this job. We recommended that they sketch the vehicle symbols with pencil, writing the colors next to each sketch (see page 19). Of course, they shouldn't look directly at the vehicle as they were copying its symbol. At night, at their leisure, they could redraw the symbols in color and then hand them over to the leader of their division.

In a few days, a good number of German vehicle symbols were waiting at my house, along with other drawings, for the day the caïque would leave.

✻   ✻   ✻

That's where things stood when Alexander Kairis called me one afternoon, urgently asking to meet with me. Knowing, from Popi Sakelaridis, the reason for this request, I told him to come to my house immediately.

Kairis was one of those truly educated people. He had studied law and was practicing, but at the same time he was dealing with theoretical studies and exploring various legal matters. He was familiar with the international cultural movement and worldwide literature, and he kept himself completely informed about them. His German was perfect. He was studious, inquisitive, and methodical without being pedantic. He had a broad perspective and fertile spirit, combined with a most delicate sense of humor. He was a humanist and had a philosophical disposition.

Alexander came from noble lineage. He was descended from Theofilos Kairis, the great wise man from Andros island who was also one of the oldest members of *Filiki Etaireia* (Society of Friends, a secret society that struggled for liberation from the Turks). His father was a physician, as was his brother Nicos, who was at that time an assistant to Prof. Louros at the university.

Alexander wasn't one of those people who would work with his country's enemies just to make a profit, even for significant economic gain. Neither could he possibly be charmed ideologically by the Nazi system of harsh German universal domination. This is why those who knew him wondered how he could be working for the Germans.

Ten minutes later, Alexander Kairis was in my office. I hadn't seen him for a long time, even though we had been childhood friends. This first meeting of ours during the occupation has remained deeply etched in my memory.

When Alexander shook hands, he'd look you straight in the eye with a particularly friendly and honorable expression. However, this look always seemed to have a barely perceptible shadow of melancholy. He wore dark-framed glasses. He was dark-skinned and somewhat tall. He was simple, thin, and agile. There was nothing noteworthy about him to someone who didn't know him, aside from his most amiable personality. At this time he was 29 years old. His handshake gave a pleasant first impression. It conveyed stability and honesty.

He lingered, holding my hand in his. "I am relying on you very heavily," he said. "I have a feeling that I am coming to the right person." I just looked at him encouragingly and let him continue.

"From the beginning of the occupation, I felt the need to offer some sort of service. As you know, I am not the heroic type. In the war, I served in naval offices and I was happy that I wasn't on the front lines.

"But with the occupation I felt a sudden depression. It was something like claustrophobia. I still feel it now. It is a need to clear the way, to pass through, and breathe free air again. Moreover, we now see the horrible German brutalities all around us that become more dreadful every day…"

Then Alexander came to his main point. "Now, not only do I feel a need, but I really *can* offer services to our country, services which I believe would be exceptionally useful.

"I've been working for some months now at the German Headquarters of Southern Greece, next to the commander of the engineering forces. Slowly I have managed to have more and more serious evidence pass through my hands. I am a *Kaufmännischer Angestellte am Leitender Pionierführer beim Befehlshaber Sudgriechenland* (Commercial Employee of the Engineering Command by the Commander of Southern Greece).

"When they offered me this position, I immediately thought that I could prove useful from in there. However, my anxiety has increased rather than decreased with each passing day. To whom will I be able to give all this valuable information? I thought that it would be easiest for me to approach the resistance.

"I am also concerned that when this war is over, I could end up with the stigma of having been a German collaborator without being able to give any proof of my intentions..."

Alexander fixed his eyes on me again. "Rigas, I am certain that you can help me. Some time ago I suddenly thought of you, and as the days went by I became more and more certain that you would be able to help me find a solution to my problem. I had also said something to Popi Sakelaridis. In any case, today I decided to come talk to you directly."

Kairis's tone suddenly became imperative. "Rigas, a way must be found for my information to reach Allied hands. Most of it would be impossible for the Allied staff to acquire from any other source. It is confidential and most important..."

Although I was prepared for all that Alexander Kairis told me, I remember that my reaction to his approach was one of shock. He didn't speak to me at all about the trust I would have to have in him to commit myself to such a matter. If I had lost this trust, as had so many of his friends who had even stopped saying hello to him, it would have been useless for him to attempt to dissuade me. However, his burning look at that moment begged for an answer.

"Alexander," I said to him. "I thank you for your trust. I'll bring up your points and get back to you. Come to Popi's house tomorrow evening at six. If you have any information, bring it with you. I'm sure your collaboration will be approved..."

I held back my emotions and enthusiasm with difficulty. I forced myself to stick to the general path we were following, hiding from Alexander my position in the organization as I did from all the others except Mitsos Rediadis. That's why I didn't immediately give him a definite answer.

I did, however, make sure to give him some immediate satisfaction. And what I told Alexander was plenty for him. He was assured of my respect, and something more. He was assured that he had at last found the organization and the means he had sought for so long.

Alexander jumped up and grabbed my hand in gratitude. And I noticed that his eyes misted with tears.

I waited to see Alexander the next afternoon with unbelievable anxiety. In the meantime, I had told the good news to Mitsos, who would be waiting for my phone call to receive Alexander's information that very night and to send it along to the wireless set.

Popi Sakelaridis lived in an apartment building on Drosopoulou 90 and Limnou Streets. At exactly 6 o'clock, I met Alexander going up the stairs to the third floor.

Our friend, who opened the door herself, didn't expect to see us together. "Are we the first of the guests?" Alexander joked.

In a short while, we were alone in the living room. Popi had withdrawn, quite discreetly.

"Alexander," I said to him, "our organization is called Service 5-16-5. This title is secret. You will not repeat it to anyone. Our exclusive occupation is espionage. Only those who are useful to us for the collection and transfer of strategic information become members. Not only do we *not* wish to extend to the public, but we avoid doing so. This is why you, especially, with your position being particularly delicate, will work alone and not come into contact with anyone but me.

"We have all the means to transfer our information directly to the Allied staff almost daily. We have a wireless set and caïques at our disposal. When you have information you will call Popi from an outside telephone, telling her that you are coming to see her. She will contact me. Since she is in recovery, your visits here are completely justifiable, as are mine. You will never call me directly. Keep in mind that due to the service in which you work, you may be watched. It is quite possible that your movements outside of work are already being followed.

"For reasons of general safety, you are obligated to follow these instructions to the letter. You alone will make up Division 3 of our service and your code number will be 'C1.' So, welcome, and good luck..."

Alexander was utterly enchanted. "Thank you," he said. "Thank you for everything. I feel like a new man."

He took some pieces of notepad paper out of his pocket. They were densely written on. I began to read his notes and I was impressed that he had compiled them in telegraphic style. I could send them just as they were.

"There will be much more in the future," he said. "For now, I just made rough drafts of what I had on hand."

Alexander's "rough drafts" were impressive. He mentioned where ships formed into convoys, the dates and times of convoy departures for the shores of Libya, the number of participating ships, the kinds of cargo, and the type and number of escorting war ships. He mentioned the route, speed, cargo, and destination harbors of particular ships that were to depart for various islands. He mentioned the types of auxiliary material that had been sent to Crete in the last three months.

Alexander took his notes again for a moment and, smiling with a ceremonial air, signed them "C1."

I laughed and said it wasn't necessary for him to sign his notes in the future. He was the only one in his division and we would know him. He would only use his code number if he was forced to send us an unexpected message without personal contact, just as we would use it if we needed to speak about him in front of other members of our service.

I used this opportunity to explain the basic reasoning behind our security measures to him and the need to follow them to the letter. These measures, which we had devised with great care and refined gradually as we gained experience, still had plenty of imperfections. For a little while at the beginning, all of our notes went to the telegraph just as they were, written in our own handwriting. Then the system improved and changed radically. But we paid for our initial imperfections later on, and in a very harsh way indeed.

Our evening came to an merry end around 8 o'clock. Popi brought us exquisite appetizers, for that time, and good wine, from those that her folks had found with great sacrifice so that she could get stronger. We joked as we saw her coming in and out of the room silently like a cat. She said, laughing, "We should write a stirring novel together entitled *The Great Spies and **Cata Hari**.*" [1]

I, however, had to leave. Mitsos Rediadis and the others were waiting. I would barely make it on time to turn in the notes for the night's transmission.

❊   ❊   ❊

---

[1] Mata Hari was a Dutch dancer who became a German spy during World War I. She became famous when she was captured and executed by the French.

That night I sat alone in my desk chair for many hours. With the little petroleum lamp lit — the electricity had been cut off — I smoked the paper-boxed occupation-era cigarettes in the dim light.

I was trying to weigh the situation within our organization given the latest developments and to figure out the right measures to gauge our potential and our responsibilities.

After so many attempts, temporary excitement and bitter disappointment, we finally had the satisfaction of having the necessary means at our disposal, surrounded by people for whom resistance to subjugation was an innate need. Our crazy dream that had become a passion had begun to be realized.

Our work was going in the right direction. We had the correct internal structure and our divisions were staffed with the suitable people.

The selection process had succeeded from the beginning, when I was searching for someone who could coordinate his efforts with mine and stopped at my invaluable collaborator, Mitsos Rediadis. Together we sifted through every detail before coming to any conclusion and putting it into action. Mitsos, as a second-in-command, was perceptive and precise. I felt an additional safety valve next to me.

We had the transmission team with our wireless set operator, Nicos Paliatseas, full of youthful fire and enthusiasm, Nicos Menegatos, our Allied services liaison, and the captains of the caïques. One of them, the captain Stamatis Tratras, would one day bravely face the firing squad beside our other companions. The dangerous transfer of information from Piraeus to Athens, and then from us to the wireless set operator, was in good hands. Our young liaison, George Zentelis, had proven himself precise and inexhaustible.

We had a finger on all the movements at the Piraeus harbor, having the harbor authorities as basic members of our organization. Harbormaster Antonis Bachas and his second-in-command Dimitris Samantzopoulos were top leaders who could guarantee that our network would function properly. We also had the leader of our Harbor Division, Manolis Koutsoudakis, an old sea dog who knew the people and details of all the Greek harbors and seas like the back of his hand. He had his own contacts and supplied us with information from all over Greece.

We had our pilots, too. Kostas Moros, Captain Kostas Damoulakis, and Captain Petros Drakopoulos, who was fated to be the last of our organization executed by the Germans at the end of 1944. We also had the chief boatman, the old man Savatakis, who would put down whatever he was doing as soon as he got a piece of information and run to give it to his superior "so that it would still be warm" as he liked to say. All of them were seasoned captains hardened to the sea. They were ghosts of the harbor who knew everything and everybody in the sailing world, and they developed a further network of informants unknown to us.

Through the technicians of Stavros Vrachnos's General Information Division, we drew plans of the Germans' fortifications, anti-aircraft installations, and the symbols on their vehicles. We observed the movements of enemy units, their encampments, and the storing of military materiel and fuel throughout the entire Attica basin.

Stavros commanded his sector with precision and drive. His brain continuously bore plans of action, and he untiringly gathered all types of information himself and tried to extend his network into the provinces through different people who worked in the countryside.

Stavros had an exceptionally good team in Athens. He had four chemical engineers, Nicos Kriezis, George Eleftheriou, Dimitris Thanopoulos, and Thanos Savas. Savas connected us with the ship manufacturing factory "Hambakis and Savas," which had been requisitioned by the Germans. He had Antonis Embeirikos, an executive of the cement factory "Atlas," and his colleague, George Kambanis, who was a Captain in the merchant marines. All of these technicians made drawings of enemy installations, storage facilities, and every kind of construction on the coast and inland. They were literally scouring the area, making drawings and gathering all kinds of information. From there on, our network broadened to many useful informants, following the instructions we had given and our triadic security structure.

We also had special companions at our disposal like Commander George Hatzigeorgiou, who connected us with valuable navy informants, and Aristeidis Papadopoulos, the city police officer in charge of the Confidential Archives Department in the Subdivision of General Security. From his contact with the Germans and Italians while on duty, or from the confidential and non-confidential orders that reached his hands, he was briefing, warning, and informing us about a great variety of matters, knowledge of which was invaluable to us.

Popi Sakelaridis had mobilized Francisko Petrits, an enthusiastic youth who gathered information on the railroad transports along with his partner, George Leousis, an employee of the Bank of Greece who also met me personally. They watched the trains that reached Athens and Piraeus and provided quite frequent reports.

Finally, I had my meetings at Popi's house with Alexander Kairis, the new important member of our service who opened the doors for us to the German Headquarters of Southern Greece, to the top secrets of the Germans, to the heart of the enemy.

This new acquisition to our service was a landmark development. Playing on the trust he had built up with the Germans, Alexander Kairis was stealing their secrets right out of their hands and facing real danger head on. However, he developed for us a new, extensive, and irreplaceable source of information that was worth every danger and every sacrifice.

This was the entire structure of Service 5-16-5 as I brought it to mind that sleepless night, stopping on faces, examining situations and possibilities, and moving on to plans for the future.

As our breadth grew, our responsibility increased. One administrative mistake could cost many lives. Starting tomorrow we would have to review the security system once again and identify the points we should revise and improve.

We had to send instructions to the divisions and give them a basic picture of the type of information we sought so that they wouldn't move in pointless directions. We had to coordinate their work so that, as much as possible, they would not waste time or expose themselves to unnecessary risk by confirming information we already knew to be reliable. On the other hand, suspect information would have to be verified by the concurrence of different sources.

The morning hours found me still in my desk chair with my cigarettes finished. The lamp's petroleum was exhausted and the flame was flickering. Outside, the day had begun to break.

By now my mind had gotten away from the closed circle of subjects that had occupied it all night. I thought about the Greek resistance as a general whole. I pictured and gloried in the pride and stubbornness of our people, who, despite the destruction, still insisted on ruling their own fate. And I reveled in the beauty of our disproportionate, yet passionate, secret war.

Happy is he who doesn't stop struggling, even if all around him seems lost. Happy, because he remains untouched by the most horrible sufferings and the heaviest oppression and has the supreme privilege of feeling free.

With such thoughts and pulsating feelings, I encapsulated the visions of that superb vigil into these verses.

We are watchful.
We carve our deliverance from slavery
Day and night
Without breath, without air,
With the rope tight around our necks
We struggle.

We are watchful.
In our minds, in our souls,
In our hearts, is Greece.
We hold the sacred torch high.
Steadily toward the harsh goal
We advance.

We are watchful.
The rhythm of our breath,
We rule in the storm.
The fierce tribe does not scare us
— Soul does not consider number —
And we strike.

New Inspection and Security Measures. The First Results. Actions of Our Harbor People.

By now we were advancing toward the winter of 1942. Our work was proceeding at a steady pace with an almost automatic rhythm.

The divisions had acquired considerable experience. It was now a simple task for me to prepare messages for the wireless set and packages for the caïques from their well-written notes and perfect sketches that accumulated on my desk.

For some time now, the new methods we had put into practice had been yielding wonderful results.

The system we had followed from the beginning to identify our informants — signing notes with the letter of the division and the initials of the informant, mixed with misleading letters — turned out not to be complete enough. Many times, the initials of the individual who came fourth or fifth in the chain connecting him to the center were lost in the mass of the initials of all the other members. Our orders that they not associate with one another and, if possible, that no more than three ever know each other — what we called the triadic system — made it still more difficult to identify a specific informant from his initials when the administration needed him.

So I sat and thought of a new system which, when put into practice, proved simple and precise. The letters of the divisions would remain as they were when we included Kairis:

A. Administrative Division — the leader, the second-in-command, and those directly connected to them: the wireless set operator and the liaisons. Popi Sakelaridis and her people also belonged to this division.

B. Harbor Division — Leader: E. Koutsoudakis.

C. German Headquarters Division — A. Kairis.

D. General Information Division — Leader: S. Vrachnos.

E. Division of Independent, Collaborating Individuals – G. Hatzigeorgiou, A. Papadopoulos, the liaison N. Menegatos, and the captains of the caïques.

F. Division of Contacts with Resistance Organizations — Trusted individuals who gave us information and connected us withother organizations such as *Ethniki Drasi* (National Action), *Stratia Sklavomenon Nikiton* (Army of Enslaved Victors) PEAN (*Panellinios Enosis Agonizomenon Neon*, PanHellenic Association of Fighting Youths), *Apollon* (Apollo), *Ellinikon Aima* (Greek Blood), *Iera Taxiarchia* (Sacred Brigade), *Ethniko Komitato* (National Committee), and EAM (*Ethniko Apeleftherotiko Metopo*, National Liberation Front).

The leaders and members of the divisions could, in principle, initiate new members into the organization if they deemed it useful, but always in accordance with the triadic security system.

Members would be given numbers based on the order in which they joined the organization, and they would write them after the code of their division as follows:

1. Division leaders were assigned the numbers A1, B1, C1, etc.
2. Members would have the number of the leader followed by their personal numbers. For example, members of B1 would have the numbers B11, B12, B13, etc., and members of D1 would have the numbers D11, D12, D13, etc.
3. If B12 created a team, its members would take the numbers B121, B122, B123, etc.
4. Team members who acquired double-digit personal numbers would enclose them within two dashes. For example, member 17 of B12's team would be written as B12-17-.

As an example, suppose we received a note with the encoded signature D1314 and wanted to contact the informant.

1. We would contact Number 1 from Division D, namely Stavros Vrachnos.
2. He would contact his Number 3, D13, Eleftheriou.
3. Eleftheriou would contact his Number 1, D131, Savvas.
4. Savvas would contact his Number 4, namely the informant D1314, who might be completely unknown to the center. Savvas would send this informant to meet with us according to our instructions.

Thus, regardless of how far away from the center an informant was, we would have the ability to find him by analyzing the multi-digit code number that connected him like a chain to the center. This system gave us the ability to supervise our entire organization, all the way out to its most distant corners.

Another perfection to our security system, put into effect a few days after Kairis entered our service, concerned how notes were written. Such notes were sent from the divisions to the administration, and from the administration to the wireless set and the caïques.

We procured thin paper which, as Vrachnos verified in his laboratory, dissolved immediately in stomach acids. Not one message now circulated written in the usual way. Instead, all were written on this paper in block letters. The letters were not written with a continuous pen stroke, either. We left spaces between their main strokes so that the handwriting could not be recognized. I composed the texts to be broadcast from the notes sent by the divisions, rewriting them in this stylized way. Mitsos polished the notes from our harbor people and handed me transmission-ready texts, written as I've described. Soon we were all well-practiced in this writing technique and were able to write messages with it quickly.

Messages were transported on crumpled wads of paper that one could swallow if necessary, and which none of the emetic medicines the Germans gave in such situations could bring back to the surface intact. Of course, the notes that went to the wireless set were burned as before, immediately after being broadcast.

Another matter we settled was the keeping of a journal, which was indispensable to our work. Often the need arose to determine whether a particular piece of information had already been transmitted or if certain parts of a message had been altered in some way, prompting us to ask why. For such cases, and many others, we felt the need for a journal.

I asked Stavros to make me a secret ink that we could reveal as many times as we wanted but that would erase immediately. In a few days I had two bottles of liquid on my desk. One was for writing watery, invisible letters. The other was for lightly moistening a cotton ball, which when dragged across the letters gave them a faded blue color for a short while. They quickly disappeared after you read them.

I had a rather large book collection in my office at home, so I chose a book in which the letters would dry without a trace. That is where I kept our journal, writing between the rows. One would have to try all methods of developing in every one of my books to find it. I kept the little bottles among other various household pharmaceuticals and cosmetics.

We also made sure to have a danger signal, which we advised our principal members to memorize well: "Madam Eleni is having a party and is expecting you tonight." This signal would be given to Mitsos or to me only from an outside telephone and only in case we were threatened by a serious danger. We appointed intermediary telephones for those who didn't have direct contact with us or who knew us only by pseudonyms.

Exactly one hour after the call, we would meet the person who sent the danger signal outside of the then very well-known blue apartment building on Exarchia Square to learn what was happening.

❋　❋　❋

In the meantime, our work had begun to bear fruits without us even knowing it. One by one, messages started coming in that told of casualties we had inflicted on the enemy with our information. In the beginning, there were unverified rumors. Later, we got information from captains and fishermen returning from trips who had seen or heard things. Finally, there were responsible reports to the country's port authorities or to the official German services.

Many ships whose departures and journey details we had announced were torpedoed by our submarines or sunk by Allied planes. *Danubio, Foscolo, Valkan, Bulgaria, Reomirus, Agatha, Citta di Genova, Henrietta...* One by one, the ships we had watched load their cargo or embark with enemy divisions, and for which we had pinpointed the details of their courses and voyages, ended up with their military cargo at the bottom of the sea.

The names of the ships listed above are taken from a journal kept by our harbor people. From all the ships whose sailings we reported to the Allied services, we verified that 55 were destroyed before they reached their destinations. I will list all the names from the journal later.

War is hard and forms a completely different consciousness in people. We celebrated like madmen every time we learned that along with valuable enemy materials, hundreds of people had lost their lives due to us. It was not only the psyche of the war and the reward for our efforts that kindled this wild joy inside us. It was the thirst for freedom. It was the protest and the revenge.

By destroying we were not only helping the war effort. We were spiritually delivered and were opening the door to the general deliverance. We were lifting our heads to the conqueror, reversing the terms of domination. We were taking back our blood...

Then the harbor division informed us that five Spanish ships were smuggling war contraband. They traveled undisturbed, under the protection of the neutral Spanish flag, transporting German war materiel.

We noted their cargo loading and broadcast the details of their itineraries at least five times, stressing to the Allies that these ships had to be hit by all means. It seems that the Allied staff was bound up in studying the international law for such cases. In the meantime, the Spanish ships were coming and going and nothing was happening.

The harbor people were just short of blaming us for the delay. They became wild. Koutsoudakis and Bachas protested vehemently. "We ask so often, for so many details for the *Bulletin of Ships' Movements*, that we are running the risk of being discovered. Observing the cargo loading and verifying the Spanish ships' itineraries will soon be impossible for us. The Germans are systematically following our movements."

Finally, after our persistent urging, the Allies gave in. The five Spanish ships, one after the other, disappeared into the liquid abyss. They, too, went on our list of 55 ships.

Our harbor people raised the same alarm for a floating dry dock in Lavrio. It provided considerable assistance to the German transports by repairing ships that would otherwise remain unused. We repeatedly reported its activity and position. In the end, British planes destroyed it, too.

Antonis Bachas and Dimitris Samantzopoulos often proposed plans for sabotage, but we always replied that they should be sensible. Sabotage was not part of our work, and we were not ready to move in that direction. Perhaps the greatest deterrent to me was that every time I heard about sabotage, I immediately thought of German reprisals against the unarmed population. I would have been deeply shaken if we carried out sabotage and the Germans shot innocent hostages.

However, the harbormaster and his second-in-command could not be restrained. So their leader, Koutsoudakis, seemed to "play" in between. He respected and agreed with the views of the center, but he did not hesitate to bombard us every so often with plans for mining and blowing up the harbor.

Finally, we gave our consent for limited sabotage under the condition that it couldn't have immediately visible results. This type of sabotage wouldn't result in any retaliation unless the Germans happened to find out about it.

Given this condition, the sabotage of fuel was put into effect, and with great success. In a series of reports that Koutsoudakis presented to us after the war, he stated:

> From the fuel storage warehouses, the tugboats and related services at least 30 tons of coal and 100 oka [about 300 pounds] of liquid fuel were dumped into the sea or made to disappear daily.

Our harbor people systematically interfered with the enemy transports, creating every possible obstacle to their departure. As Koutsoudakis said in the same report:

> Several times ships ready for departure for urgent and important missions were delayed a very long time. Trips were even sometimes postponed or canceled due to these delays, because it was not possible for their escorts, which was ready to depart, to wait any longer.

Among other proposals, Bachas asked us what he should do when people known by the harbor division, but strangers to our organization, asked for assistance with sabotage in the harbor. The answer could not be given easily. Such assistance could draw the Germans' attention, and if the sabotage continued they would realize the complicity of our people, arrest them, and thus destroy the valuable information work of our Harbor Division. On the other hand, we could not refuse to assist the work of the saboteurs, which we knew, for better or worse, was usually carried out under orders from the Allied staff.

Finally, we answered the question by saying, "Examine the seriousness of the sabotage proposals and only assist those that come from organized services and not single individuals. Always present the sabotage proposals to us for approval. When you provide assistance, work obscurely. Never participate directly in their execution."

In another of his reports on sabotage, Koutsoudakis described the efforts of the Piraeus Harbormaster, Commander Antonis Bachas:

> *He showed exceptional energy during the mining of Piraeus Harbor. He supervised the mining work himself and met repeatedly with the electrical engineer of the Piraeus Harbor Organization, George Makris, who produced a detailed plan for him. This was given to us and we presented it to the organization...*
>
> *To allow the sabotage to be carried out within Piraeus Harbor, or in the vicinity, Bachas retracted the harbor guards on duty using various pretexts. This made the work easier to carry out and prevented the culprits from being caught. The clearest proof of his effectiveness is that while serious acts of sabotage were carried out within Piraeus Harbor and its outskirts, none of the perpetrators were caught or betrayed by the Port Authorities. Due to this, Bachas was reproached by the Germans more than once. For the sabotage of the steamships* Sita di Barri *and* Orion *in particular, blame was placed on him, nearly causing him to be captured along with the Harbormaster Samantzopoulos.*

It seems that Antonis Bachas was not as fascinated by his espionage and information mission as by these parallel efforts which had immediate and striking results. Every time we approved some type of action like this, he always went a bit further and opened some new sector of activity.

Thus, slowly, a whole sub-service was created in our Harbor Division to deal with acts developing within the framework of our basic activities.

Antonis Bachas was in constant motion. He got involved with the caïques that transported officers and others to Turkey and Egypt. He assisted in their staffing and supplying them with petroleum and food. He supplied them with false documents of ownership, of departure, etc. He replaced every officer in the Harbor Services who resisted these measures or lost courage, and that is how "hundreds of Greeks" crossed over to freedom "before the eyes of the German guards," as related in Koutsoudakis's report.

Antonis Bachas grew bolder as he succeeded, and as he got bolder he neglected certain security measures. He allowed division members to telephone from the Harbormaster office about various urgent matters that concerned us. He allowed his service car to be used to facilitate our members' movements when they had to verify or transfer some information as quickly as possible. He gathered the division members in his office and spoke to them with fiery words about the execution of their mission.

Perhaps some type of very natural and very human weakness for this situation fostered these risky activities. It seems that Antonis was bothered by the attitude of many Greeks toward him, which could otherwise be excused because they didn't know his secret actions. Simply because he agreed to be Harbormaster, they thought he had sold out to the Germans. Over time, this accusation, became unbearable to him. Without even realizing it, he therefore began to succumb to the temptation of dropping hints about his patriotic actions in certain circles.

The psychological concessions one's conscience makes to deeper and insatiable demands can be strange. Bachas had accepted the responsibility not to speak with anyone about his secret mission, and he wasn't speaking. However, some things unintentionally escaped from him which gave satisfaction to his subconscious desires: he let certain operations become more daring and more obvious from day to day.

At that point we were forced to try to somehow rein him in. We sent word to him that "when boldness does not keep up with one's prudence, it can destroy our whole operation." We also instructed him to be "more careful."

At first, Bachas was terribly embittered. He had given his whole being to the struggle and served it with feeling. His results were exceptional. It was not what he was expecting to hear from the leadership of the secret service.

There were some debates within the circle of his division and, in the end, he realized that we were right. Besides, we conveyed our congratulations and our admiration for his effectiveness so often that one necessary suggestion, even if it was intentionally delivered sternly, should not have hurt his feelings.

Antonis Bachas was an object of our pride and he knew it. He therefore continued with his heroic offerings, full of self-confidence. One day he would win the position he was worthy of in the conscience of the people.

For the time being, there were other important compensations that gave him the strength to face the unjust humiliations: he saw the big enemy ships leaving the harbor and he knew that somewhere on the open sea destruction was waiting for them.

This was enough for him.

ACTIONS OF OUR TECHNICIANS. QUESTIONS OF THE ALLIED SERVICE. IN THE CONFIDENTIAL ARCHIVES OF THE GERMANS.

Our technicians did not have the satisfaction of seeing actual results from their brave efforts. They did not have the joy of cheering for any specific destruction they caused the enemy. They never received congratulations for a specific Allied success. In this respect, their work was thankless. However, their attitude remained positive and calm. They knew the worth of their contribution.

The work of Division D, the General Information Division, was laborious and dangerous. Our technicians had no pretext or authority to justify their approaching the enemy units and their work. They had to sneak into forbidden areas and remain well hidden or risk some imaginative excuse to approach more noticeably. What's more, their lack of communication and the systematic inspections at German and Italian blockades on the approaches to Athens made it difficult for anyone to approach the restricted areas. It was much more difficult to make sketches without coming under suspicion.

Now that winter had settled in, the cold worked with the permanent hunger to make our job even more difficult. Our technicians, not seeing any military results to reward their efforts, started to get discouraged.

"We are constantly in peril," Stavros Vrachnos would say to me. "And we haven't seen even one aerial bombardment of the targets we suggested. The sketching of fortified areas, the copying of vehicles' symbols, the observation of encampments and storage areas, all these contribute to constant stress. We need the satisfaction we can only get from an immediate and obvious military action due to our efforts."

Stavros was right. When one daily exposes his life to danger to contribute to a certain goal, he can be excused if he impatiently searches for tangible evidence that the goal is being achieved. Otherwise, the doubt gives rise to justifiable disappointment.

But what could we do? I told Stavros to call his people together and reason with them something like this: "The information from Division D is essential for the staffing plans of the Allies, who must definitely know about the fortifications, storage, and movements of the enemy. The sketches will certainly be valuable when they attempt, as we hope, to land in Greece. At that time they will definitely bomb the targets we have suggested. They will hit the antiaircraft batteries. They will destroy the beaches' minefields, the barbed wire fences, and the machine gun emplacements. That will be the moment for our technicians to celebrate."

For the time being, though, they would have to work and wait. Their reward would have to be the simple satisfaction of executing their mission. We knew how valuable that was to our struggle, and how much damage it would later cause the enemy.

To organize their work, the members of Division D had divided the coastline into sections. They sketched the Germans' shore fortifications and those deeper inland.

George Eleftheriou sketched the area from the School of Nautical Cadets in Piraeus to Alexandra Square. Dimitris Thanopoulos sketched from Alexandra Square to Trocadero Center, past the air force installations and the reservoir in Old Faliro. Antonis Embeirikos and his partner George Kambanis sketched enemy fortifications and encampments from Trocadero to Vouliagmeni.

Nicos Kriezis, who worked in the requisitioned factory *Chromatourgeia* in Piraeus, sent us information on the industrial and sanitary materials loaded there and the countries they were being shipped to. These materials, such as the steel bottles of pressurized gases that were loaded in great quantities for Crete, were of great importance to the enemy.

Thanos Savvas, of the requisitioned ship repair factory *Hambakis and Savvas,* gave us invaluable information about the enemy ships under repair: armament, thickness of armor plate (if any), engine power, maximum speed, and type of cargo. He also reported the date that each ship's repair would be completed so that we could continue to follow it. He also helped Eleftheriou with the sketching of installations and fortification projects in the region.

From then on, all of these members, along with newer partners they recruited under our triadic system, followed enemy units throughout Athens and Piraeus and the entire surrounding region. They noted the enemy's number, his armament, warehouses, vehicle symbols, and mechanical means, sometimes with surprising detail and always completely verified. Some of this information we transmitted immediately by wireless set, but most of it included sketches and was therefore sent by caïque.

One day, Stavros gave me a topographic sketch of trenches the Germans had dug and camouflaged under olive trees, next to Kifisias Avenue, not far from Paradeisos. These were full of fuel and other military materiel.

A few days earlier, I had asked Stavros to send one of his people to sketch these trenches in such a way that our airplanes could recognize their location and destroy them. I instructed him to chose a member of his team with a simple and sympathetic appearance who could go to Paradeisos by bicycle, unhinge a joint in his chain, and ask the German sentry to allow him to pass through to a workshop far back in the field to repair it. While making his way to the shop, he should try to memorize the trench positions and approximate their dimensions.

The sketch that Stavros handed me was excellent, and above it was written: "The noted distances were measured with complete accuracy." At the bottom were the distinguishing letters D11 and D111.

"Wait a minute," I said. "We're not going to send them exaggerations. Of course the sketch is accurate, but it would only be completely accurate if we had taken a measuring tape to measure the trenches."

"It *is* like we measured with a tape," Stavros answered, smiling. "It is completely accurate. I sent two men with bicycles, Embeirikos and Kambanis. They passed by the trenches again and again, counting their pedal strokes right in front of the unsuspecting Germans. Then they measured how many centimeters the bicycles cover with each pedal stroke, and they sketched the trench on a map of the area, measured with complete accuracy…"

❋ ❋ ❋

One night, I received a message at my house from Nicos Paliatseas: "Allied service asking if German vehicles with following symbols have arrived in Athens region: Circle of yellow eggs. Black tree. Green four-leaf clover. Urgent."

I immediately instructed Stavros to mobilize his people. "They must drop whatever else they're doing," I said. "Divide Athens, Piraeus, and the surrounding areas into sections and conduct a systematic search for these three symbols. We must send our answer as soon as possible. This is the first time Division D will mobilize to answer specific questions from the Allied service, and they stressed that this matter is urgent."

Stavros and his team mobilized energetically. They literally blanketed Athens and the country, but they did not see any such symbols anywhere.

The Allies asked this same question almost every night. It seems they needed to find out as soon as possible whether certain German units were going down to reinforce the Libyan front.

Meanwhile, we mobilized our entire organization. The fact that we hadn't seen these symbols was not enough to make us certain they hadn't reached our area. Perhaps these vehicles were centralized somewhere and would not circulate until they were ready to depart. We had to look in camps all over the countryside, the covered freight on railroad cars, and the holds of loaded ships.

Paliatseas bombarded us with messages: "They are urgently asking for an answer on the symbols... They are asking why the answer is being delayed..."

Some ten days had gone by when, one night, our liaison Zentellis returned from a meeting with Paliatseas and reported to Rediadis, "Our meeting today was quite irregular. George [that's how Zentellis knew Nicos Paliatseas] started yelling at me in the middle of the street. He told me that the 'service' is pressuring him for an answer, and the bottom line is that he is responsible *because he is the wireless set operator.*"

The next night I went to the rendezvous instead of Zentellis. Paliatseas saw me from afar as I headed towards Metaxourgiou Square and he slowly advanced toward Chios Street. We changed alleys several times and I approached him.

Our good Nicos realized, of course, what I wanted him for, and he felt badly. He tried to make excuses. "Forgive me for yesterday, but their messages made me nervous. They made it sound like we're neglecting their question..."

"I'm sorry Nicos," I said sternly, "but anyone who doesn't know how to obey orders and control his nerves puts all of our lives, and the success of our work, in danger. Every order has a purpose, and you have an obligation to respect those orders. You know very well that any type of discussion with the liaison is forbidden, and you started yelling in the street. The liaison was not supposed to know who you are, for your own safety, and you revealed that you are the wireless set operator. From the way you acted, I fear that you might also have spoken to others. You must understand that if some day calamity befalls us, it will be because of your disobedience."

Paliatseas was truly just a boy with a deep sense of responsibility, revealed by his anxiety over the reply that we had to send the Allied service. He took my remarks very seriously. With his head bowed, he whispered through his teeth, "I am not disobedient... I am not disobedient... you should not have spoken to me like that," and he started to cry.

Alexander Kairis

I told him to stop crying and to pay attention to me. I explained why we were taking all these precautionary measures.

"We know how much you care about your mission," I told him, "and that you are worthy of the task. We trust you. But even though we have the same trust in our liaison, we still gave him a false name for you and hid your position from him. If some day the Germans catch one of us and torture him, he mustn't know anything. That's the only way we can be sure he won't have anything to reveal even if he bends. The administration takes this and many other things into consideration, without being able to explain everything to everyone. This is why there are orders that we must follow to the letter, and even more so when we are under stress for some reason, because it is then that our reasoning can betray us. Only faithful adherence to orders will save us from real trouble.

"We know that all your actions are inspired by enthusiasm and conscientiousness. However, you must control your spontaneity and outbursts, just as we all must."

Nicos Paliatseas had come to his senses and was listening to me with rapt attention. His child-like face was full of understanding and devotion.

"You will see from now on," he said. "You will never have another complaint against me again. I beg you to believe that I have never, until today, neglected any of the precautions you taught me or those I learned in the Allied service. I am rarely out during the day, I don't frequent clubs, I avoid my relatives, I never talk about my work, and nobody knows where I live. I don't have friends, and the only people I talk to a bit are Menegatos when he is in Athens and a barber, an old friend of mine, when I get my hair cut in the Academia Platonos area."

He was a truly wonderful young man, this Nicos Paliatseas. He lived this monotonous, joyless life at 22 years of age, normally a crazy and carefree year. Instead he was exclusively focused on his mission, and with this he filled and enjoyed his life...

In a few days, we were finally able to send an answer.

We had discovered vehicles with the "circle of yellow eggs" gathered in Lavrio. Some "green four-leaf clovers" had appeared in Athens. The "black tree" hadn't appeared anywhere at that time.

※　　※　　※

Meanwhile, by combining the harbor information with that from Kairis, we were exceptionally up-to-date.

At least 24 hours before each departure we telegraphed overseas every detail about the ship, its cargo, its final destination, if it was to sail alone or with a convoy, the general composition of the convoy, its probable speed considering the slowest-moving vessels, and a detailed description of the escorting warships.

Our network for information on fortification construction and enemy movements had begun to spread all over Greece. We received the most interesting and most detailed information from Thessaloniki, Volos, the Dodecanese, and the Ionian Islands.

That's when, with Alexander Kairis, we proceeded one step further.

We always met at Popi Sakelaridis's, who continued to have problems with her health and was in bed most of the time. Other friends, unconnected to our organization, were usually there, too. If the Germans happened to be following Kairis, these gatherings gave our meetings an innocent cover and removed any possible suspicion.

So while Alexander's brother Nicholas analyzed some type of gynecological surgery or Nicos Karidis read and commentated on some poet, I would find the opportunity to have a few words with Alexander in a corner and receive his messages.

"What are you two mumbling about?" I remember them asking us one night as they read poetry by Kavafi.

"We're discussing 'quality,'" Alexander answered with his endless humor, playing on one of the poet's phrases.

One such evening, Kairis spoke to me about the "confidential archive of the Germans."

"First of all," he said, "entrance to there is strictly forbidden. Whenever I try to create some official reason to come into contact with the confidential archive they always find a way to keep me away. It's one floor up from my office. But during lunchtime, I often sit in the office completely alone, finishing my work. No German has ever appeared on these two floors during this time. They all go to lunch together.

"It would not be difficult for me to go up to the confidential archive during that time. And it is worth the trouble for me to try. Of course, I wouldn't have time to sit in there and copy papers. But I could take some documents, bring them to you, and put them back in their place the next day. There is a treasure in there."

There was no doubt that the proposal was exceptionally intriguing. The confidential archive of the German Headquarters of Southern Greece must be a true treasure trove. However, if from one day to the next someone on duty looked for one of the missing documents, or if anyone returned while Kairis was in the confidential archive, that would be his end.

I said this to him, and he simply smiled. "I know," he replied, "but these things are part of the ... risks of the profession."

This man was incredible. "Listen," I said. "You'll bring the documents here to me, we'll photograph them, and then you'll take them back immediately. You'll remove the documents as soon as the Germans leave and put them back half an hour before they return. We can photograph much more than we could copy in 24 hours, and this way you'll enter the archive much less frequently."

This is what we did beginning the very next day.

Alexander brought as many documents as he could fit in his pockets. We told Popi's parents that we were staging a play. They knew we did whatever we could to entertain Popi in the long period of her illness and left us undisturbed.

At lunchtime we locked ourselves in Popi's room, set up the camera, turned on the lights, and started our work.

Popi, who didn't know anything about this phase of our collaboration, was at first surprised. Then she became fascinated. She felt as if she was living in a story. She loved her friends, she loved her country, and she hated the conqueror. All of this, in the intense atmosphere of the work she saw before her, moved her deeply. When we finished and were getting ready to leave with the papers and film in our pockets, she kissed us both. We all felt a strange excitement, full of emotion.

"I want to cry," she told us. I remembered that I had seen her cry even before our country came into the war, when we suddenly heard on the radio that the Germans had entered Paris. At that time, foreign subjugation shook us as an unacceptable reality, but in a general and impersonal sense. Now we were moved and encouraged by the decisive and unrelenting effort for the liberation of our own people and our own country.

That night, when I developed the films in my bathroom and read the photographed documents with a magnifying glass, I was sure that the result was truly worth every risk and every sacrifice.

The confidential archive of the Germans took us from the present to the future. I held in my hands the plans for future troop movements, future shipments of materiel, future airports, and fortification work that they had not yet begun. Now we were hitting deep into the enemy's foundations.

I quickly prepared the telegram we would send that very night. I also hid the films so we could send them via the caïque.

Spiritual and Intellectual Resistance, 1942-1943

Can an era of slavery be seen as "beautiful?" An era in which a conqueror's incredible violence and inhumanity scared and shocked the 20th century?

In olden times, every conqueror, with rare exception, was violent and cruel. But cruelty was part of the spirit of those times. Children were raised in an atmosphere of tyranny and war. They grew accustomed to torture and execution as daily and normal consequences of their lords' uncontrollable moods not only in war, but also in peace. Rulers and subjects alike were spiritually and physically prepared for the violence that was an integral part of their lives. They were always ready to impose it as sovereigns or to receive it as slaves. In military conquests, harsh rule was the natural relationship between the tough victorious and the tough defeated peoples.

In modern times, people have softened, even though they haven't become completely civilized. The lives and deaths of citizens no longer depend on the moods of sovereigns. Laws forbid torture. Executions are not a public spectacle. Slavery is illegal. And war, captivity, and spoils are governed by international rules that are usually respected, at least publicly.

Therefore, the inhumane despotism of the Germans and their Axis allies, formally ordered by the Nazi regime and sadistically carried out by unbridled lower agents, the occupations with their unchecked violence, the intentional destructive deprivations, looting, Middle Age tortures, reprisals against innocent people, and group executions of hostages including women and children, were all monstrous phenomena which could have crushed and exhausted the unprepared, enslaved Greeks.

Still, this horrible era in Greece was beautiful...

A creative breath was in the air, full of self-confidence and pride in refusing subjugation. The fighting spirit of liberation boiled from within a thermal well with thousands of vents and spilled out in burning torrents.

People found countless ways to get into the battle, to lend a hand, to strike the enemy. Using whatever opportunities presented themselves and their own individual abilities, temperament, spiritual strength, and level of education, each opened his own combative path. Sometimes prudent and controlled, sometimes passionate and impetuous, with fists and every type of gun, with spirit, knowledge, and inspiration, always spontaneously, always boldly, facing danger with decisive deliberateness.

This is how the resistance was born in enslaved Greece, emerging from the indomitable Greek temperament. Long-standing tradition had taught Greeks that even under the most oppressive slavery one can find a way to undermine and neutralize tyranny.

Conquests in our land have gone on for centuries. Our cities and villages, our mountains and shores, are full of Roman structures, Frankish and Venetian castles, and Turkish mosques. This is what remains of the conquerors. The rulers themselves didn't stand the test of time.

The Greek race has a strong fiber. The deprivation, torture, and death, the humiliation and debasement, together with the many unpleasant remains bequeathed to us, have sharpened our reflexes and fortified our resolve.

An explosion was always brewing during the long periods of apparent inaction under slavery. Our generation had the good fortune to experience one such explosion, ignited at the very beginning of the occupation. It was an explosion of incredible brilliance and breadth. We reveled in its every moment. To offset the pain and deprivation and threats, we drew true beauty out of every facet of the struggle. A boundless faith enveloped us: faith in ourselves, faith in our generation, and faith in the future. We faced the zenith of a tragedy, but its every instant was a victory.

From the day the Germans first entered Athens on April 27, 1941, the resistance was directed toward two complementary goals. The first was to confront and wear down the enemy by all possible means. The second was to organize ways to inform and guide the Greek people to maintain their fighting spirit and intensify their resistance activities. This second effort included organizing ways to help Greeks and British escape abroad and to care for the unfortunate and the persecuted fugitives in our homeland.

The first goal was pursued with the unanimous participation of the population. Almost all Greeks faced the invaders with intense hostility. Greek youths mobilized quickly and effectively. All those who were forced to stop fighting openly in the war tried to find ways to strike the enemy at the epicenter of his domination. Fighting hand-to-hand with an authoritarian sower of life and death, they attempted to steal and transmit his secrets, sabotage his transports, materials, machinery, and construction projects, or wage guerrilla war to tie down and destroy his forces.

The second goal, keeping our people informed and guiding their efforts, was pursued by the intelligentsia. It was a job of great responsibility. With a mercurial people like ours, who soar to great heights and tumble downhill with equal ease, it was important to get things off to a good start. Their enthusiasm and national pride, which had prevailed during the wartime, had to be maintained, and the disappointment they might suffer from the rampant wretchedness and coercion had to be neutralized. The subjugation and collaboration that might grow out of an instinct for self-preservation in moments of despair had to be prevented. Every action potentially harmful to the nation had to be exposed to public indignation. National unity had to be maintained, and the spirit of cooperation had to dominate.

This is how most of the first pioneers started out in the Greek resistance, which had countless difficulties to overcome before it could be organized and produce results. They tried their hand at various types of resistance — and changed courses as circumstances dictated — until they found their most productive roles.

The first year was marked by sporadic individual efforts and disorderly, haphazard actions by ad hoc teams. The general lack of resources and experience was clearly evident in these early struggles.

The Greek resistance became more organized and productive during the second year of the occupation. By the autumn and winter of 1942-43, the resistance had reached its peak. The people's exasperation and rage, intensified by the deprivation and tyranny of the occupation, amplified the initial motives for action: love of homeland, passion for freedom, and national pride. Resistance exploded in a myriad of ways and in all directions with an unlikely intensity. This was the time when the patriotic resistance was most effective, before being hampered by internal opposition and disputes which later soiled our hands and our history with brotherly blood.

This was also the first time since the beginning of the war that the military news from abroad filled us with true enthusiasm. In the past, we had desperately clung to any clear pause in the continuous German advance as a reason for optimism. We wanted to see, and we did see, every respite in the enemy's successes as a victory of our own. The spiritual strength shown by the British (who were so tragically unprepared for the war), Winston Churchill's decisive and brilliant command, the inexhaustible resources of the Americans, and the sheer mass of the Russians, were the only assurances we could offer ourselves and others to help maintain our morale.

In the meantime, by the end of May 1942, German General Erwin Rommel had unleashed his amazing attack on the African front. On June 21, he captured Tobruk with its enormous quantities of Allied supplies, facilitating his advance. At the same time, here in Greece, we risked everything to neutralize, obstruct, or at least delay shipment of his provisions. On June 24, Rommel crossed the border into Egypt and captured Solum. Two days later he attacked and dispersed the British forces at Marsa Matrouh. On July 1, Rommel attempted a decisive hit on El Alamein. Victory here would have given him mastery of the heart of Egypt and routed the Allied and Greek forces of the Middle East. The days when Alexandria had started to evacuate in anticipation of surrendering to the German victor were some of the most dramatic days of that time.

Then, on the verge of disaster, a miracle happened. Rommel's triumphant march was halted by the 8th British Army under General Auchinlek. They immobilized the German troops and caused them to exhaust themselves with three months of attacks and counterattacks in which neither side could gain the upper hand. This gave wings to our hopes and reaffirmed our faith that our efforts had not been in vain.

After the Battle of El Alamein on October 23, 1942, however, our hopes took flight on gigantic wings. Rommel's army, the mighty Africa Corps, had been crushed by Auchinlek's successor, General Bernard Montgomery. After a heavy pounding by Allied artillery and air power and continuous battles that lasted until November 3rd, Rommel's Africa Corps fled, defeated, toward the desert.

This victory also had particular significance for Greece. The 1st Greek Brigade under General Pausanias Katsotas and the Greek Air Force of Palestine took part in the attack and performed admirably, while our Navy destroyed the enemy's supply lines and protected Allied movements.

In Greece, we learned the news from hidden radios and shared it with any stranger we happened to meet. Even though the censored newspapers were silent, news traveled at an amazing rate by word of mouth, causing widespread excitement. Soon afterward we could read accounts of current events in the secret press.

The powerless and exhausted people gained life from this broad combination of good news and open discussion. They walked the streets with renewed vigor. They happily drank the chickpea coffee in the coffee shops. They joyfully crowded into the "gazozèn," the buses with chimneys that burned wood instead of gasoline. They cheerfully waited in the soup kitchen lines to get the day's gruel, the grocer's soup, or some beans...

"Have patience. The beast is his death throes. A bit more and we will have destroyed him. Freedom is near..."

❋ ❋ ❋

The first gripping news of our internal struggle was created by the final heroic act of Kostas Perrikos in the early autumn of 1942. It was a deed that led to his death.

At noontime on Sunday, September 20, a powerful explosion shook the center of Athens. I was on my way home soon afterward and saw the demolished, still smoking building at the corner of Patision and Gladstonos Streets. The building had housed ESPO (*Ethniki Sosialistiki Patriotiki Organosis*, National Socialist Patriotic Organization), a mélange of pro-German scoundrels and idiots trying to form a Greek legion to fight alongside the Germans on the Eastern Front.

The Germans, in a state of frenzy, blockaded the street. Passers-by, filled with gleeful satisfaction, hurried to distance themselves from the scene, fearing that reprisals and arrests of hostages would begin on the spot. The next day we learned that about 30 members of ESPO, and over 40 German officers and soldiers, had found their deaths in the ruins.

All Athenians knew that ESPO was a dirty business and a national danger that had to be annihilated. There was a general outcry to punish these traitorous enemy collaborators and to create an example for other unscrupulous rascals who might be thinking of collaborating with the enemy for their own advantage. The destruction was a fierce slap in the face of the almighty conqueror from his slaves.

The ESPO explosion had a huge impact both internally and abroad, on our allies as well as on our enemies. Talk in Athens and on the Allied radio stations highlighted this dramatic event in our secret war for a long time. However, sorrow didn't take very long to cast its shadow on all this excitement. Six weeks later, the Germans arrested Kostas Perrikos.

Along with Perrikos, the Germans arrested three other PEAN administrators, Athanasios Scouras, Dionysios Papavasilopoulos, and Nicos Ailianos. They also arrested staff members Antonis Mitilinaios, Dimitrios and Petros Lois, Julia Bilbas, Aikaterini Bessi, Spiros Galatis, and the three Katevatis brothers: Ioannis, Gerasimos, and Dionysios.

For me, Perrikos's arrest was the first blow that touched me personally. I remember how, every now and again, our organization discussed the possibility that we could be discovered by the Germans. We tried to anticipate our attitudes and how we would react if we fell into enemy hands. But no matter how hard we tried to prepare ourselves mentally for such a situation — and even accomplished to some certain degree — there was always considerable distance between theory and reality. As I later had the opportunity to prove many times, a man faces danger to himself with far less concern than danger threatening a loved one.

In the case of Kostas Perrikos, I had to use all my energy to calm my shaken nerves and to consider his arrest a normal consequence of our struggle. I didn't have any delusions about his ultimate fate. From the moment he was in enemy hands, Perrikos was already dead. We had to focus on the fact that Perrikos had succeeded in achieving his goal. Whoever risks willingly must be ready to pay. We had to set every sorrow aside to maintain our optimism and our fighting spirit.

We tried to learn as much as we could about this bold operation. We wanted to learn as much from its successes as from its possible imperfections which may have led to Perrikos's and his collaborators' discovery. We concluded that the weak point in Perrikos's amazing plan was a lack of secrecy. Kostas Perrikos had an explosive nature. He saw all Greeks as his brothers. He embraced them. He tried to pour his enormous emotional reservoir into their souls and draw, as far as possible, all those he met into the sacred struggle. He had the ability to enrapture everyone around him, but he spoke too often and too openly. In his drive to enthuse and captivate, he uncovered his secret activities.

Kostas Perrikos paid no heed to the danger in trying to expand his struggle as broadly as possible. Though his boldness proved fruitful, he paid for it with his life.

Below is an excerpt from an article which one of Perrikos's close colleagues, the chemist Takis Mihailidis, wrote specifically for this book. He took part in the explosion and describes it in vivid detail.

THE BLOWING UP OF ESPO BY THE P.E.A.N. DEMOLITION CREW ON 20 SEPTEMBER 1942

by Takis Mihailidis

There was a four-story stone building at the corner of the Gladstonos and Patision Streets. The flags of Germany, Italy, Japan, and Greece were hung on the mezzanine floor. A large inscription said "National Socialist Patriotic Organization ESPO," and beside it was an advertisement that read: "Greek youth, join the pioneers of the New Order."

It was a voice of the Axis, a nest of enemy agents in the middle of Athens. Their goal was to recruit a legion of Greek volunteers to fight at the eastern front and work in the German military industry. They thought they could achieve that goal by exploiting the starvation and degradation of the Greek people.

PEAN, the PanHellenic Union of Fighting Youths, took on the task of stopping this corrosion. Its leader, Kostas Perrikos, entrusted study of the problem and execution of the attack to the organization's demolition crew. This crew consisted of Antonis Mitilinaios, a telephone company technician; Nicos Mourtos, a technician; Spiros Galatis, Takis Mihailidis, Spiros Stanotas, and Nicos Lazaris, university students; Petros Lameras, a coffee shop owner; and Mrs. Julia Bilbas.

The "target" was the four-story stone building mentioned above which was in the heart of Athens, barely 100 meters from Omonia Square. There were shops on the first floor. Between the first and second floors was a mezzanine level with a side entrance on Gladstonos Street. This level contained law offices, tailors' shops, a dentist's office, and other offices. The ESPO offices were on the second and third floors, served by the main entrance on Patision Street. An office of the GFP (*Geheime Feld Polizei*, the German Field Police) was on the fourth floor.

Antonis Mitilinaios and Spiros Galatis devised a comprehensive plan of action after repeated checks inside and outside the building. The final plan decided upon by the administration was as follows.

The operation would be carried out on a Sunday morning for two reasons. (1) The shops and offices would be closed, thus avoiding casualties among the innocent occupants. (2) Every Sunday between 9 and 11 AM, the ESPO administrators held a regular weekly meeting with their members. Of course, the operation could have taken place at night, which would have been easier, but then the guilty members of ESPO who had to be punished would escape. The building would be blown up using a "handmade" bomb made from 10 kilograms of dynamite. It would have a slow-burning fuse calculated to detonate in about six minutes. A noteworthy advantage to attacking on a Sunday morning is the impression it would make on the population.

How the bomb would get into the building and where it would be placed tormented Mitilinaios and Galatis. ESPO's entrance on Patision Street was guarded and each visitor had to show his identity card. The guards were extremely vigilant, because just one month earlier a detachment of the PEAN demolition crew consisting of Mitilinaios, Mihailidis, and Mourtos had blown up the offices of OEDE, a similar traitorous organization at 7 Katakouzinou Street.

BOMB PLANK

For these reasons, the other entrance was favored. In other words, the bomb would be brought in through the Gladstonos Street entrance and placed on the ceiling of the mezzanine level, just under ESPO's offices on the second floor. On this mezzanine level, at the end of a dark hall and outside the dentist's office, there was a corner with a ledge near the ceiling, 20 centimeters deep. We would place our bomb on that ledge and hold it in place with a plank wedged diagonally between it and the floor. Thus the bomb's explosive wave would have a direct impact on a triple support.

The operation was scheduled for September 20, 1942. The team's meeting place was Kaniggos Square at 9:00 AM.

At 8:00 that morning, Mitilinaios and Julia Bilbas receive the bomb on a side road off Kaniggos Street. It is inside a basket and covered with green vegetables.

A first reconnaissance is made. Near the mezzanine entrance on Gladstonos Street, a fisherman is secretly selling his wares on the black market. One of the law offices is open and four people are having a discussion inside. The ESPO offices are packed with followers.

Mitilinaios reports to Perrikos. They decide to wait for the four people to depart the law office so that they will not be sacrificed needlessly. Every so often, someone checks on them. We wait an irritating two-and-a-half hours. Two-and-a-half hours holding a 10 kilogram bomb, revolvers at the ready, in the center of Athens, to spare the lives of four innocent people.

By 11:30, however, we see the ESPO meeting coming to an end and the traitors about to leave. There is no time left. Perrikos orders the operation to proceed. Mihailidis's cover team of Mourtos, Lazaris, Lameras, and Stanotas take their places around the Gladstonos Street entrance to cover the operation and the retreat with their revolvers.

Perrikos had set up his headquarters in the confection shop "Astoria" across the street. Julia Bilbas starts out, carrying the bomb in its basket covered with green vegetables. Mitilinaios and Galatis approach from the opposite direction. Acting completely normally, exactly as planned, Bilbas hands them the bomb. At the same time, Lazaris returns from the last inspection of the mezzanine level. At that very moment, God intervenes and the four in the law office who were unwittingly causing the delay leave the building.

Mitilinaios and Galatis ascend with the basket containing the bomb. They proceed to the end of the dark hall, remove the bomb, and carefully put it in its place. The escape route is open and covered by the others. It is a few minutes before noon.

Mitilinaios lights the fuse. The two of them calmly descend the stairs, come out, and head toward the Astoria where they find Perrikos and Bilbas. The cover team withdraws as well. The fuse is burning. Mitilinaios and Perrikos look at their watches.

12:03 PM, September 20, 1942. A loud, muffled noise is followed by a deafening explosion, an intense vibration, and a dense cloud of black smoke. The confusion and panic are so great that the Germans sound the sirens, thinking it's an air raid.

The explosion buried 29 members of ESPO, 43 German officers and soldiers of the GFP, and one passing Greek priest in the ruins and fire that ensued. It also wounded 27 members of ESPO, five German soldiers, and eleven Greek citizens who, by chance, were passing by. The leader of ESPO was blinded, and he succumbed to burns a few days later.

The building's collapse destroyed telephone and electric wiring. The area was blockaded, and pedestrians and vehicles were prohibited from approaching for ten days. The fire department was kept busy for two days. It took five days to retrieve all the dead from the ruins.

This sabotage was characterized by the London and Moscow radio stations as the greatest in an occupied country up to that point. The result was the immediate end to even idle talk about the dispatch of Greek volunteers, either as soldiers for the eastern front or as workers in Germany. ESPO disbanded. No traitorous organization ever appeared again.

It is important to mention here that Perrikos's PEAN paid a heavy toll of blood for this sabotage.

On January 7, 1943, Ioannis Katevatis, Dimitrios Lois, Athanasios Scouras, and Dionysios Papadopoulos were executed as hostages even though they had previously been discharged after enormous efforts on their behalf.

Julia Bilbas was executed in Germany. Takis Mihailidis reported that she was beheaded with an axe.

Spiros Galatis suffered the frightful hardships of the German concentration camps and died soon after the liberation.

Nicos Lazaris was killed by ELAS members in December 1944.

I will speak later about Perrikos's execution on February 4.

Takis Mihailidis's article includes two more noteworthy points.

(1) Two days after the ESPO explosion, EAM circulated a proclamation renouncing the act, stating that it was in opposition to the popular interest and a provocation similar to the arson of the Reichstag. Abroad, they claimed that EAM itself had carried out the sabotage (*The Actions of EAM in Greece*, London edition, 1943).

(2) Not one distinction of any sort was granted to any of the executed members of PEAN!

❋　❋　❋

October 28, 1942. Athenian individuals and organizations had been preparing for weeks to celebrate the day Greece answered the aggression of two all-powerful empires with proud defiance. This was the day Greeks decisively set out to die defending their borders and succeeded in utterly humiliating the army of Mussolini. Six months later they stunned the hordes of Hitler, who had decided to add his overwhelming strength to capture the little stronghold Greece.

The occupation authorities tried to act in time to prevent this national celebration and the demonstration we were preparing for them. All troops in Athens were put on high alert from the eve of the appointed day. Everywhere there were tanks and military attack units, especially in central and crucial locations. The Italians stationed their cavalry at Sintagma Square. The clash that was brewing fanned the fires of our enthusiasm.

I decided to try to get a complete picture of the celebration so that I could describe it in a special telegram that evening.

Early that morning, I dressed myself with particular care. My pants had a fresh crease and my well-ironed gabardine coat looked like new. My shoes were well shined. My calm demeanor and impeccable appearance gave me the look of anything but an enraged revolutionary. That's how I proceeded toward the water pump truck that was headed for the crowd on Kaniggos Square. The German who was operating it moved the hose so that he wouldn't soak such an elegant gentleman. By excusing myself politely, I also got past the belt of German soldiers that had formed behind the Technical University. There I saw the armored vehicles that were waiting on the side streets. Undisturbed, I found myself at Areos Field and at the Cathedral, at Sintagma Square and at the Tomb of the Unknown Soldier. I walked among the Germans' machine guns and the Italians' horses like a peaceful person who had lost his way. But all the while I was fighting the inner voice telling me to run, to scream, to strike.

And I saw. I saw the statues of our national heroes crowned at Areos Field. I saw the Germans' tanks and armored vehicles and I heard them echoing like thunder under the downpour of the stones the Greeks rained on them. I saw the Italian cavalry at Sintagma Square charge a group of invalids and their nurses as they walked in pairs holding laurel wreaths. Manhandled and beaten up, this group still managed to reach the Tomb of the Unknown Soldier and place their wreaths there. All of Athens resounded with patriotic songs. Everywhere there were gatherings with flags, flowers, and laurel. Treetops were decorated with the Greek colors. The walls were painted with patriotic proclamations and slogans. I saw students on their knees in the University courtyard, singing the National Anthem while Italian carabineers attacked. I then saw these same students charge through the enemy ranks and crown the statues of Rigas Feraios and the Patriarch Gregory. I saw people fall outside the Cathedral, hit by German machine gunfire. I saw laurels and candles placed where the soil was stained with the blood of those who fell.

My hand was still shaking as I wrote the telegram that evening, the only one we sent in our nightly broadcast. The Allies answered the following evening with words filled with admiration and wonder, and we heard descriptions of that unforgettable October 28th from the radio stations in London and Cairo.

These open, public demonstrations gave the oppressed an outlet for their need to release anger and show national pride, even at the risk of their lives.

Parallel to the mass demonstrations were the ones by intellectuals and artists, our creative people. The bold cry of protest was a vital need for them as well, and they expressed it publicly by signing their works with their own names. This was an open resistance without any kind of cover. It brought its prime movers face-to-face with the conqueror. I relate here much of the struggle-filled offering I experienced first-hand, especially works by my friends whose creation I witnessed personally.

Writing these lines, I have next to me one of the more valuable relics in my book collection, *The Akritika* by Angelos Sikelianos, a collection of ballads about the frontier guards. This is one of 100 copies handwritten by Spiros Vasiliou in late 1942 and enriched by him with beautiful illustrations.

The book contains five long poems and an equal number of black and white, NeoHellenic woodcuts in the Byzantine style. (The first of these is on the cover of this book.) There are ten big quadruple-sized pages in a cardboard cover. The titles of the poems, the first letters of the stanzas, and the decorative vignettes at the end of every poem are red. Inside the front cover it says: "100 numbered copies of *The Akritika* were written by hand and each was signed by the poet." It also says: "The woodcuts were carved by painter Spiros Vasiliou." And at the bottom is added: "Written for Rigas Rigopoulos." On the facing page is the signature: "Angelos Sikelianos."

Every time I hold this relic in my hands, I feel the same pulsations as when I first saw it. It is a gift that these two spiritual master craftsmen, with phenomenal daring, gave to Art and to Greece.

In his first poem, "Styx's Oath," Sikelianos speaks with dead warriors about redemption:

> *... until, while dancing the Kleftiko [1] and the Sirto [2] deep*
> *within herself,*
> *at one moment, you burst her fetters*
> *in just one instance of delight,*
> *Your heartbeat,*
> *in just one pulse of homecoming, your dance,*
> *the eternal dance of Greece.*

In the second poem, "Unwritten," Sikelianos raises faith in Justice and hope in the Eternal in spite of the tragedy that encircles us. This Dionysian, but also deeply Christian, poet raises an anguished prayer to Jesus in the hour of disaster.

> *Give to me too, Lord ...*
> *... give me*
> *for one moment, Your holy serenity,*
> *so that I can stop, unruffled, among*
> *the rotting carcasses...*
> *so that something can suddenly shine deep inside me, ...*
> *A reflection of the Eternal, but with*
> *the harsh lightning and hope of Justice!*

The wonderful "Hellenic Funeral Supper" is an appeal to Dionysus, the most ancient attendant of exaltation. The poet addresses his companions at an ancient Greek table with the souls of the dead fluttering around. Holding his goblet like a chalice, he excites all those around him and finishes with a tremendous appeal.

---

[1]Kleftiko: A dance of the klephts, mountain dwellers who fought the Turks.
[2]Sirto: A traditional Greek circle dance.

O Dionysus — Hades's holy attendant,
support our hearts with Your black wine of pain,
strengthen them, keep them untouched,
for that moment when suddenly Your cry,
Your earthquake-like roar, will raise us with the dead,
To a sacred attack!

Written during a Christmas vigil in 1941, the fourth poem, "Dionysus in the Cradle" is an amazing example of Sikelianic Helleno-Christian Dionysism.

Night — oh Great one, night mother among the nights of
Centuries,
Night-cradle of the Titan infants ...
can it be that a child is born again tonight,
the God of all Ages?

   Yet, oh mother Night ...
I hear the howling of wolves filling You,
mournful, drawn-out, shrieks, I hear
great fast packs of wolves passing by
... but where are the guards
who keep watch at the sacred borders, to defend
the holy infant from the wolves? Tell us, where are they?

In the last poem of the *Akritika,* "Solon's Apology," Angelos Sikelianos identifies with Solon, who once pretended to be insane to incite Athenians into reseizing Salamis.

... And when I saw around me
the crowd of Athens
I screamed, "Salamis,
you hear me, await,
Onward, let us rescue her
and she is ours again,
Lads, the struggle is small
but the victory is sacred!"

As far as I know, this was the first time in the history of Greece and perhaps the entire world that a leading poet collaborated with a leading painter to confront their country's conqueror face to face, defying his omnipotence and pouring out the beatings of their hearts to their enslaved brethren.

In addition to the *Akritika,* Spiros Vasiliou worked tirelessly and circulated a large number of illustrated patriotic articles in a big, open, quadruple-sized format. Each had an illustration drawn with tempera on the left, and an article written with India ink on the right. I have many of these "folios," each containing powerful and inspirational compositions that bring to life excerpts from Solomos ("Women of Messolonghi"), Makryiannis ("The Song of Makriyiannis" and "The Death of Goura"), A. Antoniadis ("Kritiis"), and many more traditional ones: "Lamentation of Handakas," "Rise, Sun," "Kleftiko 1942," and "The Cretan:"

... and the hope of freedom shook my whole being,
and I yelled, oh divine and blood-soaked Homeland.

With skill, certainty, and showy Greek tradition in his brush-strokes, reconciling classic style with modern fashion, Vasiliou captured on paper not only his pain and rage, but also his faith and boundless optimism. He worked as quickly as he could to offer as much as he could, and always signed his combative works, carefree, at the bottom of the page.

❋   ❋   ❋

On November 16, 1942, at the Strait of Kafirea, a Greek submarine attacked a convoy whose formation, departure, and course had been reported by our organization. However, our submarine was then destroyed by a German warship with depth charges.

Our Harbor Division sent us this news, which they had directly from the German authorities. They also told us that an enemy ship had been sunk the same day. They told us its name, but I no longer remember it.

Later, we learned that the Greek submarine was the *Triton*. The convoy consisted of a huge tanker, the *Celeno*, and a 9,000 ton cargo-vessel, the *Alba Julia*, escorted by one German destroyer and two smaller patrol boats.

After a fierce fight, the commander of the *Triton*, Lieutenant E. Kontogiannis, found himself a German prisoner. After liberation, he reported that he had torpedoed and (according to his information) hit the cargo-vessel *Alba Julia*. In official German reports there is no mention of any loss of their vessels. We concluded that if the *Triton* did sink an enemy ship that day, it must have been the tanker *Celeno*, for two reasons. (1) We had transmitted information about the departure and course of the convoy the *Triton* had met. (2) The *Celeno* is listed among the 55 ships that the leader of our harbor division, Manolis Koutsoudakis, reported had been sunk after we transmitted information on them. In addition, the *Alba Julia* is not mentioned in any of Koutsoudakis's reports.

That day is vividly etched in my memory. I remember how Mitsos Rediadis appeared at the Bank early that morning to give me the still unconfirmed news that one of our submarines had been hit by a German patrol boat. I asked to leave the Bank immediately so we could verify the details and send a telegraph message during the special extra listening time that the Allies had allocated to our wireless set. I even remember quarreling with my department head because I was leaving my work unfinished and left without his approval. I also remember how that same night, as we did so many other times, we cheered and celebrated the destruction of an enemy ship. At the same time, however, our spirits were sorrowful, because by then we had verified the sinking of our own ship and the loss of so many of our men.

The officers and men of the *Triton* were true heroes. The Germans themselves reported that these men had continued their attack even when their submarine was half-destroyed by depth charges. Choking from chlorine fumes, they finally surfaced not to raise a white flag, but to continue assaulting the enemy with cannon fire, hand grenades, and pistols. They continued to fight until most of them had been swept away by enemy fire and their own ship, which had been rammed twice and was engulfed in flames, began sinking out from under them. My friend, Lieutenant Christos Solliotis, fell into German hands along with the submarine's commander, Lieutenant Kontogiannis. Solliotis risked going down with the ship to prevent it from being seized by the enemy. Working amidst the chlorine fumes, he made maneuvers designed to intentionally accelerate its sinking. He was pulled from the sea as he was swimming over to save two wounded crew members.

* * *

On November 25, EDES and ELAS partisans under the command of General Napoleon Zervas, working with British saboteurs, blew up the bridge at Gorgopotamos, northwest of Athens. The news spread like wildfire and was published in the secret press. The Greeks celebrated and Churchill characterized the deed as "the most important sabotage in Europe." Rommel's Africa Corps had to go six weeks without the valuable supplies that needed to cross that bridge.[3]

This was followed by more sabotage to rail lines. These events compelled the Germans and Italians to initiate the "cage" system, in which each engine pushed a cage car in front of it filled with Greeks who had simply been picked at random to serve as human shields. In the event of sabotage, these people were doomed. They would be blown up first, and if they didn't die from the initial explosion they would be shot on the spot.

* * *

In September 1942, Major Yiannis Tsigantes arrived in Athens by order of the Allies. We learned of his arrival from friends and acquaintances who saw him. We worried for him. Tsigantes was a dashing man who fought the secret struggle in the old tradition of a bold Greek officer who doesn't hide, doesn't take cover, and doesn't fight on his belly behind a mound. Instead he charges the enemy, sword in hand, using his passion to inspire others to follow him into the attack.

This was the Tsigantes whose arrival in Athens was known even to the rocks. This was the Tsigantes who walked among Germans and Italians as if he was in his own house, enjoying the contempt he showed them and the danger he faced. Thus he went on until one day in January when the Italians invaded his bachelor pad on Patision Street. He was betrayed, so they say, by the jealousy of a woman.

Tsigantes was stout-hearted even in death. He probably could have escaped while the Italians were checking other apartments in the building, but he stayed to burn his records so that names and secrets wouldn't fall into enemy hands. Only when the Italians entered his apartment and smelled the burning paper did he try to escape, shooting his way out. But it was too late. He killed two Italians on the spot and wounded a third who died shortly thereafter at a hospital. He wounded two others less severely, yet he didn't succeed in escaping. No one had the courage to face him head-on, but a wounded Italian hit him from behind. They took him into custody, badly wounded, and interrogated him for four torturous hours. He breathed his last breath at 5:30 that same evening, January 14, 1943. The enemy wasn't able to get even a single word out of him.

We learned these shocking details from our friends who published the secret newspaper *Ellinikon Aima* (Greek Blood) and who had met personally with Tsigantes. A few days later, in the edition of February 1, 1943, the story was published in greater detail. At least four people in our organization had predicted such an end. We discussed it many times both before and after the event, trying to draw conclusions and extract lessons to improve our own tactics and security system.

---

[3]This is what we knew at that time. We now know that this sabotage was organized by a special mission of British officers (code-named the "Harling Mission"), which had much broader activities in occupied Greece in collaboration with the Greek Resistance.

But how Tsigantes's heroic example stirred the people's will to fight! Athens was turned upside down. Once again the walls filled with fighting slogans. Those who hadn't taken part in the resistance up to that point felt badly. Everyone wanted to feel worthy of the man who had sacrificed his own life for the cause and died in action.

* * *

This was indeed a beautiful time. Despite the fact that Communism played its frightful game behind a patriotic mask, the struggle took on a grandiose air. The national organizations began to coordinate their efforts, putting aside their secondary disagreements.

In June 1942, the first edition of *Eleftheri Skepsi* (Free Thought) appeared. This was the secret newspaper of *Ethniko Komitato* (National Revolutionary Committee). The main article on its front page, entitled "Our Struggle," read:

... As we make a clear struggle at this time only for liberation, we also look beyond the end of the struggle to our National Freedom. This "beyond" is not the same as what, unfortunately, some blind and sordid Greeks desire. They seek to occupy the country's government, ignoring the current national tragedy. They work dishonorably and criminally, splitting the nation and undermining its unity by seeking signatures on petitions for the future they foresee. ... They seek the proclamation of a plebiscite and elections to establish party dominance immediately after the truce and before PEACE is signed.

Our vision of "beyond" is different! It is the time when bells will sound proclaiming the truce. On that day we Greeks, united as one, standing shoulder to shoulder, MUST start another great struggle leading to the complete realization of our Great National Ideals." ...

With these combative words, Nicos Grigoriadis, George Vichos, Yiannis Zacharakis, and our other friends in *Ethniko Komitato* inaugurated their participation in the struggle of the secret press to make our people understand that only "united as one" would we see the realization of our dreams for our nation.

The other secret newspaper with which we were on friendly terms, the more journalistically complete Ellinikon Aima (Greek Blood), was published twice a month. In its fourth edition, published on July 20, 1942, and under the heading "United Towards Victory," *Ellinikon Aima* presented its position:

"Ellinikon Aima" does not represent any political party, movement, or particular policy. It developed out of the expressed or hidden desires of all enslaved Greeks everywhere. It is not aligned with, nor does it reject, anyone — except traitors. ...

"Ellinikon Aima" believes that until this war is brought to an end, any thought concerning the future is superfluous. It believes that until the last barbarian no longer walks our sacred ground, our minds and thoughts must focus only on how to get rid of him. Everything else is insignificant detail which must not, under any circumstances, distract our attention from our one and only goal: Victory.

Spiros Vasiliou: Karaïskakis's Death
(from the October 1, 1942, issue of Nea Estia*)*

> *Certainly, "Ellinikon Aima" could participate in the fruitless*
> *paper war being waged between national newspapers over issues*
> *of regime and politics and even social matters. All of these are, of*
> *course, interesting in their own way, but this interest is very lim-*
> *ited under our current conditions. Today, the struggle is national,*
> *and only national. Let us win. Let us liberate our country. We will*
> *sort out the rest among ourselves." ...*

The article ended with these lines from Solomos:

> *... would that foreign Nations*
> *do not speak their thoughts about us*
> *knowing that they hate each other*
> *freedom does not suit them!* [4]

This article agreed completely with my personal beliefs and the course that I had always followed. Excited by reading it, I remember how I had hurried to congratulate my friends Dinos and Spiros Vovolinis and Rikos Piniatoglou.

---

[4]Verses from Hymn to Freedom, whose first few verses were set to music and adopted as the Greek National Anthem.

　　　　✳　　✳　　✳

The secret press was one of the two public outlets for the spiritual combativeness of that time. The second was open action. Oblivious to the consequences, our intellectuals recklessly slipped under the net of censorship and published articles and illustrations of a patriotic nature. Like the secret press, this type of struggle, though not directly combative, helped sustain continuous agitation by the Greek public. It broadened and fortified the general resistance to the point that its contribution to the struggle became truly invaluable.

I experienced this peculiar battle of our intellectuals, not only through personal contact with my friends, but also through its concentrated outpouring in the pages of Petros Haris's literary magazine, *Nea Estia* (New Hestia). It was not only admirable that Petros Haris dared, but even more so that he actually succeeded in printing, right under the noses of the German censors, articles, poems, and illustrations that throbbed with the desire for freedom, the exaltation of the struggle, faith, and optimism.

Nea Estia filled the role of the resistance press. It provided a platform for symbols of liberation. It boldly and openly stirred the enslaved Greeks' emotions. The courage of the publishers and the stirring works signed by eminent intellectuals and artists captivated and enthralled the literary public.

Petros Haris gave the signal for this spiritual crusade just four days after the Germans entered Athens. The main article in the May 1, 1941 issue of *Nea Estia* began with these inspired words:

> *A chapter of Greek history has closed. But the new one that has opened is not completely sunken in the dark, even though it formed under the heavy shadow of national disaster, ruins, and grief the likes of which Greece has not seen or felt for more than 100 years. In this much-tortured land, not only is there the abundant light that makes the ruins look more bare and deplorable. There is also another light, imprisoned in personal worlds, in consciences, in anguish, in curiosities, in bottomless thoughts, in liberation visions. It is precisely this light that must fall on the new chapter of Greek history. ...*

All of Athens was talking about *Nea Estia*'s signals and the "liberation visions" of its contributors. The Germans only minimally understood this wonderful work. It seems that the old German spirit had been totally extinguished by their military machine.

As you turned to the second page in every issue of *Nea Estia*, you would always find a woodcut at the left by the omnipresent Spiros Vasiliou. Its clear-cut Hellenic style alone was enough to quicken your patriotic pulse. Underneath each piece was a folk verse or other well-known text that clarified its meaning.

We utterly marveled at these illustrations, relished the words, and scrutinized them to identify their hidden meanings. Most of the time those meanings were completely obvious. Fearlessly, Vasiliou delivered all types of messages that touched and electrified us.

On New Year's Day, 1942, under an illustration of a goatherd with his flute and goats, but also with his *kariofili*[5] and an unsheathed sword, this folk verse appeared:

> *Would that I were in May a shepherd, in August a vineyard guard, and in the heart of winter a wine seller.*
> *But it would be even better if I would be an Armatolos in the*

mountains and a Klepht[6] in the plains.

From then on, every issue contained a symbolically combative illustration with an explanatory verse.

In the issue of October 1, 1942, Vasiliou referred to an historic appeal for cooperation and harmony. In a wonderful cyclical composition he depicts Karaïskakis,[7] who seems to have just died. His companions surround him and are lifting him up. A priest stands nearby. (See the reproduction above.) Underneath was Makriyiannis's[8] simple description:

> Then, in a short while, I learn that Karaïskakis was hit.
> I go over there, we gather, we watch ...
> In between jokes, he tells us,

"I am dying, but you must live in harmony and defend the homeland."

In the issue of January 15, 1943, Spiros Vasiliou advised us to pound the enemy without hesitation with a verse from a Greek proverb:

> In the month of February, prune
> and do not consult the moon.

This is what the innocent couplet says. The illustration above it has all the appropriate symbols. It shows a night dimly illuminated by a pallid new moon. On the flat roof of a little peasant house, a woman keeps watch all around while the man below holds a knife and ... prunes.

On the third page of *Nea Estia*, to the right of the woodcut, you would always find a poem. Many times it was innocent, but other times it was full of patriotic messages and slogans. On New Year's Day 1942, we found the "Prayer to the Guardian Angel" by Kostas Ouranis and we indeed made it our prayer.

> ... Angel, with the herbs and with the infinite ways
> let us wander in magical and untrodden places,
> may we fool witches, and overcome obstacles.
> Dragons with fiery tongues may we lance,
> may we open haunted palaces without keys
> fighting, alone, against brave armies ...

We drank of those verses and felt ready to overcome all "obstacles," to lance thousands of "dragons" and, "fighting alone," to throw ourselves on all the "armies" of the world.

June 1, 1942, brought new shocks with a dramatic poem by Konstantinos Tsatsos, "Earth and the Tree."

> It lashes,
> the north wind of January,
> with his gray wings
> the lone tree
> in the mountain's saddle...

---

[5]*Kariofili*: a rifle used by the Greeks during the Turkish occupation and the revolution for liberation in 1821.

[6]*Armatolos and Klephts*: two bands of rebels of the same origin fighting the Turks during the entire Turkish occupation. The armatolos were klephts the Turks tried to attract and neutralize by granting them police duties. They never stopped collaborating with the klephts and openly joined them in the revolution.

[7]Karaiskakis: A leading figur in the Greek revolution against the Turks.

[8]Makriyiannis: Another leader of the same revolution, who wrote his memoirs.

The Tree's branches are dry and petrified. Its bushy, sweet-smelling foliage has scattered in the mud. The Tree seems dead. But it continues to stand erect...

Hard like spite,
there, before the dark sky...

And suddenly "in a respite from the cosmic rage," the Tree speaks to the Earth:

My beloved
as long as You are there, ...
I am a solid body. ...
As long as You are there,
my great bosom
that does not end,
let all the eras pass;
as long as you exist, the hidden
and inexhaustible Source,
everything blooms for me
and everything awaits me.

The next day, I went to Kostas Tsatso's house to see him and to express all the emotion that his verses aroused in me. I didn't know what secret role he had in the resistance. But I knew that the Germans had removed him from his University professorship due to his intense national activities, and had only canceled his arrest later to avoid commotion from students who worshipped him. I saw now that Tsatsos hadn't let up, but continued to provoke the enemy.

The August 15, 1942, issue published *Aristodimos* by Panagis Lekatsas. This is a story of the ancient Spartan who was the only one of Leonidas's 300 men to survive the battle of Thermopylae and return to Sparta. The first person he meets is his mother, who renounces him:

The mother you first met at the fountain
did not give you water. "My son," she said,
"if I had a son, he would have honored me
as my father honored his mother...
Unwavering is the great law that
generations supported with rivers of blood:
"Where you are appointed, you shall stay, and there is no road
for you to return to Sparta, other than
the one of victory, or the one of death...

But Herodotus, from whom Lekatsas got the idea for this poem, after mentioning the cowardice of Aristodimos at Thermopylae and also recalling that "returning to Sparta he was disgraced and dishonored," adds, "But the same man, in the Battle at Plataies, redeemed the blame ... and became the best."

Thus Panagis Lekatsas, in concluding his wonderful poem, urges all those left behind who still have not fought for the homeland to repay their debts like the ancient Spartan:

But you are of the Spartan stock;
the obligation of your shame will
awaken your first bravery...
Come along and tell your mate
to bring your blind steps
to the line of the defenders
where you shall straighten,

> *and eagle-like in your shining armor,*
> *surrounded by the great Sun,*
> *bang on the Earth, pinned at the chest*
> *and cry out to Sparta "I am yours."*

On the morning of January 27, 1943, the poet Miltiadis Malakasis died. Over his grave, Angelos Sikelianos recited a farewell full of love and daring. His eulogy was published in the February 1st issue of *Nea Estia*. "*Milto, as you leave for the world below,*" Sikelianos yelled ...

> *With a branch of an almond tree in your hand,*
> *you go to Hades to announce the Resurrection! ...*
> *With a branch of an almond tree in your hand,*
> *Oh great Lyrist, announce also for us a victory,*
> *You, who in Your deep-voiced song*
> *did not separate beauty from fighting for freedom!*

The March 1, 1943, issue of *Nea Estia* announced, "Greeks have mourned heavily since February 27. KOSTIS PALAMAS HAS DIED.[9] The next morning the Greek consciousness surrounded his coffin and became the heartbeat of the nation."

The day of Palamas's funeral was a day of national emotion. The anonymous masses mourned him with the same feeling as our literary and artistic nobility. With equal exaltation, thousands of men, women, and children, youths and elders followed his coffin, identifying the free soul of the poet with the spirit of their own freedom.

At the end of the funeral, standing over the coffin at the apex of emotion, Angelos Sikelianos raised his epic voice above the general lamentation once again.

> *Trumpets, sound! ... Bells, thunder,*
> *shake the whole country, from one end to the other...*
> *Drums of war, moan! ... Terrific flags of Freedom,*
> *unfold yourselves in the air!*

His fervent voice thundered and shook the church dome. The pounding of his fist on the coffin could be heard all around as he yelled:

> *On this coffin stands Greece! If we raise a mountain of*
> *laurels*
> *to the heights of Pilio and Ossa,[10] if we built it up to sev-*
> *enth heaven,*
> *whom would it cover? If only my tongue could name him!*

Step by step, Angelos Sikelianos raised the verse to the pantheon of eternity where "Orpheus, Heraclitus, Aeschylus, and Solomos accept the sacred, triumphant soul." Ending, he repeated his initial verse, transformed into a stirring signal for a general charge toward liberation:

> *Trumpets, sound! ... Bells, thunder,*
> *shake the whole country, from one end to the other...*
> *Triumphal hymn, moan! ... Terrific flags of Freedom,*
> *unfold yourselves in the air!*

The people lifted the coffin up high and carried it to the open grave waiting to

---

[9]One of the greatest Greek poets.
[10]Mountains in northern Greece.

accept the venerated remains.

A German officer proceeded to lay down a wreath on behalf of the conquerors. Terrible swearing from Marika Kotopouli, our renowned tragic actress, answered this unacceptable gesture.

And then, led by Giorgos Katsimbalis, a friend and spiritual supporter of the poet, a thousand voices shook the calm grove of the dead, raised as one in our National Anthem.

OUR LAST DEEDS FROM NEW YEAR'S TO EASTER

In the first few months of 1943, the months that preceded our discovery and destruction, Service 5-16-5 acquired a fast and steady pace within the general tension.

We were pretty well-organized, and each of us had found the way to coordinate with the others. The entire network was functioning like a well-oiled machine. All divisions were working intensively.

All kinds of information reached us from all parts of Greece, after it had passed through several layers of control. This expansion into new areas occurred automatically, mainly through the efforts of the Harbor Division and their more distant informants. The central administration was not involved, except to give instructions of a general nature, orders for specific investigations, or answers to questions.

From Thessaloniki we regularly received information on the movements of military units and ships. From harbors like Patra, Volos, Kavala, Rodos, and Hania, we received notes and sketches on shipments, departures, fortification projects, mine laying and anything else that could be considered interesting.

Our caïques sailed almost regularly to and from the shores of Tsesme (Turkey) and our wireless set was in full operation, but we still didn't have the capacity to transmit all of this information.

I sent a message to our liaison, Nicos Menegatos, who regularly went to Turkey with the caïques, to ask for a second wireless set from the Allied service. Paliatseas would provide us with a second wireless set operator.

Our divisions, beside reporting general observations and matters within their jurisdiction, which was by now routine, delved deeper and deeper into the Germans' most tightly kept secrets. Stavros Vrachnos's division warned us of the concrete ships the Germans were building in strict secrecy in a forbidden area of Perama (near Piraeus), in an attempt to overcome the serious lack of metals that plagued them. Koutsoudakis's and Bachas's harbor people charted the secret channels that allowed safe passage through the Germans' minefields.

Alexander Kairis, from his confidential archives, got us the code symbols that the German ships and airplanes used to recognize each other by day and night.

The way we transferred documents from the confidential archives to be photographed improved considerably.

In the beginning, as I described previously, Alexander Kairis would first contact Popi Sakelaridis via telephone and would then set out to carry the documents from the beginning of Panepistimiou Avenue, next to the Athenian Club, to Ioannou Drosopoulou Street, further up from Agamon Square. In other words, the round trip from his office was about six kilometers, and often he had to walk because there was no public transportation.

Most of the time, I then had to bring the documents to my house and bring them back to Popi's later, because other people were often at her house, preventing us from photographing there. So quite often Kairis would just barely make it back to his office in time. Our new method of photographing the documents was simpler and much faster.

The Germans left for lunch at 1 o'clock. Alexander would take the documents, which he had often pre-selected, to the Bank of Greece on the next block. Alexander had free access to the Bank at any time as part of his official duties, so he could justify his presence for any of a thousand reasons.

At that time the second floor of the Bank building joined the back of an old house that faced Stadiou Street. A zigzagged corridor and narrow stairs led from the main building to the Health Department and other minor services.

There was a toilet there, with its tank mounted high up the wall and a chain to flush it. Behind the tank was a cavity in the wall, an excellent hiding place completely unseen to the eye. It could only be reached by sliding a hand between the tank and the low ceiling.

I found this hiding place by chance. Here I hid a small revolver I carried in certain situations or gave to other members of our service.

Alexander placed the documents there and then walked around the Bank doing his work or chatting with acquaintances and friends. Sometimes he would pass by my desk, and sometimes he wouldn't. But when he had papers to be photographed, he would pass by a certain column in the huge hall, scratch his ear, and I would confirm that I had seen him by straightening my tie.

In those times I was free to leave the Bank at any time, because I represented the Bank of Greece in other banks to authorize withdrawals from blocked deposits. So when Alexander signaled me I would immediately take the documents from the hiding place and go to my house to photograph them. I would also take my pistol. Under no circumstances could these documents be allowed to fall into the hands of the Germans, as that would surely spell Alexander's end.

The trip to 67 September 3rd Street was brief enough. I returned the documents to their hiding place well before 2:30 when the Bank personnel would leave. Each time I burned with anxiety until I got a chance to read them. But I would only develop the film later, in secret even from my family, groping with the chemicals in our darkened bathroom.

Many times Alexander left the Bank at 2:30 with the regular workers and with the documents in his pocket. Calmly, and with the most innocent look in the world, he would leisurely go to eat and return the documents to their place before 4:00 that afternoon.

During one such transfer I had a really close call which actually turned out to be quite cute in the end.

As I walked up Patision Street one afternoon — there was no transportation — I ran into my sister Popi, who was also returning home. We walked together and chatted, arm-in-arm. I must have had a strange air about me. I was thinking that I was putting her in danger for no real reason just by having her next to me. She asked if anything was wrong. I told her that I was carrying a pistol and that it would be better if we separated. "It's better if we stay together," she said. "The Germans will think we are a couple and they won't bother us."

We had just crossed Stournara Street across from the Technical University and she had barely completed her sentence when a heavy hand hit me on the shoulder and a German voice seemed to be ordering me with inarticulate babble. "Hey, hey…"

How did God give me the composure not to flinch or to put my hand on the pistol or to make any kind of suspicious movement? I just turned calmly and looked at the German soldier who was holding a cigarette in one hand and a pipe in the other. He was dead drunk.

"*Steck's da hinein* (put it in there)," he told me, showing me his pipe and giving me another push.

I smiled at him. "*Ne Brüderlein*," I responded, "*gut war der Wein?*" ("Eh, little brother, was the wine good?")

He stopped, confused. "*Ich habe geglaubt dass du ein blöder Grieche bist* (I thought you were a bloody Greek.)"

My sister turned white as a sheet, and she only knew about the pistol... I slapped the German on the back amicably.

"Give me your cigarette," I told him, and I put it in his pipe.

"*Ich bin besoffen* (I'm smashed)," he admitted.

We walked on together and I carefully pumped him for information. He told me that he had just arrived from the Russian front with a unit of armored vehicles, the name of the unit to which he belonged, and where his unit had camped and camouflaged themselves. Thus I was able to add some things to my telegram that night.

On Epirus Street, where I wanted to turn to go home, I had a damned difficult time getting rid of him. I had told him that I knew Athens well, and he insisted that I show him a good time. Finally, I convinced him that we should make plans for the next day so that I could bring a second girl with me. With that agreed, we separated forever with enthusiastic handshakes.

A similar incident amused us in the end, but caused us to endure a rather tense 48 hours.

One afternoon, Mitsos Rediadis came to my house all shaken up and told me that an Italian took George Zentelis's identification card the night before in Piraeus.

Zentelis was returning from his meeting with Koutsoudakis, loaded with notes. The Italian stopped him and asked various questions in broken Greek, like where he was coming from, where he was going to, what kind of work he did, etc. He then inspected his identification card and finally kept it.

"Come back here the day after tomorrow at 8 in the evening and I'll give it back you," he said.

"What do you think we should do?" Mitsos asked me. "If he goes to the rendezvous tomorrow night, they might arrest him. If he doesn't go, he will surely become a suspect even if he is not one already."

We considered all of the possibilities. We did not know why the Italian had stopped Zentelis and why he had kept the identification card. If they had followed his moves and considered him a suspect, why didn't they take him to interrogation at their headquarters? Why did they give him two days? Were they going to follow him to see who he contacted after they first tripped him up with the identification incident? In any case, we could not leave him without cover. We had to protect our liaison at all costs.

Finally, we decided that Zentelis should go to the rendezvous but that he should be tailed by a team under Rediadis's leadership that could respond quickly if needed. We drew up a detailed plan. Rediadis was to watch Zentelis as he met with the

Italian. Two others were to loiter on the street watching Rediadis, chatting between themselves.

If there was immediate danger, Zentelis was to run both hands through his hair. Rediadis would then repeat this signal to our men. This would mean "attack." Both would start to run, pretending to chase Rediadis, but would fall with all their might on the Italian and any others with him. This would give Zentelis a chance to run away. If they weren't able to escape themselves, they would explain that they were chasing somebody who owed them money and would beg forgiveness. Rediadis would return immediately to inform me of the outcome.

The next night, from 7:30 on, I paced the house like a caged lion. I couldn't stand still. It was already 10 PM and Mitsos still hadn't shown up. I blamed myself, realizing now that the plan we had put in motion was frightfully dangerous. Finally, the doorbell rang and Mitsos came in, choking with laughter. The more he saw my perplexed look, the more he laughed, walking towards my study and making broad hand gestures that meant, "Where should I begin? We laughed till we cried!" When we had closed ourselves in my study, he turned and looked at me. He uttered a crude word to let me know just what kind of man the Italian really was... Apparently the manly Zentelis suited his amorous tastes!

"You see, the gentleman didn't have the time yesterday, and so he kept the identification card to force the young man to return today. We followed them through parks and squares for over an hour. It took Zentelis a while to understand what the Italian really wanted. He finally succeeded in getting rid of him and came toward me, triumphantly waving his identification card. As an exercise, it wasn't bad. Everything went according to plan. If Zentelis had signaled us, we certainly would have liberated him."

❋   ❋   ❋

February 4, 1943 was a day full of emotion for me. Storms churned inside me from clashes of exaltation and pain. It was the day we were informed of the liberation of Stalingrad. It was also the day Kostas Perrikos was executed. I learned about both almost simultaneously, one from the hidden radio, the other from information acquired by our Service.

People poured into the streets to celebrate the great victory of the Allies. The news spread like wildfire. The entire German 6th Army had been destroyed. 100,000 Germans surrendered and were taken prisoner by the Russians. I found myself outside among happy faces, among people who saw this distant demolition of the enemy as a harbinger of their general collapse and our speedy liberation.

And I swallowed the sobs that welled up in my throat for the loss of my friend, the idealist and the fighter. Three more heroic young men joined him in death, like honorary attendants.

I tried to add the pride of sacrifice to the joy of victory.

Kostas Perrikos was my partner, even though we belonged to different organizations. I had collaborated on his newspaper since its first edition, and he had worked with me on our first transports of information and in so many other matters concerning the common struggle. It was my first personal loss.

I learned that Kostas Perrikos died bravely, just as he had lived. Proud of his deeds and his sacrifice, he expressed his entire bold and patriotic credo in three powerful phrases: "I die as an officer of the Greek Air Force. I have done my duty.

Long live Greece." The firing squad officers saluted him before carrying out the execution.

This unconquerable power which elicited the respect of his enemies is what Kostas Perrikos wanted to bequeath to us, not lamentation. Power that would be transformed inside us into passion for more intense and effective action until the final victory.

So that night we celebrated the first great defeat of the enemy and the last great victory of our friend.

❋   ❋   ❋

The next day at the Bank, still upset by the previous day's news, I had a brisk argument with the head of my division. The result of this clash almost created very serious obstacles to the work of Service 5-16-5 and could have cost me my own personal freedom.

The reasons for the argument and all that followed characterize the position all of us held toward the enemy's wretched Greek collaborators.

The episode started in the Popular Bank, where I went each day as a representative of the Bank of Greece and where I worked for a while with Dimitrios Konstantinou, the Director at the time. This freedom to leave the bank allowed me to spare some time for the work of our organization, something that was particularly important. The two of us, together with a secretary who introduced the cases, constituted a first-level committee that approved or disapproved applications for releasing bound deposits in accordance with the current regulations. When there were issues that exceeded my level of authority, I took the relevant applications back to a second-level committee at the Bank of Greece.

Among the applications that appeared that day was one from a Greek engineer requesting the release of a large sum for the construction of cement bases for German anti-aircraft artillery around Athens. Naturally, the release was mandatory and within the limits of my authority. The Director of the Popular Bank signed his approval and gave it to me to countersign.

I refused. "I will not sign, Mr. Director, for a scum to cooperate with the Germans. I will not countersign the sentencing of Allied airplanes to destruction."

The man, who was no less a patriot than I but much more self-controlled, tried to calm me down and get me to be more reasonable.

"Would that we could reject it," he sighed. "Allow me to give you a bit of advice, as an older man and a friend. Don't create problems that could cause you incalculable harm without achieving anything in return. You know very well that the release will be approved."

"It will be approved, Mr. Director, but without my signature. I will refer the application to the second-level committee."

The Director made some additional attempts to change my mind, but I ended up taking this document with others that actually did concern the second-level committee and handed them all together to my superior at the Bank of Greece.

The Head of the Deposits Division at that time was Christos Staikos, who later became a Director. Much later, when he learned about my activities in those days, he expressed deep regret for unwittingly creating obstacles for me.

On this day, however, as soon as he saw the application that I was to have signed, he returned it to me. When I again refused to sign it he threatened to ask for my removal from the special exterior service, which he did finally accomplish.

Not being free to move around in the mornings anymore was a real blow for me. The time that I could spare for our organization during my uncontrolled absences from the Bank was precious and indispensable.

The Governor of the Bank at that time was naturally a friend of the Germans, but also an old family acquaintance. I thought that no matter what he might do to help his career, he would never betray me.

I decided to play all my cards and ask him for help. After all, I reasoned, being the advantage seeker that he was, he might also want to be on good terms with the Resistance, especially at that time when events had begun to turn in our favor.

Of course, when I appeared in his office, I did not reveal my true activities. I had an underground newspaper with me which I placed before him, telling him that I was involved in its publication and that my morning freedom was necessary for this work.

"I am certain that, as a Greek, you will want to help us," I concluded.

The Governor jumped from his armchair.

"Get this newspaper out of here," he roared. "I manage this Bank and all of this is irrelevant to your work here. See that you do your job properly. I will ignore the rest."

On that day, the war between us began. The Governor threw me into some division on the second floor, a location that hindered my movements even further. I retaliated harshly by instigating and leading strikes and openly opposing him in unionized movements. This provided an outlet for my rage against all enemy collaborators. Either he had to give in or I had to leave from the Bank so that I could continue with my mission.

When Neubacher, Hitler's all-powerful delegate, reached Athens as the Reich's Representative Minister for Greece and found us on strike in the Bank's big hall, he asked that a three-member delegation be nominated.

The strikers demanded my participation, and I found myself among the three representatives. The two others were the President and Vice President of the Employees' Association. We presented ourselves to Neubacher. The Governor and the General Secretary at the time — who shortly thereafter became the Assistant Governor and later Governor of the Bank — were also present at the meeting.

Neubacher spoke first, through an interpreter. "As soon as I got off the plane," he began, "I was informed that there is a revolt in the Bank of Greece against the Authorities of Occupation. I came with the best intentions to work on the economic problems of the Greek people, whom I respect. I am, however, a German patriot. And I am a strong man. I will not hesitate to choke the life out of every type of resistance to the orders of the Reich, just as I have done elsewhere. I order you to return to your work immediately so that I will not be forced to resort to extremely harsh measures."

The President of the Association, Angelos Leousis, answered first, describing the wretched financial situation of the employees, whose wages wouldn't even buy two days' worth of food due to the continuous acute inflation. This, he explained, is what forced them to go on strike.

Truly, drachma prices at that time went from thousands to millions and billions from one day to the next due to the lack of consumer goods and the constant issuing of paper money. There was a soup kitchen for the Bank employees, but most were family men. How could a whole family live off the inadequate supplementary portions and allowances?

The Vice President spoke in the same spirit.

When it was my turn, I spoke like the others through an interpreter. A bad interpreter with stage fright, whose German I corrected purposefully so that Neubacher would realize that I spoke his language very well, but that I preferred to use my own.

I stressed that he was misinformed that the strike is against the Authorities of Occupation. It is against the apathy of the administration toward the living standards of Bank employees. "We thank you," I said, "for your good intentions. If you also prove them in deeds, assuring the employees an acceptable standard of living, this type of strike will not be repeated."

Knowing that the Governor himself had met Neubacher at the airport, I concluded, "As for the Greek who hastened to squeal on his compatriots as soon as you got off the plane, saying that the strike is against the Authorities of Occupation, we are certain that you, as a German patriot who respects the proud Greek people, will not classify this squealer among the Greeks whom you respect, and you will not honor his words with your trust."

These last words, which the interpreter was unsuccessful in translating, were translated, with great pleasure, into good German by the General Secretary — who intervened in the matter and who was eyeing the Governor's position for himself — while the Governor's knees were shaking so terribly he needed to support himself on his desk.

Neubacher listened to the translation attentively. He then turned and fixed his eyes on mine. Perhaps my fortune, too, was being decided in that moment.

"Very well," the German said finally, "I will go down to speak to the employees."

I did not yet know if we had won or lost.

The conclusion of this scene has been described by Elias Venezis, a member of the Academy of Athens, in his book entitled *Chronicle of the Bank of Greece*:

> *Faced with the indomitably brave stand of the personnel on all national issues, even Neubacher, the Reich's financial dictator, was forced to capitulate. He spoke to the gathered employees to promise them and reassure them.*

The employees' existing concerns were thus temporarily settled. But the Governor was furious with me and threatened gods and demons. He threatened to fire me immediately, but he had no authority to do so. He threatened to transfer me to a provincial branch office, and I sent word to him that I would hold him responsible for my personal freedom if they arrested and held me hostage for being a reserve officer, which we knew they often did in the provinces.

The Bank directors and the department heads presented themselves to the administration and stated that if measures were taken against me, that would mean persecution of a representative of the employees' union and trouble would follow.

In the end, the Governor found a maneuver that he thought would save his prestige. On February 23, he notified me of my transfer to the branch office in Larisa and simultaneously granted me a 20-day leave. At the same time, he announced to the employee representatives that he would transfer me back to Athens when my leave was over.

I don't know what kind of ruse was hiding behind this game. In any case, when I received the two documents I notified the administration that I did not ask for leave and that I had no intention to use it, nor did I accept the transfer to Larisa.

So I just stayed in my office, without any consequences. I even left the Bank whenever I wanted with relative freedom. Perhaps, however, this event later enabled the Germans to pick up my trail, because I was already known to them. From then on, I later learned, they characterized me as dangerous and kept their eyes on me. This was my mistake.

* * *

The successes of our organization at that time lifted us to such a point that our natural sorrow from the hardships of slavery was replaced by supreme satisfaction and an excessive feeling of invincibility.

We saw the despots in our land who flaunted their decorated uniforms and stomped their black boots, and we despised them. We felt we had a hold over them and were gnawing at their foundations day by day until the moment we would see their shining military edifice crumble. This feeling of secret superiority that boiled inside us and was difficult to contain gave us self-confidence and audacity.

Thus, when the Allied service telegraphed us to ask whether the Germans had requested that the Italians allocate military divisions to them and the Italians refused, Alexander Kairis opened a dialogue with his chief in the German service. He began by openly criticizing the Germans' oppressive policies in Greece as having no effect other than to intensify the Greeks' reactions and to increase espionage against the Germans.

"Your measures are ill-considered," Alexander said. "The executions don't stop the Greeks, they enrage them. People who could have been your friends do whatever they can to sabotage you and steal your military secrets, which have reached the point of circulating on the streets."

The German was beside himself. He flew into a rage and reacted violently to Kairis's criticism. But Alexander insisted.

"Is it or is it not true that your allies, the Italians, refused to allocate the military divisions you asked them for?"

"Where did you learn that?" roared the German.

"It isn't at all difficult to learn something that has become widely known. I have told you, and I want to prove to you, that your secrets are circulating on the streets. I challenge you to tell me honestly whether this fact, which today is known to all Greeks, was or was not a military secret of yours."

"It was a secret, God damn it," the chief swore, "and I don't know what idiot let it leak. But you will not convince me that if we were more tolerant the Greeks would stop undermining us. We are surrounded by spies and our only defense is to strike your stinking resistance wherever and however we can."

This is how Kairis pried from authoritative lips the verification the Allies were looking for. But the German respected Kairis's "honest devotion" to such a degree that, as we will see, he later appeared in court as a witness for his defense.

* * *

During that time, friends at the German-controlled Athens radio station asked me to give a talk on the *Children's Hour* for middle school-aged children explaining, in simple terms, how to write a poem. I thought that I could perhaps use this opportunity to pass verses with patriotic implications through the censorship, like the ones that enthused the Greek public so much back then.

In a few days, speaking over the microphone about rhyme, meter, and stanzas, I gave some examples using known or improvised verses whose "special" meaning was rather obvious.[1]

To illustrate meter, I read two lines of Solomos's[2] poem *Destruction of Psara*:

> *On the blackened – crest – of Psara*
> *Walking – Glory – alone.*

Then a couplet, full of optimism for a nation destined to live:

> *The boat that has days*
> *Is not frightened by reefs.*

Next, a quatrain, again with a boat metaphor, alluding to those who every so often escaped to freedom:

> *Boat, little boat*
> *With the small white sail,*
> *Won't you take me inside*
> *To sing a sailing song.*

Another quatrain, from a popular war song, clarified the meaning of the previous one:

> *Mother give me a blessing*
> *And let me give you a kiss*
> *For I leave at dawn*
> *And march to fight.*

One more example referred to our boys, whom we awaited to return victorious:

> *The swallows will return*
> *One day in the spring*
> *And the air will be full*
> *Of joy in the branches.*

The last verses implied bad news for those who had invaded our land:

> *And all the best dive*
> *And all the bully boys*
> *But the sea is deep.*
> *Alas for the divers.*

Many who heard this broadcast stopped me on the street to shake my hand, and a lot more called me on the phone. In those days, people got excited about even the slightest act of defiance.

Supportive public reactions like these led me to reveal myself once more on the radio...

I had finished a poem at that time that was somewhat longer than any I had written up to that time. It was a triptych entitled *Spirit and Nature (Ode to the Land of Olympus)*. It was a hymn to the immortality of beauty and spirit, amidst the tempests that struck Greece.

The poem begins with a series of cosmogony images on the summit of Mt. Olympus. This is where Spirit is born, and from where it spreads throughout the

---

[1] In the original Greek, these verses rhyme. They demonstrate several combinations of meter and the structure of stanzas.

[2] Dionysios Solomos(1798-1857). A great Greek poet who wrote he long poem "Hymn to Liberty," of which the first verses were set to music and became the Greek national anthem.

universe. Images of harmony, serenity, beauty and truth follow.

Finally, the frightful tempest breaks…

But the country hides "an immortal germ in the earth." "The rock stands," "the tempests pass,"…

> *And serenity returns*
> *And the Spirit illuminates*
> *Ever deeper*
> *Ever greater.*
> *Eternal symbol*
> *That stands out*
> *In the time's turmoil.*

I really loved this poem. I read it to my family, my companions, and my friends. It brought joy to my father, who by then was near his end. My mother and sisters, who experienced only the darkness of the Occupation without the exaltations of its struggle, felt intense emotion. My close companions showed their enthusiasm in every way imaginable. My great friend, the poet Angelos Sikelianos, often made me read him these verses. He always preferred to listen to a poem rather than reading it himself, enjoying its sound like music that colored the meanings. I remember him, one day when I was reading his verses to a close circle of friends, conducting me with his hands like a maestro, so that the subtle shades of the poetic sounds would not be lost.

Overwhelmed by the sensation this poem created in my circle and believing it would move a broader audience similarly, I decided to publicize it.

Without thinking about it very much or discussing it with any of my friends, I went back to the German-controlled Athens radio station, passed the poem by the unsuspecting censors, and recited it over the microphone myself.

My brief introduction on Ogyges, the first mythical King of Attica, that the announcer read before the poem, predisposed the listener with images that obviously symbolized the resistance to foreign invasions and the strong fiber of the Greeks.

What followed is indescribable. Phone calls, outpourings of emotion, congratulations, encouragement to continue, recommendations that I be on my guard…

In our organization: alarm. The self-controlled Mitsos Rediadis was raging, and he roared like a dragon. Stavros Vrachnos was enthused, but skeptical. Alexander Kairis was enchanted. Popi was terrified…

And I was happy and proud. I had unloaded feelings that had been building up inside me for a long time. But deeper inside I harbored uneasiness. I began to understand that I had overdone it, and that such actions endangered my main mission.

It was natural that the feeling of superiority that emboldened us would also take root in Antonis Bachas, the Piraeus Harbormaster. Bachas had considerable power in his hands, but, as mentioned earlier, had the type of character that disdained self-control. If one considers that the role of his division in our organization was such that he would justly throb with pride with every sinking of an enemy ship, and if one recognizes that almost every recent telegram we sent with information on the departure of a convoy or the movement of an individual ship was followed by one or more sinkings, one could easily explain and, in a way, excuse his foolhardy self-confidence and his dangerous displays of enthusiasm.

Bachas had a mortal hatred of every enemy collaborator. We all loathed these scoundrels who fortunately were few among the heroic vast majority of our compatriots. However, facing the unjust public outcry of those unaware of his secret mission who considered him a friend of the Germans and a traitor, Bachas had all the more reason to be enraged by the real enemy collaborators, who thought he shared their beliefs and was an accomplice.

One day he therefore decided to flex his muscles, not only to blow off steam, but also to rid his area of unwanted observers.

He shoved two harbor people known to be friendly with the Germans into isolated positions that lacked responsibility, thereby rendering them harmless. At the same time, he reassigned some others for purely service reasons to neutralize the Germans' suspicions.

The Germans summoned him for questioning the very next day.

"Mr. Harbormaster, you relocated two of our friendly officers," they said.

"I did not relocate only two. I relocated many officers and petty officers."

"Yes, but you must take back these two in particular."

"I have no objection," said Bachas. "I didn't know that they were ... our people."

And then this daring man attempted to take one more risky step.

"If you'd tell me who else you trust, I'll position them as best I can to make sure that such an error is not repeated."

The superior German officer gave him a piercing look.

"That will not be necessary," he answered tersely. "If the situation arises again, we'll send you our orders."

When we learned about these events, we judged that Bachas had yet again overstepped the boundaries of safety and had provoked the Germans' suspicion without any tangible benefit. And because we had all begun to "overdo it" in this manner as of late, we transmitted an advisory notice to the divisions emphasizing the need to be careful, that we must not become carried away by our zeal, and that we should not underestimate the intelligence of our adversaries.

Reflecting on Antonis Bachas's actions, I realized that I was criticizing and restraining others without taking care to avoid similar breaches myself. At that point I abruptly stopped every type of risky public action.

This is how we passed, little by little, the harsh winter of 1942-43. We went into March, a month that I remember as freezing cold. Perhaps we felt the cold more intensely due to the lack of energy-giving food and practically non-existent heating. I remember wearing an overcoat when I worked in my study at home. I also wore wool gloves from which I had cut the finger-tips so that I could grip pencils and papers. The only fuel we could find was pressed olive pits that we burned next to my father's bed. On bitterly cold days I also burned a bit in my study in a beautiful old brazier.

We were also upset that March due to the civil mobilization the Germans had threatened and the constant strikes that followed. The actions of the communists, who undermined our struggle materially and morally, had also intensified. Under the heel of the conquerors we heard slogans for friendship with the Bulgarians and the autonomy of Macedonia. The Greek units in the Middle East had rebelled.

April came and sweetened the air. More calmness, better moods, greater optimism. The communists were somewhat more restrained. Our food supply improved somewhat due to the combined efforts of the Greek, Swedish, and International Red Cross, the Turkish Red Crescent, and shipments of considerable loads of foodstuffs.

Menegatos returned from Turkey with the caïque and brought us the second wireless set we had asked for.

One night I met our wireless set operator, Nicos Paliatseas, outside the barbershop he frequented on Academia Platonos and he gave me the pleasant news. He also explained some technical details.

"Menegatos is keeping the wireless set hidden in Piraeus," he said, "and he is waiting for instructions. We could install it on the ground floor of the house with my wireless set and thus use the same antenna. But even if you decide to install it elsewhere we'll find a way to camouflage the new antenna as we did the old one. It's just that in another location we won't have the advantage we enjoy here of confusing the enemy's radio detectors by being mixed with foreign broadcasts, a fortunate coincidence until now."

Then Paliatseas spoke about a friend of his who was a good guy and a good patriot and who could become the operator of the second wireless set.

That same night, I discussed the matter thoroughly with Mitsos Rediadis. We decided not to install the second wireless set in the house in Nea Smirni, but to search for another house somewhere nearby.

With this approach we would, of course, have to face the danger of curiosity in the new environment and the difficulties of installing a new antenna. However, we would have greater assurance that our mission would continue if the enemy found our tracks. It would be good to keep the second wireless set independent of the first. We decided, however, to install the new machine in that same general area so that it would hopefully be in the same zone that was protected from the radio detectors.

We also decided to check out what the new wireless set operator had been doing during the Occupation as best we could.

Paliatseas assured me that, according to our general guidelines, he hadn't breathed a word to him about our organization or about his own participation in the resistance. But he considered the new man completely trustworthy.

All good spies, however, appear trustworthy. We had to be sure that he was not an enemy counterespionage agent, that we did not risk later being betrayed to the Germans, and that he did not belong to any of the communist organizations which lately had dropped their masks and were openly fighting every national organization.

For all of these reasons, we would somewhat delay putting the new wireless set into operation. When we did start using it, we would contact the new wireless set operator only through an experienced liaison, in full isolation from all others. In addition, we would keep him under constant observation.

We entrusted this verification and surveillance on Stavros Vrachnos's division, and Nicos Paliatseas started looking for the house we needed the very next day. He was to judge its technical suitability. We would rent it for the new wireless set operator, who would be the only one to present himself to the owners, saying that he was a student from the provinces.

During these first days of April, when, as always in that season, Athens smelled fragrantly of bitter-orange blossoms, we lived the exhilaration of Spring with particular excitement, planning our new ventures. But in those very days, the Gestapo was methodically tightening its unrelenting grip, advancing step by step to ensnare us.

These were the last days of beauty, joy, and optimism. To these I owe the reserve of my spiritual strength, which I would soon need to face the successive blows we took with composure and to limit our destruction as best I could.

For a few days, I would continue to enjoy the fertile Spring. The gloom of slavery, for me, had disappeared. I saw the road ahead unobstructed and in bloom, illuminated by our successes and our expectations.

The Spring conspired with my 29 years, my patriotic enthusiasm, my poetic exaltations, and even with the beauty of a young girl who for some time now was completing my emotions, mollifying the clash that was soon to follow.

For a long time I savored the wonderful taste of those last enjoyable days before that frightful Holy Thursday of 1943.

Now, with the new wireless set and double broadcasting time at our disposal, we could move with greater potential and give a boost to our activity. We sent relevant messages to the divisions and gathered abundant material for the wireless sets and for the caïques's next trip to the Turkish coast.

Stavros Vrachnos's General Information Division started to spread into the provinces. They created new networks and technical teams to observe enemy movements in the countryside and create engineering drawings of the enemy's military installations.

The latest movements of enemy units in and around Athens were recorded. New maps of coastlines and many sketches of the symbols on German vehicles were delivered to me. In a report written for me just after the Liberation, Stavros Vrachnos gives a characteristic description of this considerable expansion of his division shortly before our organization was discovered by the Germans.

> *What is unfortunate is that once the organization of our Division had been perfected and our information collection network had expanded in every direction within and around Athens and Piraeus, and once similar networks began to be organized in the provinces, as you know, by people of similar moral values and effectiveness, the events of the Spring of 1943 followed and suddenly interrupted our activities.*

Popi Sakelaridis's two team members, Petrich and Leousis, tracked the military railroad transports and handed me daily reports. This division was the only one that did not expand beyond its initial stage. Popi had been bedridden for quite some time, and she probably needed a serious operation. Thus, despite all her admirable good intentions, she could provide no more help for the time being.

We had to organize ourselves better with regard to railroad information. There was a great deal of mobility in this area, and our means of gathering information were inadequate. In an attempt to create a specific division for this purpose, I approached Basil Leontopoulos, at that time the Director of SEK (Railways of the Greek State), through the intervention of my venerable friend Admiral Hors. I faced understandable reservations from someone who did not know me. I had to put more energy into developing this sector.

Alexander Kairis was excited. He passed documents and notes to me almost every day, in our usual way via the toilet at the Bank, and when I would meet him at Popi's he would blame himself for not being able to do more.

The Harbor Division worked miracles. Koutsoudakis would send a stack of notes and drawings to Rediadis every day, and Rediadis would bring them to me in turn.

Our pilot, Captain Kostas Damoulakis with the signature B13, sent us tremendous information: engineering drawings of the coastal anti-aircraft defenses around the harbor and in the area of the Saronic Bay, of the barbed wire placements at the Harbor entrance, of the anti-magnetic field and safe channel in Keratsini, of the mine fields from Fleves Islet to Tourlon in Aigina, and from Perdika in Aigina to the Methana peninsula.

Pilot Kostas Moros, with the signature B14, noted all departures and arrivals and all of the enemy's casualties from Allied submarine torpedoes and airplane bombings.

The pilot Captain Peter Drakopoulos, a sixty-year-old sea dog with the signature B15, sent us convoy formations, movements of enemy troops, and the entrenchments on the islands and reinforcements of their garrisons.

Antonis Bachas, together with his second-in-command, lieutenant commander Dimitris Samantzopoulos, directed and coordinated this entire effort. Samantzopoulos expanded his actions into other sectors as well, following his chief's example. He equipped caïques and enabled escapes to Turkey and Egypt, all the while maintaining a vigilant eye on the enemy's military movements. He enabled sabotage and helped prepare the demolition of Piraeus Harbor with explosives.

All the details of these exploits are included in the reports that the leader of the Harbor Division, Manolis Koutsoudakis, submitted to me in January 1945, shortly before his death. The hardships of the Occupation and the pursuit of the Germans had seriously shaken his health.

To construct a concise picture of Service 5-16-5's effectiveness, I collected elements from the records I was holding, writing with invisible ink between the lines of a book, and made a list of all the ships that had been sunk after we sent the Allies information on their departures and itineraries. This list was complete, but I was forced to destroy it when the Germans were on our trail.

I present here a similar list based on Koutsoudakis's reports submitted to me in 1945. In those reports, a good number of the ships were omitted. On the other hand, ships for which we had repeatedly telegraphed departure and itinerary information, like the *Simfra* and the *Louloudis*, are listed. However, these ships were sunk by the Allies later, owing to information that our harbor people managed to send even after our organization was essentially destroyed. Two vessels hit by saboteurs are also listed.

Koutsoudakis's reports state that "...these ships were *basically* as follows..." In other words, he didn't include them all.

The reports also say that "...these ships were tracked with the utmost care, insuring that all information was accurate. The result was that *nearly every ship serving the enemy's military needs in Greece, either Italian or German, was destroyed.*"

Another excerpt characterizes the great damage the enemy suffered from these sinkings: "...from the positive information we supplied about their departures, the steamships *Louloudis* and *Livenza, each carrying a full 18,000-ton load of war materiel, were lost with their cargos and all hands.*"

Thus, according to the list I have in my hands, the following ships were sunk by the Allies after information was provided by Service 5-16-5 and its Harbor Division on their departures and itineraries:

1.	*Citta di Savona*	29.	*Artemis Pitta*
2.	*Citta di Genova*	30.	*Sifnos*
3.	*Citta d'Agrigento*	31.	*Caliari*
4.	*Foscolo*	32.	*Petrakis Nomikos*
5.	*Danubio*	33.	*Creta*
6.	*Macedonia*	34.	*Elli* (tanker)
7.	*Thessalia*	35.	*Vicente*
8.	*Prosperina* (tanker)	36.	*Leopardi*
9.	*Celeno* (tanker)	37.	*Reomirus*
10.	*Palermo*	38.	*Susana*
11.	*Italia*	39.	*Agatha*
12.	*Argentina*	40.	*Silva*
13.	*Cambanella*	41.	*Lola*
14.	*Anita*	42.	*Vesta*
15.	*Calino*	43.	*Gertrud*
16.	*Crespi*	44.	*Doxa* (sailing vessel)
17.	*Isora*	45.	*Henrietta*
18.	*Tzar Ferdinando*	46.	*Madalena*
19.	*Valcan*	47.	*Olymbos*
20.	*Zimfra*	48.	*Pier Louigi*
21.	*Santa-Fe*	49.	*Citta di Livorno*
22.	*Tanais*	50.	*Burgas*
23.	*Louloudis*	51.	*Rigel*
24.	*Livenza*	52.	*Kithira*
25.	*Elsi*	53.	*San Issidro*
26.	*Ardena*	54.	A floating dry dock in Piraeus
27.	*Bulgaria*	55.	A floating dry dock in Lavrio
28.	*Drague*		

One of these ships, the Spanish steamship *San Issidro* which served the enemy by smuggling transports and whose departure and course we had signaled in advance so many times, was sunk on April 4, 1943 by the Greek submarine *Katsonis*, commanded by Captain V. Laskos.

Admiral P. Konstas, the commanding officer of the Greek submarine fleet in the Middle East at that time, wrote about this Greek success in his book *Hellas of the Decade 1940-1950*, page 234:

> The submarine *Katsonis* *attacks near the Cyclades and sinks the large cargo vessel* San Issidro *which sailed under Spanish flag but carried out war contraband transports for the Germans, information which a wireless set (of the Organization 5-16-5) had transmitted to us from Greece.* [Added as a footnote: *This organization, "Service 5-16-5," otherwise known as E.P.E., was under the leadership of Rigas Rigopoulos and provided a great deal of service through the information it supplied.*]

Further down, Admiral Konstas describes the sinking of the Spanish ship and the order that had been issued — after our persistent telegrams — to ignore the protection of the neutral Spanish flag.

I put the list of sunken ships in one of my desk drawers, intending to copy it over with invisible ink into the book where I was keeping our records. All of my desk's hiding places and drawers were full of incriminating notes and drawings from each of our divisions as I was working intensely to prepare them for transmission. But this list of ships, which has been lost but at that time remained in my desk drawer, created enough troubles for me.

Soon I sorted out the information that was to be transmitted via the wireless set. I composed the message texts, always writing them in capital letters, and sent them to Paliatseas.

Then I divided the information to be transported via the caïques into two parts. The first contained information that was more urgent or that was ready to go just the way it was without elaboration. These I wrapped in tarpaper and sent to Menegatos, who left immediately on the *Santa Teresa* for the Turkish coast. This must have been around the 10th of April.

The *Santa Teresa* was to return to Piraeus before Easter, which fell on April 25th. At that point I would give Menegatos the second part, to be sent with Captain Stamatis Tratras aboard the *Chrysanthi.*

❋   ❋   ❋

The arrival of the new wireless set from the Allied service was a reward for our work and a landmark event in the history of Service 5-16-5. Mitsos and I decided to send a summary report that would give us the opportunity to bring up certain information we had transmitted months before, but for which we had not seen the follow-up offensive actions we expected from the Allies. We also wanted to bring up a few ideas for even better collaboration in the future.

I signed the report "R17 – Chief of Service 5-16-5." The number 17 corresponds to the letter "R" in the Greek alphabet, and thus the report was signed with my initials. We decided that I should use this coded signature so that I could prove my position in the organization if I ever needed to contact the Allied espionage services personally. We redrew some of the plans of enemy installations which we had sent with previous dispatches. I even drew many German vehicle symbols in color onto the thick gray paper we used at home to black out the windows. These drawings also later caused me serious trouble.

Finally, on Holy Wednesday, April 21, 1943, I received notice that the *Santa Teresa* was back in Piraeus. I rolled up the material I had for the new dispatch, wrapped it with tarpaper as usual, and sent it to Nicos Menegatos.

I still have today the note I wrote about this package so that I could later make an entry in our invisible archive. The note lists the contents of that fatal package, which the Germans found in Menegatos's hands:

> *Map of a section of the fortifications from Piraeus to Vouliagmeni. Map of the fortified seashore of Githeion. Map of minefields in the cruising lanes of the Aegean Sea. Map of dry land minefields on Rodos and two other smaller islands. Plan of trenches in the area of Paradeisos where the Germans stored fuel.*

More than 100 symbols of German vehicles. The texts of many of our previously transmitted telegrams. A report on the general capabilities of Service 5-16-5, with imminent perfecting of the network in the Eptanisos and about organizing a railroad information network.

The strenuous work of these last days fascinated me. I was living in an enchanted atmosphere of intense action. I saw dedicated people around me who gave themselves to the struggle wholeheartedly without feeling privation, without regard for danger, and with a simplicity that epitomized the true meaning of greatness.

Now that I had arranged the current dispatch, I tasted the satisfaction that each important stage of our work had given us. I savored the serenity and relief granted by each completed action. I rejoiced in the vibrant journey that my companions completed around me despite countless dangers. I felt pride in the new Hellenic generation whose wonderful achievements I had the privilege of following day by day.

Gripped by the excitement that engulfed me and by my visions for the future, I lay awake — as I often did back then — for a large portion of the night. It was my last night of true freedom. I echoed my heart's pulses in verses.

What a Joy to be born in this Land ...
What a Joy to be born in these years ...

The house of the wireless set at 23 Sevastias Street, Nea Smirni

THE PERSECUTION

THE GERMANS ON OUR TRAIL. ARRESTS. EXECUTIONS.

Holy Thursday, April 22, 1943. A day full of light and emotion under a bright, cloudless blue sky.

Calm and serene, we will go to church to witness the divine drama.

Calm and serene, we will follow the passions of our so human-like Lord.

We will live His suffering from moment to moment and we will share His divine meekness, drawing from His strength and waiting with Him for Resurrection.

> *Today is hung upon Tree,*
> *He Who suspended the land in the midst of the waters.*
> *A crown of thorns crown Him,*
> *Who is the King of Angels.*
> *He is wrapped about with the purple of mockery,*
> *Who wrapped the Heavens with clouds. ...*
> *We worship Thy Passion, O Christ.*
> *Show also unto us*
> *Thy glorious Resurrection.*

My family and I were getting ready to go to church for the Twelve Gospels when the phone rang.

"Eleni here." It was Eleni Limberopoulos. "Nicos called me to say that 'Madam Eleni is having a party and is expecting you tonight.' "

I didn't understand what she was saying. Who has a party during Holy Week? And then it hit me: it was our danger signal.

Nicos Paliatseas, who did not know my name or phone number, was contacting me via the emergency channels we had set up.

"What time did Nicos call?" I asked.

"Just now, a few minutes ago."

It was shortly after 7 PM. In one hour, as we had prearranged, I would have to be in front of the blue apartment building on Exarhia Square to learn what sort of danger we were facing.

The hour's wait was terribly hard for me. Something horrible must have happened for Paliatseas to give the danger signal, but without knowing the details there was nothing I could do. I simply had to muster my patience and wait.

I called Mitsos Rediadis to put him on alert, but he wasn't home. I left a message saying that I urgently needed to speak to him and that I would come by his house later.

Then I went to church with my mother.

At ten of eight I was at Exarhia Square. Nicos Paliatseas was already there, waiting for me. We advanced, separately, through the dark alleys around the Square, and then I approached him.

"The Germans came into the wireless set house," were the first words out of his mouth. "They got Menegatos. I escaped over the back fences." He then filled in the details.

"Menegatos came home late last night. He was delayed in Athens and couldn't make it to Piraeus. He stayed in my room for quite some time and watched my nightly wireless set transmission. He helped me put the machine back in its hiding place and went downstairs to sleep. In the morning, he came back up to my room and his old aunt brought us some coffee. Around 10 he was getting ready to leave, and we checked the street from the window as usual. Something was going on. German soldiers were guarding the corners and others were passing below and looking up at the houses. We thought they must be looking for someone, unless a radio detector had located the area of our wireless set and they were now looking for antennas so they could zero in on the house where it was hidden.

"We relit the fire in the kitchen stove so that I could get rid of the wireless set and the code if we had to, and we waited. It got to be past noon, and still nothing happened. The Germans remained at their posts. They had cordoned off the block and were waiting. Somehow we had to find out whether they were looking for the wireless set or just watching someone.

"Menegatos had an idea. We filled a big bag full of clothes and asked the old woman to take it as far as the church. We watched from behind a curtain. As soon as the old woman reached the corner, the Germans stopped her. They opened the bag and searched it. Then they let her go. This convinced us that they were looking for the wireless set and we thought they might start searching the houses at any moment.

"In fact, shortly thereafter, cars with more soldiers arrived. It was then that I decided to destroy the wireless set. I kept only the crystals so that I could perhaps build another one, and I hid them deep in the ashes that had accumulated in the depths of the kitchen stove. I threw the box into the fire along with the code and plenty of wood to build a real blaze. I covered whatever remained with the ashes.

"In the meantime, Menegatos decided to leave. He figured they would let him pass, as they had allowed the old woman and plenty of other pedestrians to.

"As soon as he stepped out the door, they fell upon and arrested him. I lunged through the kitchen door to the back yard. As I was jumping the fence into the neighboring yard, I heard the Germans go into the house. I jumped another three fences, passed through another yard, and escaped via a back street."

"Do you have a place to stay tonight?" I asked him.

"Yes, I still have a room in Kallithea where I used to live. Or I can stay with my friend the barber in the Academia Platonos area."

"Does Menegatos know about the room in Kallithea?"

"No, nobody knows about it."

"OK, Nicos, listen to me very carefully," I said. "The slightest mistake now could cost us our lives. We have no idea where this evil started. Maybe we even have a traitor among us. From now on you must not meet with anyone but me. You will lock yourself in your room in Kallithea and you will only come out at night to see me. You absolutely must not to go to the barbershop in Academia Platonos for any reason. If we have been betrayed, or if Menegatos talks, the Germans could learn of this shop. Go now, and I'll meet you tomorrow night at 9:00 sharp at the corner of Kiriakou Square and Elpidos Street. If I don't show up by 9:05, leave and return the next night at the same time. Good-bye, Nicos, and be careful."

Rethimnou Street, where Mitsos Rediadis lived, was not far from where Paliatseas and I had separated. I dropped in and found him home.

Mitsos listened to the story calmly. We tried to draw conclusions from Paliatseas's words about the possible source and scope of the danger.

The Germans had spent several hours in the neighborhood of the wireless set, which showed that they didn't know its exact location. But they had definitely pinpointed the area.

When the old woman left the house they searched her bag, but again they didn't seem to know the exact location of the wireless set. They would certainly search any suspicious package to prevent the machine from escaping.

It was obvious that the Germans were looking for something, and when they got tired of waiting they brought in reinforcements to search the entire area under suspicion.

The fact that they arrested Menegatos as soon as they saw him, and then immediately rushed the house he had come out of, meant that Menegatos must have been known to them. However, they didn't know exactly which house he was in, and that's why they waited for so many hours.

Thus Mitsos and I pieced together a picture of what must have happened.

The wireless set couldn't have been located by radio detectors. Or if this had happened, it must have been combined with a more specific surveillance of us by the German counterespionage service. The Germans must have been watching Menegatos, knowing his link to the wireless set and with some espionage network they were trying to uncover.

Menegatos hadn't suspected anything. A little before the curfew, when he decided to go and sleep at his uncle's house where we kept the wireless set, he took the usual security measures we all took in these situations. He turned a few streets, watching his back, and only went into the door when he was sure that no one was around to see him. So those who were following him must have suddenly lost him, but still knew roughly where he was.

They decided to stand guard so that they could catch him when he came out again, and they cordoned off the area. Maybe they then contacted the radio detectors to focus their search in that sector. Maybe the last nightly transmission had been pinpointed.

The next day, they continued to block the street, but they let people circulate freely, hoping that Menegatos would come out at some point. Perhaps they preferred to try this easier tactic first, or perhaps special teams were not available that morning for a house-to-house search. It seems that they decided on the search in the afternoon, but then Menegatos fell into their hands and the house with the wireless set was discovered.

We still had to figure out how the Germans learned about Menegatos. Who could have informed them? How did they know that the espionage network around him was worth the intense effort they put into capturing him?

These and many other questions would remain unanswered for the time being. But among the things we had to face was the possibility of a traitor in our organization or very near it. This would have to be someone who, despite all the security measures and the very limited contact circle we had put into effect, knew something about Menegatos's secrets and had betrayed him to the Germans. Surely this person — if he existed — would have to be closer to the foreign service detachment to which Menegatos belonged than to the side that was purely ours. But this didn't mean that the danger wasn't more widespread. We couldn't know where the Germans' searching would end, especially if Menegatos talked. He didn't know many things about us, but he did know the type of information we transmitted, and from there the Germans would be able to get to specific people, from them to other people, and so on, and the arrests would broaden.

Therefore, our first job would be to cease all contact between everyone until we saw what developed. It would be even better if every member ceased all contact even with their close friends for a short while, to avoid being compromised or exposing others.

However, one of us had to disappear completely and get abroad as soon as possible: Alexander Kairis. If the Germans found any of the information he had given us, they would immediately realize who the informant was.

Menegatos's other acquaintances were the captains and crews of the caïques. But only Menegatos saw them, and we didn't know where they were. Only our harbor people could possibly find them and warn them of the new danger. Of course, Menegatos knew me personally, but only by my code name, "Captain Nicos," without any further details.

So Mitsos took charge of informing the Head of the Harbor Division, Manolis Koutsoudakis, and the liaison, George Zentelis, to cease all operations and all contacts immediately. Koutsoudakis would transfer this order to the members of his division, attempt to find the caïque crews, and keep us informed. I took charge of warning all the others.

The very next day we began moving in all directions to shut down the entire mechanism of Service 5-16-5, which had been put into operation with such intensity and enthusiasm. We hoped these actions would snuff out the danger at this point. We couldn't know that we would soon face a chain of frightful developments.

I spent all of Holy Friday trying to find and warn my companions, but the Holy Day made it hard to find anyone either at home or at work.

I searched for Alexander Kairis at his room on Ipitou Street. He wasn't there. Perhaps he was in the suburb of Ekali at his parents' house.

I finally succeeded in finding Stavros Vrachnos where I least expected him: in the chemistry lab of the Technical University. He listened carefully to the story of what had happened and concluded, "I don't think we need to hide right for the moment."

I agreed. "I'm the only one who has contact with your division, and only one other person in the entire organization, with the code number A2, knows of your existence."

I was talking, of course, about Mitsos Rediadis. "But I think that neither he nor I faces an immediate danger," I went on. "In any case, if A2 needs to contact you, you will know him by his code number and you can trust him as you trust me."

Stavros immediately set out to warn his people.

Meanwhile, Popi Sakelaridis had been brought to Areteion Hospital to be operated on by Alexander Kairis's brother Nicholas. Due to the events that intervened, the operation didn't actually take place until much later.

Around midday, I left my house with the book in which I kept our invisible records between the lines. I also took some pieces of information that we hadn't had time to transmit and some poems of mine — some of which had been published in the secret press — and went to the hospital.

Popi's condition made me cautious.

"It looks like the Germans have suspected something about our organization," I told her. "We have to take certain precautions."

"Tell me exactly what's going on," she answered. "It won't hurt me, because I feel completely fine. Besides, I imagine the worst, because if it was something small you wouldn't have mentioned it."

I was forced to tell her the details. At least the problems were with people she didn't know, so she didn't have to suffer the pain that problems with her own people would have caused.

I told her of our decision to suspend all contacts between members for the time being. She took charge of contacting her people. She told me that Alexander was indeed in Ekali, where he would spend Easter with his parents. She knew this from his brother Nicholas, whom she said I could see in a little while after he finished visiting his other patients.

"Watch out for yourself, too," she said. "Make sure you get rid of any evidence that might be in your house."

I told her I had already thought of that, and that I had brought our records and some other information with me. I would take these to some friend with no ties to our organization.

"No," said the brave girl, "leave these things with me. The Germans will not come in here. Besides, I will put the papers in one of the little pillows that I always have near me. I will keep the book next to me, with the others that I read. No one will touch them." So I gave Popi the book and papers.

In the meantime, Nicholas Kairis had entered the room. I told him that I was thinking of going up to Ekali that evening to see Alexander and their parents. My friends had invited me many times to spend a couple of days with them in the countryside.

"Stay with us for Easter," Nicholas said. "In Ekali you can enjoy the holiday as if there was no Occupation."

I thanked him, saying that I wanted to spend the Resurrection and Easter with my family.

We said good-bye, looking forward to meeting again that night. Alexander would have to find some kind of excuse to say good-bye to his family this very day, so we could hide him somewhere in Athens and get him out of Greece as soon as possible.

❋   ❋   ❋

The Kairis family gave me a warm welcome at their villa in Ekali where they spent the Occupation.

I felt terribly uneasy, seeing them welcome me unsuspectingly, with such joyful expressions. They were even concerned that I had shown up on a day of great fasting and they were unable to treat me the way they would have liked. They insisted that I stay with them through Easter so that we could eat lamb together, something rare in those times. Alexander's real love for me had diffused throughout the entire family.

I was trying to figure out how I could get Alexander alone to talk to him, when he himself suggested that we go see the room where he insisted I stay at least for that night. He didn't want me to go back to Athens on the wood-burning bus after dark.

There was a smaller house in the same yard where the two boys had their own apartment. With childish glee, Alexander took me there and the two of us went inside.

"Alexander," I said, "I have some really bad news. That's why I'm here."

His joyful face became serious. He looked deep into my eyes, as he used to do, waiting for me to continue.

I described the situation in minute detail. I told him about the conclusions we had been able to draw, about our fears, and about the dangers that threatened him in particular.

"I fear that Menegatos will talk," I continued. "The Germans have a way of getting secrets out of even the most resolute. He must know plenty of the things we transmitted, much of which could only have come from you. If the Germans discover this information they will immediately suspect you. Perhaps the papers in our last dispatch have already fallen into their hands from who knows where Menegatos hid them. I just sent that package to him the day before yesterday, and I don't think the caïque has left yet. Many of the papers in that package incriminate you. You might as well have signed them."

Alexander was obviously deeply concerned. He lit a cigarette but remained silent.

"Alexander, you absolutely must disappear today," I concluded. "For you, the danger is immediate. Together we'll find a secure house where you can hide for the next few days. Then we'll arrange to smuggle you to the Middle East."

Alexander paced the room. I let him ponder the situation for a while, unbothered. Finally, he stopped and looked at me again.

"Rigas, on the Tuesday after Easter I will go to my office," he said simply. Then, he started to slowly unravel his thoughts as if he was talking to himself.

"Everything you've said is possible, but most likely nothing will happen. The papers in our last dispatch must be well hidden if they haven't already been turned over to the captain, who may have already left for Turkey. I can't imagine them falling into the Germans hands. From what you've told me, Menegatos is not the wireless set operator, he's the liaison. He has no reason to let on that he knows the texts of our messages. On the contrary, he will keep away from the subject completely to avoid incriminating himself further and making his position worse…"

"Don't count on this, Alexander," I interrupted. "Logic does not stand up to torture. The Germans torture you until they destroy every ounce of spiritual and mental resistance. They break your nerve and morale completely. They turn you into a human rag and then they extract, little by little, everything you wanted to hide from them. The people who can withstand such an interrogation are rare."

Alexander seemed to be listening to my words without digesting them. He continued, following his train of thought as if I had never interrupted him.

"Besides, why should they particularly suspect me? Couldn't a German in their service have been bribed and be disclosing the secrets? There are so many of us in there, and my superiors trust me more than they trust a lot of their own. They consider me a fanatic friend."

And then, with a shocking calmness, preventing another interruption, Alexander Kairis finally brought the deeper source of his reaction to the surface.

"But even if these doubts did not exist, there is always the basic reason that obliges me to return to my work..."

The words of Alexander Kairis from here on have historic significance. They are the sort of words that prevail over time, that survive eras, and that are worth passing from generation to generation to build national traditions. Since then, these words are indelibly inscribed in me. I transcribe them here almost verbatim.

"The information I bring directly from the German Headquarters is invaluable and irreplaceable. Some way will be found for our organization to continue its work. But if I abandon my position, a considerable void will be created in our overall mission.

"We dedicated our lives in the very first moment we started this struggle. Can any of us be certain that he will survive to the end? I, at least, believed from the beginning that it would be improbable to get through all of the dangers we face alive.

"So, the only issue that remains is how can we hurry to offer more. That is the heart of the matter.

"This is why I will definitely show up at my work on Tuesday."

I tried with all my might to change his mind. I exhausted all my arguments. I emphasized that a great number of people in our organization besides himself are in vital positions and likewise provide us with critical information. Anyway, I stressed, there are also other organizations in our country — the same and even more important than ours — which certainly transmit a massive volume of information daily to the Allied services. Finally, I pointed out that as valuable as his information may be, it is not logical for him to risk his life — with a good probability of losing it — and have his services ended in such a way.

Alexander calmly smiled at this last argument.

"But there is also the probability that I will live and continue..." Then, trying to calm me, he added, "Don't exaggerate the danger. Calm down. They will not get to me. They are not as smart as you think."

I clearly saw that this amazing man would never give in. But in a desperate and probably naïve effort, I tried to sting his innate sense of integrity by playing my last card.

"Alexander," I said, "when you presented yourself to our organization and we accepted you, you undertook the obligation to obey orders. The leadership has decided that you are no longer to show up at the German Service. This is an order."

Alexander smiled once more and put his hand on my shoulder.

"We are such old friends, Rigas... Such things have no place between us."

That night I stayed in Ekali, although my good friend told me at one point that I could still catch the last bus if I wanted. Perhaps inside he started to fear that the Germans might come to arrest him that very night and he was tactfully trying to distance me from him.

We retired fairly early to the room in which the two boys had set up my bed, too, so that we could all be together.

Maybe it was our nervousness that turned that night into devilish merriment. We acted like we were drunk, without having had a drop of alcohol. We played like children, with Alexander leading the silliness and dragging the usually calmer Nicholas into the frivolity. Jumping on the beds, we started a pillow fight and fortified our-selves behind the mattresses. We started throwing all kinds of things that were big-ger and bigger, until Alexander lifted an armchair and threw it at my head, scream-ing like a banshee. Later, when Alexander wrote to Popi Sakelaridis from prison — he would never write to me directly — he would refer to me in code as "my excep-tionally beloved 'armchair-stricken-one.' "

Our laughter echoed inside the little garden house late into the night, until it slowly abated and we fell into a deep sleep.

In the morning, I left for Athens. Alexander went with me to the bus stop. We did not speak about the matter that was on both of our minds.

We kissed each other before we parted.

Then, as the bus was leaving, I turned and looked at him through the window. He was waving to me and laughing.

It was the last time I ever saw him.

Holy Saturday went by quietly…

As always, I went to work early in the morning. Somehow or other I rummaged through my desk papers until 12 noon. We had a half-day holiday, and I went home early.

Mitsos Rediadis came in the afternoon. He had arranged everything as we had agreed. I told him about my efforts. Service 5-16-5 was now at an absolute standstill.

We had one more thing to do, but we needed Paliatseas's help to do it. We had to get hold of the second wireless set, which we had not yet put into operation, install it somewhere even temporarily, inform the Allied service about what had happened, and explain the temporary — so we hoped — suspension of our services.

I went to meet Nicos Paliatseas at Kiriakou Square at 9 that night. Occupied with Kairis, I hadn't gone the first night, and I could imagine his impatience as he waited for me. When he saw me approaching from afar, he proceeded onto Elpidos Street. We took the usual security measures, walking through the dark narrow pas-sages at a distance from one another and then we met.

The dear boy was overjoyed to see me. Since the dramatic events he experi-enced two days earlier, he had not spoken to a soul in a full 48 hours. He was weath-ering his emotional storm locked inside his room completely alone.

I asked him about the second wireless set. He had no idea where it was. "I know that Menegatos has it hidden in Piraeus," he said, "but I don't know any other de-tails."

We walked on a bit in silence. So we had to give up on making immediate contact with abroad. If only our harbor people could at least find the caïques. Our only hopes now lay with them.

"Maybe Socratis knows something about the wireless set," Nicos said suddenly. He had spoken to me before about a Socratis Tselentis. He, too, belonged to the Allied services and was in contact with Menegatos. We did not know how the Allies used him, or even if Tselentis had anything to do with the relations between our service and abroad. Maybe he was connected with the caïque dispatches. Anyway, Nicos knew where he lived.

I didn't let him go, because I feared that the Germans may have already gotten to Tselentis. We would have to see how things developed and then decide what to do next.

"In any case," Nicos said with his boundless enthusiasm, "as soon as we find the wireless set I will reinforce the antenna at my house and I can begin normal transmissions again. Luckily, I have a copy of the code that I burned in Nea Smirni. I hope things will soon be straightened out so we can get going again."

I enjoyed and admired the simple bravery and the lively spirit of this young man. But for the time being, special care was needed. I said that I, too, hoped we would soon be back in operation, but I warned Nicos once more to watch himself, and we agreed on the time and place we would meet Monday night.

"If either of us does not show up at the rendezvous," I said — after all, we are only human and one of us could become ill — "the other will wait a bit and then return to the same place at the same time every night until we meet."

We said good-bye.

"Good Resurrection…"

"Good Easter…"

We exchanged these wishes out of habit, without any hope that they would be fulfilled.

That night, my family and I went to church to sing the *Christos Anesti* (Christ Has Risen) and to bring Father a candle lit from the Holy Light.

I spent Easter Sunday with my family, at my father's bedside. My mother had bought half a lamb from a black marketeer, paying for it with things from the house.

Thus we had a decent Easter.

I didn't want my family to notice that anything unpleasant was happening to me. I maintained hope that I would overcome the difficulties, and that our life would continue as it once was.

Monday also went by calmly. I met with Mitsos and later with Stavros, and we decided we would have to approach some trusted people outside the organization to see if they would hide in their homes people being sought by the Germans or who were in any way at risk. We had to secure some safe houses just in case.

I also took some flowers to Popi in the hospital to lift her spirits. I told her that Alexander did not consider the danger immediate, and that he would go to his office the next day. She did not like this idea at all.

Various acquaintances came to the house that afternoon and I asked two of them if they would give asylum to a friend of theirs who might need to hide. They side-stepped the question. As a matter of fact, one of them reasoned quite logically that if this was needed for me personally, friends' homes should not even considered, because those would be the first places the Germans would search and they would find me easily.

That night I saw Nicos Paliatseas briefly and we set up another meeting for Wednesday.

Tuesday morning I went to the Bank. It was the crucial day that Alexander Kairis was to show up at his office. It was impossible to concentrate on my work.

I held onto the hope that Alexander would appear, as he usually did, and that he would come by my office so I could relax. He did not show up… The hours crawled by incredibly slowly until noon when I left for home.

It was my last day as a Bank employee. The events that followed distanced me from a job that didn't suit me and that I would never love.

On my way out of the Bank, I called Popi Sakelaridis. "Nicholas didn't show up at the hospital today," she said, "and I'm worried." I told her I would call her again in the afternoon. I was certain that Alexander had fallen into Gestapo hands.

That afternoon, I left my house and called Popi again. Her voice trembled. "They arrested both of the boys this morning. I learned this from their mother…"

"Alright," I interrupted, "we'll talk again," and I hung up the phone.

I had been expecting this for days, but nevertheless the actual event dealt me a sudden shocking and crushing blow. I knew that Alexander was doomed and that I would never see him again, but my whole being rejected this idea as monstrous and unacceptable.

But even in this state of shock, an alarm went off inside me to signal the danger Popi was facing by talking on the hospital telephone after Nicholas's arrest. The telephones there might already be under surveillance. That's why I abruptly cut her off and hung up.

My second thought was that Popi had the Service records near her, along with the papers I had given her. If the Germans learned that she was a close friend of the Kairis brothers, they would probably search her and her belongings as part of the more general search of the hospital in which Nicholas worked. I had to get the incriminating evidence away from her immediately, by any means possible.

But might I already be on the list of suspects? Everyone knew that I was a close friend of Alexander Kairis.

I began to realize that even for me there was no security. Even if Alexander did not speak about me — and I knew that he would sooner die than open his mouth — I feared that they might bring me in for interrogation and show me to Menegatos. That could be my undoing.

Maybe the Germans already knew what I looked like. Maybe they were lying in wait at the Areteion Hospital at this very moment to arrest and interrogate any friends of the Kairis brothers who might show up.

So instead of setting out immediately for the Areteion as I had intended, I decided to first change my appearance as best I could. I returned home in a hurry. I shaved my moustache and put on glasses that until then I had only used at the cinema. I put on a hat, which I never wore, to hide my distinctive balding forehead. So disguised, I set out for the Areteion.

I didn't notice anything suspicious at the hospital entrance. I passed through the front yard, hunching my shoulders a bit and bending my knees slightly under my gabardine coat to cut down my height.

I carried a bouquet of flowers to help create the impression of an innocent visitor. I entered Popi's room and found her with her eyes swollen from crying. She tried to hide her distress.

"You should not have come," she said. "The Germans have been plowing through the hospital all morning. You hung up on me, so I didn't have a chance to warn you."

"Give me the records and papers," I told her. "Quickly."

"You can't take them with you. If they stop you and search you on your way out, they will arrest you. From there on, it won't be difficult for them to read the records, and we'll suffer even greater catastrophes."

"Give them to me and I'll flush them down the toilet."

I quickly glanced down the hall, and then I took the book and the written documents and locked myself in the bathroom that was next door. I ripped everything into very small pieces and flushed them down the toilet.

Then I kissed Popi and said good-bye. "Be strong," I said to her. "You won't see me for a long time."

I left the Areteion without anyone bothering me.

❋ ❋ ❋

I walked toward the center of Athens in deep reflection. I hadn't yet decided where I would go. A thousand muddled thoughts were going through my head.

Subconsciously, I was following the less frequented streets. Maybe that way I would avoid unwanted encounters. Besides, since I had changed my appearance, I didn't want to pique the curiosity of anyone who might know me.

As I proceeded down a narrow street behind Kaniggos Square, someone grabbed my hand and stopped me. It was my dear and respected friend, Admiral Hors.

"Hey, where are you going looking so grim and glum?" he said in his characteristically pleasant air.

"I fear that the Germans are searching for me, my Admiral," I answered. "It would be best if I didn't go home. Do you perhaps know anywhere I could stay?"

He looked at me, startled. "As long as there is my house, why would you look for another?"

"My Admiral, I fear that I will put you and Mrs. Hors in grave danger," I replied. "This concerns the national resistance and the accusations against me may be very grave..."

"Well, why else would the Germans be chasing you?" he said, grinning. "No further discussion is needed. I'll be home within an hour, and I'll be waiting for you. Bring the essentials for your comfort and stay as long as you need to."

I didn't object further. I simply shook his hand and thanked him, very moved.

"You have no obligation," he said to me. "It is we who have an obligation to protect not only you, but any patriot in danger."

Mitsos Rediadis's house was nearby. I found him upstairs, and I briefed him on the new arrests and the destruction of the records. He was furious that I had risked going alone to destroy the records without contacting him first.

"If they caught you at the hospital," he said, "I wouldn't have had a clue about it. You've got to disappear as soon as possible."

I responded that I had already secured a safe refuge, that I was going to drop by my house for a moment to inform my family. We then set up a rendezvous for the next night.

Before I went home, I called to make sure that everything was calm. "Did anyone perhaps ask for me?" I asked my mother.

"No," she answered. "Are you expecting anyone?"

"No...I'll tell you about it," and hung up the phone.

In five minutes I was home. Besides my mother, I found my three sisters there, too. I took them all into our father's room.

"They are arresting reserve officers and I have to hide," I told them.

My family had realized that something serious was going on these last few days, but they accepted what I said without asking for details. They were simply paralyzed. Only Mother whispered a question. "My child, do you have a decent place to stay?"

"Yes, everything is settled just fine. Please, just put some underwear, pajamas, shaving things, and a toothbrush in my bag, and don't worry about me at all."

Meanwhile, I sat down and wrote a letter to the Bank of Greece. I wanted to somehow cover my absence without creating problems and arousing suspicions among the Bank's German supervisors.

I vaguely claimed that while going for a walk on the slope of the Mt. Imittos I had hurt my back and was laid up in some shepherd's dwelling. This romantic picture had the advantage that there was no way for the Bank's doctor to come and verify the event, as was always done when employees took ill.

So, for a short time, we would continue to receive my salary, which was readjusted every month by a few million or billion inflated drachmas, and was essential to us. Due to the rampant inflation, income from our rental properties had been completely annihilated, and my family's financial situation was in a horrid state.

In a few minutes, I was ready to leave. I stood before my father's bed and looked at him. His terrible sickness had by now affected his vision, and he could only discern things with great difficulty. I thought that perhaps I was seeing him and he was seeing me for the last time.

He slowly turned his head and looked at me. "Whatever you do, my child, I am certain that it is dictated by honor and duty…"

He showed me that he had understood. My eyes filled with tears. "Farewell, Father," I said. "As soon as things settle down I'll come home."

My mother and sisters escorted me to the door. My mother's damp eyes were full of worried questions. I understood what her gaze was looking for.

"I mustn't tell you where I will be staying, Mother. If the Germans ever ask, it will be better if you don't know than if you try to hide the truth. It will be better for all of us. But we will see each other frequently.

"Tomorrow night," I continued, "come to the statue of King Constantine in the Park, at 8 o'clock. Leave early, and go do some other errand first. Also take a couple side streets to be sure you're not being followed. When you reach the statue it will be dark. Proceed toward the park's little streets. I will have seen you, and I'll approach when I'm sure there is no danger. All of these precautions might be unnecessary right now, but we cannot know when they'll be needed. Therefore, we must use them in all of our future meetings."

I kissed my mother and sisters and I went out into the street. By now it was dark. Given the dangerous situation that had developed, I was trying to advance as cautiously as I could. Soon events would justify the precautions I had taken from the beginning and would continue to take from then on.

※　　※　　※

A new kind of life began for me that night. All day I would stay inside and only go out at night. The house on 32 Kikladon Street was an old three-level mansion. The Hors lived on the second floor and rented out the other two. With their boys in the Middle East, there was plenty of room.

A great privilege for me was a veranda full of potted plants at the back of the house where you descended directly into the garden. This garden was full of trees and flowers and enclosed by the blind backs of the surrounding houses. It was a hidden paradise where I could enjoy greenery and blue sky.

Another privilege was the Admiral's extensive book collection, and a third was his pleasant company. Mrs. Hors went to bed quite early, and the Admiral and I would usually talk until 2 or 3 in the morning. The Admiral's breadth of knowledge was encyclopedic, and we never ran out of things to discuss.

There couldn't have been a better way for me to spend this phase of the great adventure, garnering my emotional strength and the composure that would be needed to face the terrible phases that followed.

I saw my mother every second or third night in the usual manner. The first news she brought was that the Germans had searched my desk at the Bank. Someone from the department I worked in told her that he saw them compare my handwriting to that on a paper they had brought with them and then say to each other, "It is the same handwriting. There is no doubt."

My family was expecting a search at the house at any time. Nothing happened. But soon they verified that two or three people had our house under continuous surveillance.

The Germans must have been sure that I was not in the house. They were letting me regain my confidence and expected me to return home at some point. It was not difficult for them to find out that my father was seriously ill and conclude that I might therefore risk going to see him. Indeed, this I did, but I did not go carefree and unaware of their trap.

They also had my family under surveillance in case they came to meet me. Luckily, their agents didn't do their job well, or at least they didn't show much zeal for their work. They spent most of their time just loitering around the house.

My mother put a complex plan into effect. She went out every day and visited different shops and friends' houses. When it came time for her to meet me, she always made such visits first. Then, when she was certain that she was not being followed, she did not neglect to zigzag on her way to our rendezvous, which was always at night and in different places each time.

One of those nights, it occurred to me that the list of ships sunk by the Allies was still in my desk at home. Who knows what else I could have forgotten in there. Then I remembered that I had drawn the German vehicle symbols I sent in the last package to Menegatos on blackout paper that I had taken from our windows. It was a distinctively gray paper, faded from the sun. If the Germans saw this paper in our house and had the paper with the symbols in their hands, they would immediately know who had drawn them.

In the bathroom cabinet there were still two little bottles of the invisible ink I used for our records and the solution to make the writing reappear, as well as chemicals for film development. I sent word to my sister to burn all the handwritten papers she could find in my desk drawer, to destroy the remaining blackout paper that had covered the windows, and to break all the bottles.

It was a godsend for me to suddenly recall all of this evidence overlooked in the moments of haste before going into hiding, because two or three days later two Germans suddenly entered the house, accompanied by a Greek. My mother said that they looked everywhere, but left without conducting a thorough search. It seems that they immediately realized from seeing the empty desk drawers that they would not find anything.

Of all my companions, I only saw Mitsos Rediadis and Nicos Paliatseas regularly. I saw Nicos every other night to break his terrible loneliness and to help keep up his morale. The danger did not seem to spread, and we hoped that we would soon be able to find our second wireless set and get our organization functioning again.

Mitsos and I discussed all of our problems in dark side streets. His security did not seem to be threatened for the time being, and so he could go out and bring me news. His basic mission now was to find out and relate to me every possible detail about our imprisoned members.

❋   ❋   ❋

In a few days we got our first news about Alexander Kairis, along with some news about Menegatos and me.

I combine here the information we collected from the lawyers who undertook Alexander's defense, from the Archdiocese we asked to take an interest in his case, from Nicholas Kairis who was released about a month after his arrest, and from a barber the Germans used in the Averof prisons and who helped us repeatedly without my ever learning his name. Thus I have tried to piece together the most accurate picture I can of Alexander Kairis's arrest and the first days of his life in prison.

The Tuesday after Easter, April 27, 1943, Alexander appeared at his office as usual. Two officers of the GFP (*Geheim Feld Polizei*) who were talking with his superior approached him.

"Certain confidential information from this department was conveyed to enemy spies. Do you know who could have handed it over?" they asked.

Alexander, emotionally prepared for this situation, maintained incredible composure. "I am not aware of that confidential information," he answered with the air of a person trying to help. "Besides, there are many in our department who learn various secrets while on duty. It is not easy to identify the one who could have passed them on."

The policemen continued. "Do you think that if we found a note with a particular person's handwriting in the hands of Greek spies we would have the ultimate proof of his guilt?"

Alexander did not expect this complication. His clever mind, keenly trained by his education in law, quickly directed itself at this new development. "It would be a most serious indication of guilt," he answered.

Then the GFP officers showed Alexander a paper clearly written by his own hand. "Do you recognize this note?" they asked. Alexander looked at the paper carefully. It was an old note of his from the time when we still sent unaltered, handwritten messages to the wireless set.

"Gentlemen," he said to them, "if this paper was found in the hands of enemy spies, suspicion of me would indeed be great. However, I remember very clearly that I wrote this note under the order of my department head so that we could answer certain questions from the Crete Headquarters. The document with the questions and the copy of the answers can be found in our archives, which are at your disposal. The only logical explanation is that someone removed this note from the folder containing the correspondence or perhaps even from my desk drawer. Who this person is I do not know, and it is your responsibility to find him. As for me, everybody knows — and the general himself will certainly ensure you — that I am a most loyal friend of yours. You are obliged to investigate this matter fully before you direct such a serious accusation at me."

"We're sorry," was the GFP officers' response, "but we must arrest you. Whatever you have to say, you can say at the regular interrogation."

The forceful and quick-witted denial of his accusation had not helped Alexander Kairis in this initial clash with his opponents. They handcuffed him and transported him to the Averof prisons. The next day, they took him to Piraeus for interrogation.

While the GFP were arresting Alexander at his office, the German police were searching his house and arresting his brother.

I convey here, from a 1945 book by the British Colonel W. Byford-Jones,[1] an excerpt from what Alexander's brother Nicholas told him about those days.

> *The day my brother went back to the office, on the Tuesday, two Germans came to the house. One was a member of the German secret field police. They went through all the cupboards and drawers and they filled a great bag with all the papers they could find. They were there two hours. When they'd finished they said to me: "You must come with us." I knew then that Alexander had been arrested for being a spy. He didn't tell me what he was doing. My parents were against him working for the Germans and there was a chilly atmosphere in the house. Many of his friends didn't speak to him because of it. They regretted that after. ...*
>
> *On the next Monday night we met each other in the police office, but we couldn't speak. He was pale, strained about the eyes and looked very tired and much thinner than he was before. It was obvious they had been trying to force the names of people out of him, and get him to confess. I don't know why, but I knew that he would never tell anything. I was asked if I knew why I had been arrested, and I replied "No."*
>
> *They told me I had luck that I lived with my brother and that he had been arrested for being a spy. I said at once that he was not capable of doing that and a German said, "Your brother is the biggest agent of the British Intelligence Service." ...*
>
> *"You must say what you know about your brother. His life is lost. You must save your own." ...*
>
> *He asked me who his friends were and I told who they were, including Rigas Rigopoulos. Then the Germans said: "Do you know Menegatos?" ... I said firmly that I didn't know him. Then in came a man. I had never seen him before. We looked at each other and neither of us spoke. He was taken out and I was put in a cell. Later I was in the same cell as the man they said was Menegatos. I asked him who he was and he gave me another name. He was a caïque skipper and he didn't know why they had arrested him. He'd been there five days, and had only once eaten. ...*
>
> *Menegatos ... was tried with three other members of the gang. ... Menegatos was the only one who'd said anything, and he spoke because they'd tortured him.*

---

[1]Byford-Jones, W. (1945). *The Greek Trilogy.* Hutchinson & Co., Ltd., London. pp. 38-39.

For four torturous days Alexander resisted the frightful German interrogation. He didn't change his initial statements even in the slightest detail. He was not ensnared by their traps. He did not bend.

He faced the physical pain and moral pressure with incredible spiritual strength and alert caution. He describes the first days of his imprisonment in a shocking letter.

> *Four days, my dear, in a basement with no window, with the walls and half the ceiling soaked with moisture, the floor of black flagstones, pissed on, and, in two corners, volumes of human fertilizer ... you couldn't breathe, handcuffed the whole four days, without even a second with your hands free, without cigarette — the least — and famished — only on the third and fourth day in the evening a small piece of stale bread and water after a thousand pleas. ...*

With the same clear-cut, descriptive style, he gives an account of *"the worst of all,"* the attempt to restrain for four days and nights his natural need:

> *... Yes, my friend, try with the handcuffs to undo your suspenders and make all of the necessary movements and you will see "the impossibility of the task." I can tell you, that this was the greatest torture. ...*

And for the hours of sleep, he writes:

> *... As expected, this mattress was soaked. I shivered all over from the dampness that pierced me to the bone ... But when it was beyond me to stand on my feet and my eyes became heavy with fatigue, I would fall onto this mattress. Sometimes I would fall asleep, but in ten minutes at most, I jumped up shivering and heard my teeth chattering in the darkness. ...*

Meantime, the interrogation continued. His interrogators used all means: brutalization, hunger, sleep deprivation, threats, promises. The result remained unchanged. Persistent and absolute denial.

Some of the Germans faltered. Could it be that Kairis was truly innocent? Could it be that they were torturing a good friend in the place of an unknown spy? The tougher ones insisted, "Kairis is a spy. One of the most dangerous. Behind him is a whole network that must be neutralized."

Finally, they returned Alexander to the Averof prisons and locked him in strict solitary confinement until the day of his trial.

In another letter to Popi Sakelaridis that he managed to smuggle out of prison, he described, with his characteristic, refined spirit and innate literary style, the return to his cell after the four frightful days of interrogation in Piraeus. The following excerpt, aside from painting a vivid picture of a prisoner's life, reveals the wonderful psyche of an exceptional person.

> *Oh, when they brought me back here to "Averof's," as soon as I entered my cell and the iron door shut behind me, I felt such a warmth, such a relief, as if a bad nightmare had just ended, as if I was in a place where one is certain that he is safe and looked after. Searching in the dark — it must have been after 9 and the cells do not have lights — to find my blanket to lie down, I pushed some-*

*thing with my foot. Feeling my way, and with eyes that started
getting used to the dark, I saw that it was a clay bowl of the prison,
and it was full! ... Some merciful hand had cared to fill it for me.*

*Oh, the emotion of that moment is impossible for me to ani-
mate for you. When one is imprisoned, he is easily moved. There
are things, simple, very simple, that you see quite differently. Believe me that at that moment I did not think I would have something to eat. It was not this that moved me — although I had starved
for four days (the last two with only a piece of stale bread). Believe me, it would have meant nothing to me had I gone to sleep
without putting anything in my stomach. Besides, you know that
I'm not the type of person who worries about food — moreover,
one gets used to hunger easily. The first day he only feels some
annoying rumbling and then nothing, that's all.*

*It was the thought that someone worried for me, the thought
that someone took care of me and he thought that I might return
and perhaps be hungry — even though this someone didn't know
me, or precisely because he worried about me without knowing me
— precisely this — made me kneel in the darkness and take this
bowl into my hands, the same way one would take the head of a
loved one to kiss it, and whisper a deep thank you to my unknown
friend ...*

*At that moment, I felt that if I let myself, perhaps tears could
come to my eyes. But I did not want this. Sitting flat on the floor, on
my blanket, I slurped from the clay bowl — I did not have a spoon
— the cold bean soup, without bread, contemplating that good-
ness does exist in the world.*

*The next day I saw that the same unknown hand — and this
hand continues to be unknown to me, I am not allowed to speak
with anyone — had even cared to put a piece of bread in my cell,
something that I had not seen last night in the dark.*

*That night, although exhausted after the four days in Piraeus,
sleep did not come quickly. A long time passed, I was feeling full of
gratitude, I was feeling secure, and finally sleep found me like a
little child who falls asleep in the warm and safe bosom of his
mother. ... Dreams I cannot remember to have seen that night, but
if I did, oh, I am sure they would have been beautiful dreams, a
child's dreams, no doubt, they must have had some good witch
who saves the princess from the claws of the evil dragon, or something like that."* ...

Nicos Menegatos faced much of the same moments and interrogation methods
as Kairis.

As mentioned earlier, Menegatos was a brave man. He, too, determinably resisted the inhuman pressure. He persistently claimed that he was a captain of a caïque
and that he didn't know anything.

But the tortures annihilated him. Nicholas Kairis, as we saw, encountered Menegatos
in prison. However, he did not meet the robust, rather fat Menegatos, but a wretched
and feeble shadow of the man. That was how the interrogation wore him down.

Even in this miserable condition, he still resisted for quite a few days, until the Germans, systematically searching his house in Piraeus, discovered the package with the information and the report that we had given him for the last dispatch. With this overwhelming evidence in their hands, they discharged their last attack against him. They broke him in body and in spirit. They turned him into a rag.

Returning one night to the cell he shared with Nicholas Kairis, Menegatos summed up his despair in one sentence, "I can't dodge the bullet now." When they got Menegatos in this state, the Germans changed tactics. They started creating new hopes for him. It seems that they offered him his life in exchange for unreserved disclosures.

And Menegatos finally cracked. He gave them facts and names. It is said that he talked about the caïques and the wireless sets, Nicos Paliatseas, caïque captain Stamatis Tratras, and Socratis Tselentis. The last two soon fell into the German hands. Nicos Paliatseas followed shortly thereafter. However, we are not certain that their arrests were a direct result of Menegatos's disclosures. Subsequent information convinced us that our downfall began on the coasts of Turkey.

German espionage, which moved freely in Turkey, discovered the two caïques that transported information from Greece. They left them undisturbed to watch their movements and to get to the organization or organizations that used these caïques in Piraeus and Athens.

They followed Menegatos, who, totally unsuspecting, led the Germans to our wireless set in Nea Smirni. The circle had closed. They arrested him to extract more under interrogation. Perhaps in the same way they followed and arrested caïque captain Tratras and Tselentis, who belonged to the same Allied service as Menegatos.

The only thing that seems to be certain is that Menegatos's disclosures led to Paliatseas's arrest, because Menegatos was the only one who could tell the Germans about the place where they finally located him.

Our organization, Service 5-16-5, was not really known to Menegatos. He knew the secret code number 5-16-5, of course, but this was also mentioned in the report that fell into the Germans' hands along with Menegatos's package. In the same report, there was also the code signature "R17–Chief of Service 5-16-5," which did not say much at first glance.

Menegatos also knew my code name, "Captain Nicos." He might have said that "Captain Nicos" must be the leader of Service 5-16-5 or at least a high-ranking member. Maybe he even gave them a description of my appearance, or at least whatever he remembered from our meeting the previous year.

However, it looks as if none of these things had any relation whatsoever with the searches in my office at the Bank of Greece and at home, with the blockade of my house, and with the pursuit that followed. It is more likely that the search at the Bank was instigated by the hard core of Alexander Kairis's interrogators, those who were not swayed by his endurance and patience and who were determined to leave no stone unturned that might prove his guilt.

I was a very close friend of Kairis and the Germans learned this. Our friendship was well known, and if either of the Kairis brothers concealed my name when the Germans asked them for the names of their friends, they would have immediately raised suspicion about me.

But the Germans' suspicions were really aroused when they looked for me at the

Bank, perhaps only to ask me something about Alexander Kairis, and verified that I had disappeared the very day they arrested him. At that point, it was easy for them to take the picture of me from my Bank personnel file and show it to Menegatos. If Menegatos recognized "Captain Nicos" in my picture, Alexander would definitely be lost.

But Menegatos had only seen me once, a long time ago, at night in the grove in Nea Smirni. Besides, the Bank's picture was taken eight years before. Then, as a boy of 21, I had more hair, no moustache, and my face didn't show the lines of hardship etched during the retreat and Occupation.

Menegatos would have been doubtful. Perhaps he would have deliberately made his doubt seem greater. He was not the type to drag someone down lightheartedly and in cold blood, if he could avoid it.

We also learned that the Gestapo had in hand something written by me, which might have been found near the wireless set along with Kairis's note. There was also the report that the Germans had compared some note of mine with handwritten papers they found in the Bank and verified that it was my handwriting.

If, however, the Germans had discovered my relation to the wireless set in Nea Smirni from this note, they definitely would have presented this during Kairis's trial as a verification of his guilt, which they didn't do. I therefore conclude that the document examined by the Gestapo must have been one of my patriotic articles or poems that Alexander might have kept at one point and was found in his house during the search.

Only one fact can be considered certain, a fact that explains the organized pursuit of me by the Gestapo. By combining my friendship with Kairis, my disappearance from the Bank and from my house, my note they had in their hands, and Menegatos's disclosures, the Germans must have suspected that I was one and the same with "Captain Nicos," and possibly the leader of Service 5-16-5. The signature "R17–Chief of Service 5-16-5" on the report in Menegatos's package also would have tipped them off to my name.

The evidence was serious enough for them to organize my systematic pursuit. They even told the Kairis brothers that they could arrest the leader of the organization at any time, so their silence was useless.

In the months that followed, as we will see, I came within range of my pursuers twice and a third time they had me surrounded, but all three times they missed by pure luck. Their confidence that I would soon fall into their hands did not discourage my guardian angel.

During those calm nights in early May, Mitsos Rediadis and I would stroll the remote side streets between Areos Park, Kipseli, and Agamon Square, dissecting every new bit of information about those who were detained, trying to predict developments and do whatever we could.

We considered how we might help the prisoners, stall their probable execution, or even liberate them. Every idea that crossed our minds, no matter how improbable, had to be analyzed and scrutinized.

We studied the legal and psychological means that the defense might use or the possibility for certain personalities to intervene, such as the Archbishop or well-known people with some sort of influence, like the members of the puppet government. We considered the possibility of bribing certain Germans to release or at least help one or more of the prisoners escape, and it was then I recognized my mistake in not accepting the Allies' financial help from the beginning, so that we would not be facing — along with everything else — the lack of money that might be needed.

We even proceeded to devise a plan of attack to free Alexander during his transports from the Averof prisons to the interrogator or to the court-martial. We had been informed about the routes the automobile followed, and we debated at what points and in what manner we might attack it and neutralize its few guards.

We made efforts on all these matters in several directions. But we proceeded with great caution so that the presence of an organized team behind the prisoners would not be detected. That would surely cause them more harm than good.

In the case of Alexander Kairis, with great hesitancy I gave my consent for some people to be informed about his secret activity, because only then would they possibly agree to help him. This is when Alexander's parents learned something about his national mission. It is also when Archbishop Damaskinos was informed that it was worthwhile to take an interest in this exceptional person.

Most of the requests were made without mentioning Alexander's secret activity. We were only asking a favor for a beloved person. Some good will. One exception. My sister Popi dedicated herself to this effort. At the same time, Alexander's relatives and many friends did likewise. Andreas Logothetis, a lawyer who often visited Alexander in prison, offered him precious support. Two distinguished lawyers admitted to the German court-martial undertook his defense, Prof. John Georgakis, an advisor and friend of the Archbishop, and Prof. John Sontis.

Promises made by high-ranking Germans and assurances given by "powerful" German collaborators raised our hopes until they later proved false. Steps taken by the Church and by Greek authorities also proved fruitless. But our intense efforts continued with the hope that we would finally make some progress.

In any case, the only substantial help that I could personally offer to Alexander, after all these discussions and futile efforts — help that could only come from me — was to send this message via his family: "The leader begs him, if he is sentenced to death, to reveal his name to the Germans after they agree to spare his life in return." I added that "we are all well hidden and they will never be able to find us." Alexander would immediately understand that I was asking him to identify me as the leader of the organization, without fear of putting me in immediate danger. I believed that I was removing a great, moral dilemma for him and was releasing him from any obligation so that he could save himself.

This message was passed to Alexander Kairis one day through his lawyers. His answer once again demonstrated his supreme moral fiber and his incredible spiritual strength. "Cut the nonsense," was all he said. "You know very well that such a thing cannot be done." Alexander was not the type to go against his conscience under any circumstances.

At the same time, we tried to figure out how we might reestablish communication with the Allied service. Now that we had made sure, little by little, that there was no betrayal from within our organization, it might soon be possible to begin operating again. In addition, the Allies might be able to help our imprisoned members. Perhaps they could send money for us to buy the help of certain people. For this to happen, we needed a way to ask for it.

We envisioned two means to achieve the needed communication. The first and most ideal would be for us to find or construct our own wireless set. The second was to approach another organization, via friends, that had communication with abroad. We began to work on both of these possibilities.

We considered asking our harbor people to contact some of the escape caïques. But how could we entrust our such a confidential message to someone outside our organization? And to whom would he transmit it when he arrived at his destination? We would have to avoid this method of communication for the time being.

I continued to meet Nicos Paliatseas every other night. Lately, he came to our rendezvous terribly worried. He was upset not only over the arrests of Stamatis Tratras and Socratis Tselentis, who seemed to have been quite dear to him, but also because these arrests dashed our hopes of finding the second wireless set or using the caïques, which, we verified, had been abandoned by their crews.

When I told him that we were still hoping to communicate with abroad, and that we would perhaps do so very soon, Paliatseas regained his composure. He suggested that we try to find a trustworthy radio technician who could at least build an imperfect wireless set for our first communication, and he gave me some numbers for the wavelengths on which the machine would have to be able to operate.

That is when I thought of my friend Alkis Delmouzos with whom, as mentioned previously, I worked at the Bank and often discussed military events and domestic resistance. Alkis's brother, Panagis, was an electrical engineer, and together they had a fairly well-stocked radio factory in Kipseli. I also knew that Alkis was a member of some resistance organization, but I didn't know any other details.

One night, I went to see the two brothers at their factory. The first thing I asked about was the possibility of sending a message abroad. Unfortunately, nothing could be done. It seems that strife had developed in their organization, "Apollo." This rift eventually led to Alkis Delmouzos replacing the current leader. In any event, Alkis doubted if he could get my message transmitted abroad any time soon.

As for the manufacture of a wireless set transmitter, Panagis Delmouzos explained that aside from certain instruments they didn't have, we would never find the wavelength we needed to communicate because the numbers on the British crystals did not correspond to wavelengths or kilocycles. They were symbolic, just for the convenience of the operator.

I saw Alkis Delmouzos a few more times to see if he ever had a chance to transmit the message I left with him just in case the situation changed, but the message was never transmitted.

❋ ❋ ❋

Then I suddenly lost Nicos Paliatseas.

Five nights in a row, from 9:00 to 9:15, I walked around looking toward the corner of Aristotelous Street and Kiriakou Square, which was the point of our rendezvous. Something very serious must have happened.

I hoped he had just taken ill. But deep inside, I was sure he had been arrested. I don't know why, but it immediately crossed my mind that he must have gone to see his friend the barber in Academia Platonos despite my admonitions. There the Germans, informed by Menegatos, might have been keeping watch as they had been doing for quite some time outside my house. I knew that Nicos arranged rendezvous fairly often near this barbershop. I, too, had met him near there, and Menegatos and Tselentis knew it well. For this very reason, I had forbidden him to go there.

I called Eleni Limberopoulos, but Nicos hadn't contacted her, either.

Through a boy whom the Limberopoulos family also used to help their prisoners, I maintained contact with the barber of the Averof prisons. I sent word and asked if they had recently brought in a tall, husky young man. In response, I received a list of the names of new detainees. Paliatseas was not among them. Nonetheless, my anxiety had become unbearable.

Whatever the reason, Nicos definitely must have been in serious trouble. Perhaps he was gravely ill or wounded and needed our help. Maybe he realized that the Germans had him under surveillance and would not approach so that he wouldn't lead them to me. Maybe they had arrested him and were holding him in one of the interrogation centers. Or maybe they had killed him.

Whatever had happened, I could not simply ignore his absence. If there was even the slightest chance that I could help him, I had to do everything I possibly could.

Nicos could have surfaced in two places, at Eleni Limberopoulos's and at the barbershop in Academia Platonos. As long as Eleni hadn't heard anything, I had no choice but to go to the forbidden barbershop that was perhaps being watched by the Germans. Only there might I learn something.

Mitsos Rediadis and I discussed the matter that night and decided that I should wait at Kiriakou Square one more time, that we should ask again at the Averof prisons, and if nothing changed we should risk approaching the barbershop together.

Anticipating that the barbershop would be under surveillance by the Gestapo, I devised a plan which Mitsos and I reviewed in minute detail.

We planned to set out when the barbershop opened in the afternoon. The Germans probably wouldn't keep watch inside the closed shop during the entire midday break. So if there was a team of three or four guards, we would see them returning from their break and we could take the necessary precautions.

We would be armed. I would go inside to meet the barber and Mitsos would wait nearby to cover me in case I fell into danger. If the Germans suddenly surrounded me I would try to break out using the pistol. Mitsos would intervene only if the Germans succeeded in arresting me. Then he would advance and open fire at his discretion. Mitsos was a good shot and a passionate hunter. If he could neutralize one or two of them, it wouldn't be too difficult for us to escape. Amidst the commotion, we would both try to disappear.

This plan may sound fictional and irrational as one calmly reads it today. However, I can assure the reader that when I later went through special training and took part in commando operations, I learned from experience that much more difficult operations can be carried out successfully.

That very same night we started living in the atmosphere of alarm created by the operation we were planning.

While we were outwardly taking every logical step to avoid an encounter with the Germans, inside, without realizing it, we were practically hoping for one. In a way, we were looking to break out of our forced inaction. To blow off steam. To shake off the distasteful role of fugitive for a while and become attackers. Perhaps we could extract a bloody reimbursement for all that our people suffered at the enemy's hands.

Aside from my revolver, which I had taken from its hiding place above the toilet in the Bank of Greece, Admiral Hors had also given me a beautiful precision automatic pistol. I thought of taking both weapons on the upcoming operation. But I was bothered by the fact that I had not tried the Admiral's pistol and I did not even know if it functioned properly.

When Mitsos and I parted, I went to the Technical University to see Stavros Vrachnos, who frequently worked at the Chemistry Lab late into the night. I wanted to see how things were going with his team. I spoke to Stavros about the operation we were planning and the untested pistol I would have with me.

"Come back tomorrow night and test it here," he said. "I will turn on some motors and the shots will be drowned out by the noise. Besides, explosions are common in the laboratory."

We agreed that he would prepare an explosive mixture and set off a small explosion at the moment of the gunshots, so that if the Germans were to come, they could be convinced that it was just an innocent experiment.

"I also have something else for you," Stavros said. "If you ever need to change your hiding place, I know a house that belongs to friends of mine where you can stay safe and sound. They are a very trustworthy couple without children and without a servant." I could not imagine then how useful this house would be to me later on.

The following night, Nicos Paliatseas yet again failed to appear at our rendezvous point. We also heard nothing new from the prisons. Shortly afterwards, I saw Mitsos and we arranged to meet the following afternoon at 3:30 at the beginning of Heyden Street. We also finalized some last minute details. Then I went to see Stavros.

The laboratory was about 25 meters long. We hung a piece of wood on the wall with a small circle in the middle as a target. We started several machines, and amidst the noise I pulled the trigger twice. Only one shot fired.

I never imagined that such a small caliber pistol could make such a racket. The laboratory had a domed ceiling, and in this enclosed space you would have thought the whole university had been blown up.

Stavros set off his mixtures, broke some bottles on the floor, and rushed to the door to see if anyone was in the courtyard. Everything outside was calm.

I rushed to the target. I had the satisfaction of seeing my bullet in the center. I looked on the floor for the cartridge that must have been ejected, but I couldn't find it. I threw the wood with the bullet into the burning kiln, hurriedly passed through the university courtyard, and proceeded carefree up Patision Street.

When I looked at the pistol later, I found that the fired cartridge had stuck in the chamber. It was completely rusted. That's why the second shot didn't fire. I opened the magazines and carefully polished all the cartridges, which I had failed to do when I was cleaning the automatic's mechanism.

At the beginning of this book, I spoke about two cases in which my good fortune miraculously saved me from death. The first was in Kifisohori during the horrifying bombing, when a bomb fell next to me but didn't explode. That bomb served to chase me, you might say, away from a place that was completely blown to bits half a minute later. The second was in Nafplionn, when I fell asleep on the dock at dawn after helping load British troops all night. Thus I missed boarding a caïque that hit a mine and was blown up as it transported the last detachment to their ships waiting out in the harbor.

The same good fortune had put its hand on my shoulder once again.

Mitsos Rediadis and I met as we had agreed at 3:30 in the afternoon on Heyden Street. We were both wearing gabardine overcoats. Mitsos had his hand in his pocket, holding his gun so that it would not be visible. I was wearing a hat and glasses. I had my revolver in my back pants pocket. I had made a holster for the automatic pistol that I tied high inside my right thigh under the wide pants, practically between my legs, and attached it to my belt with a strap. I cut out my pants pocket, and from there I could reach down and draw the pistol. I thought that if I fell into the Germans' hands and they found the revolver in my back pocket, perhaps they wouldn't continue the search in that unlikely location and I might be able to surprise them later on with the automatic.

As soon as Mitsos saw me, he came to my side. I was surprised. Not only was this counter to the measures we always took, but it also went against the plans we had discussed the previous night. We were to walk separately, and not even sit together on the bus.

"I have urgent news about our communication with abroad," he said as soon as he got near me. "A close friend of one of my people is leaving, maybe even today, for the Middle East. We can give him whatever message we want for the Allied services. He is a trustworthy person. Do you still want to go through with our plan for Paliatseas today, or do you think maybe it's better to put it off until tomorrow to make sure we don't lose this opportunity for communication?"

I immediately agreed that the Paliatseas operation should be postponed, and I authorized Mitsos to meet with the person planning to escape abroad. He should speak to this person in general terms about our situation and instruct him to contact the Allied services that deal with espionage in Greece. That person would have to stress to them that we are waiting for a liaison to contact us as soon as possible. Their person would have to ask for Mister Mitsos on Dimitry Rediadis's telephone. As long as the liaison somehow mentioned the reason for his call with the correct details, no further signal of recognition would be needed.

That night I would go once more to Kiriakou Square to wait for Paliatseas. I would also inquire again at the Averof prisons to see if there was any news. But we were confident that nothing would change.

Tomorrow, at noon, we would definitely set out for Academia Platonos.

There are moments in life when you definitely sense the presence of God at your side. You feel small and powerless before His greatness. You do not judge and you do not interpret His inscrutable will. All you ask for is a church where you can light a candle and humbly worship His grace.

That is how I felt that night at Saint George Square in Kipseli, when, after waiting for Nicos as usual, I met the boy who brought us news from the Averof prisons. "There is a new inmate who must surely be your guy," he said. "His name is Nicos Paliatseas. He was arrested several days ago at a barbershop in Academia Platonos."

I tried to still my pounding heart. "Did you learn anything else?"

"Paliatseas hadn't shown up at the prisons because the Germans held him in strict solitary confinement all those days, without food and water. They interrogated him in the harshest manner without getting a word out of him. They still have the barbershop where they arrested him cordoned off, and they've placed machine guns on neighboring roofs and in windows, waiting for other collaborators to show up."

The boy soon disappeared into the night and I stood alone in a corner of the Square, immobilized by surprise and awe. First Menegatos, then Kairis, Tratras, Tselentis, now Nicos Paliatseas. What curse had befallen us? Weren't the misfortunes we had suffered up til now enough? Nicos had dodged the first real bullet, escaping from the wireless set house as the Germans arrested Menegatos, and had warned us all to take cover. Why did this beloved boy have to fall into the Germans' hands now? I revulsed from the depths of my soul over fate's unjust persecution.

But Mitsos and I should also have been in enemy hands since midday. How did the need for us to postpone arise at the last minute? Why was everything we needed to learn about Paliatseas and the barbershop revealed to me today? Just to make me definitively call off the next day's action?

If we had gone to Academia Platonos, death would certainly have been waiting for us. Outside the barbershop, we would not have seen anything suspicious to warn us of the danger. The Gestapo would surely have grabbed me as soon as I went in. If I had succeeded in getting away with Mitsos's help, they would have mowed both of us down with the machine guns...

Once more, I was seeing a supreme force intervening, turning the natural flow of events and protecting me. But why only me? I stood there on the corner of the dark Square, drowning in opposing emotions and questions. With an unfounded feeling of guilt, I thought about my wronged companions and pleaded...

I saw the church in front of me. I went up the stairs, pushed through the half-opened door, and stood in a corner. There, I slowly regained my composure. I wanted to believe that everything would work out well in the end.

But fate follows her own path, unforeseen and unexplored. Her ways, beyond every human logic and frailty, can be cruel.

On May 29, 1943, as dawn broke at the shooting range in Kaisariani, the Germans shot Nicos Paliatseas, Nicos Menegatos, Stamatis Tratras, and Socratis Tselentis...

Mitsos Rediadis brought me the news that night in front of the Evelpidon School.

Twenty-eight years have passed since then — by some strange coincidence I am writing these lines on May 29, 1971 — and in all those years I have never passed that spot indifferently. For me, each pass is a commemoration.

But at those times, my psychological state was quite different.

The intense atmosphere of the Occupation, and particularly the execution of Kostas Perrikos four months before with the emotional reactions it created in me, seemed to have forged a defensive shield that gave me the ability to face shocking events — some of which I even anticipated — with maximum self-control.

I was not shaken at that moment. I did not weep — as I did not weep soon afterward when I saw my father, whom I adored, dead. I accepted what was done and thought that at least there was still hope for Alexander Kairis, who, although he had been tried with the others, had skillfully managed to deceive the court-martial and have the decision on him postponed.

That night, Mitsos and I stayed outside very late. We even broke the nightly curfew without realizing it. We walked the narrow streets of Polygono, talking about the dead as if they were still with us. We remembered their stories and their jokes. At some moments we were even able to laugh...

The next few days were more difficult. My thoughts constantly went back to those we had lost. We learned various details about their trial and sentences, their lives during the last days in prison, and their glorious stance before the firing squad.

None of them lost heart and none placed blame on anyone else. They stood brave and united before death. The priest who stood by during the execution wrote in his report:

> They kept their calm and faced death as good Christians after they accepted the Holy Communion and piously and reverently confessed to me.

When the evidence that the Germans gathered convinced them during the trial that every denial of their guilt would be pointless, they proudly admitted their participation in the national resistance and revealed to the conqueror all the joy and satisfaction they felt for the destruction they had caused him.

An excerpt from a letter by Alexander Kairis, written on May 26, three days before the execution, gives a simple picture that leaves us in awe before the incredible composure of those condemned to die.

> ... Last Saturday, six of us were tried and sentenced together — the four [of ours] to death, one got 15 years imprisonment, and for me, the decision was postponed — all six with the same accusation: espionage. ...
>
> ... The next day, in the morning, as we were washing up in the basins side by side, despite being prohibited from talking, one of those sentenced to death whispered to me confidentially, "Last night I discovered an important machine." I didn't understand what he meant by "important machine." Was he talking literally about some kind of mechanical device or was he talking figuratively about some kind of racket or swindle?
>
> So I asked him, "In other words?" and got the reply, "A machine that runs continuously and with automatic lubrication" and I don't know what else. Of course, I had no idea what he was talking about. He added, "For so many years I struggled, and last night I found it!" The night of his sentence to death, the rascal!
> ...Of course, these are things that could make you cry. But I took the side that makes you laugh, and I laugh! ...

The "one of those sentenced to death" must have been caïque captain Stamatis Tratras.

Nicos Paliatseas, prematurely approaching death at age 23, also maintained not only his composure, but his perpetual, carefree smile as well, even when he saw the firing squad moving into position directly across from him.

As we learned from the priest, he turned to some guard next to him and asked for a cigarette. When the guard, with shaking hands, gave him the whole pack, our cool-headed young man lit a cigarette and returned the pack, cocking his head toward the firing squad.

"I don't need more," he said, smiling. "I'm in a bit of a hurry..."

As always, Nicos played with death, right down to the last minute.

Soon the four Greeks were standing before the shooting range wall, facing the German firing squad. With their heads high, full of the grandeur of their sacrifice, they refused to be blindfolded. They preferred to write the last word of their story staring Death in the eye.

The firing squad captain ordered: "Take aim..."

With vigorous voices, the four young men began to sing our National Anthem. Each salvo cut a voice from the heroic song, until the last fearless voice fell silent.

Two Last Months in Athens. Hide and Seek with the Gestapo.

In June 1943 I decided to leave for Turkey. My plan was to make personal contact with the Allied services, ask for a wireless set, operator, caïques, and necessary organizational assistance, and return to Greece as soon as possible. Service 5-16-5 could — and had to — start operating again.

Mitsos Rediadis was never suspected and was keen to mobilize as before. Koutsoudakis's Harbor Division, with the harbor master, assistant harbor master, pilots, and all the others, Stavros Vrachnos's Technical Division, with its chemical engineers and other specialists and their expansion into the provinces and islands, and Popi Sakelaridis's developing Railroad Division were completely intact. All they needed to resume operation was a signal from the central administration. They would then mobilize immediately and begin supplying us with their most valuable information.

It seems that our security measures had been effective. Our air-tight organization into triads, combined with strict security at all levels, had isolated the danger and brought the German counterespionage authorities to an impasse. Even Kairis and Paliatseas would have avoided arrest if they had followed my instructions.

Whatever the Germans managed to learn through interrogations was limited to the Allied services' network to which our wireless set operator, Nicos Paliatseas, belonged, despite the fact that he was an integral part of Service 5-16-5. Outside this special circle, a barricade of ignorance blocked the way.

In Alexander Kairis's case, things seemed to be going exceptionally well for the time being. His brother Nicholas had recently been released and was finally able to operate on Popi Sakelaridis, who since then had regained her health. Alexander had gone through two trials without a verdict being reached.

His defense attorneys, John Georgakis and John Sontis, distinguished German-educated jurists to whom many Greeks owed their salvation, defended him with true passion and at serious personal risk to themselves. It was not at all easy for one Greek to defend another in a German court-martial, particularly when the defendant was charged with espionage.

The defense centered on the argument that Alexander's handwritten note found near the wireless set had been stolen and that it was just one of the many notes he had a compulsion for keeping to help maintain exemplary order in his department. There is even a special term in German psychology for people with a mania for keeping notes on everything: *notizbuch menschen*. It is in this well-known category, the lawyers argued, that Alexander Kairis belonged.

By now, the Germans were treating Alexander well. Many things had played crucial roles for him in this turn of events: his skillful answers under interrogation and during the trials, the defense by his own German chief who continued to think of him as completely trustworthy, and the fact that while it was proven that Paliatseas, Menegatos, Tratras, and Tselentis knew each other, they did not know Kairis and they didn't even seem to know anything about him. So we could be calm about Alexander Kairis's situation for the time being.

Despite this favorable outlook, I was still concerned about Alexander's ultimate fate. This concern was another important factor pushing me to make the trip to Turkey. The Allied Secret Services must certainly have an incredible organization, and it might be very possible for them to help us save Alexander conclusively.

Of course, we must not fail to admit that there were also unavoidable points of leakage in our security system. Ignoring this would be an injustice to the memories of Paliatseas and Kairis, to whose indomitable psychological endurance we owe the fact that the Gestapo was unable to advance even one step toward us.

From Paliatseas, the Germans could have gotten to Eleni Limberopoulos, specifically armed with the knowledge that she knew the real identity of "Captain Nicos." Or, even easier, they could have gotten to me directly if Paliatseas had not had the strength to be silent and had led them to the rendezvous where I waited for him so many nights. They could have gotten to me from Kairis as well, and to Popi Sakelaridis if he had not had the strength to resist as he did. But these dangerous vulnerable points had now disappeared.

The only dangers that remained were the Germans' suspicions about me personally and their continuous persecution, things which would force me to stay in constant hiding from now on and even change hideouts as I carried on my duties in the organization. But these were things I was prepared to face.

So everything supported the notion that I should to leave for Turkey as soon as possible. There, in Constantinople, I would try to find the British Major with the pseudonym "Hatzis" as Menegatos instructed me, obtain all the necessary supplies from the Allied Headquarters, and then return to Greece.

We immediately began to work toward this goal. Rediadis notified Koutsoudakis and Bachas that they needed to arrange someone's escape to Turkey as soon as possible. We soon heard back that the traveler could depart by caïque, posed as a member of the crew, in 15-30 days. He would leave directly from the Port of Piraeus for Tsesme, Turkey. They asked for his basic features, so they could find a used identity card of a sailor with corresponding characteristics: oval-shaped face, brown eyes, etc. I would have to get photographs taken to replace the one in the identity card. The missing part of the stamp could easily be added at the Port Office. They also recommended that the traveler's appearance be made to look like that of a sailor, a man of the sea and of the caïques, because he might have to go through the usual German inspection. That's where we stumbled.

I had the pictures taken by a street photographer on Klafthmonos Square. Wearing a shabby gabardine coat with my forehead half covered by the hair combed over from the side of my head, I obtained exceptionally satisfying photographs. They were faded, with my face distorted, and made me look like someone from the cheap dives around the harbor. I also arranged with Stavros Vrachnos to use chemicals to try to make me look fierce. I would get a dark tan in Admiral Hors's garden. The last day, Stavros would harden the skin of my hands to make them appear worked.

But I didn't like any of this. I would only resort to these extremes if I really had to. In the meantime we worked on arranging my escape by other means.

Again, we turned to friends in other organizations. I personally met with two or three people who promised me they could help, but nothing came of it. I even approached the communist EAM and at least got a clear-cut refusal: "We send frequent dispatches abroad, but only with our people."

These unsuccessful efforts, the irritating waiting, the atmosphere of the executions, the long confinement indoors, and the forced inactivity began to make me very uncomfortable. I tried to react by writing verses:

Deep inside me then I had the sprout of a divine seed ...
Deep inside me now has nested a demon of evil ...

I also dedicated a poem entitled "Gratitude" to Admiral Hors and his wife, who were risking their lives for my sake. I remember the tears sparkling in their eyes as I read it to them.

One night I went by my girlfriend's house and told her that I had to disappear for a while, but didn't give any further explanation. She insisted that we see each other, at least for a bit, in the park at night. I explained that there was danger for her as well and showed her that I was carrying a gun. I did not succeed in scaring her. I gave in because I needed her company and she stood by me very bravely, my sweet friend.

Every so often, I saw my mother as well. One night, she scared me by saying, "Something terrible has happened..."

I was ready for anything. "What?" I asked her. "What has happened?"

"I wouldn't want to worry you..."

"Please tell me what is going on," I repeated more insistently. I feared a new tragedy and preferred to hear it straight out and immediately.

"My child, they stole all your suits. You have none except the one you're wearing."

"That's all? Thank God."

"But my child, how will you replace them during the occupation?"

Human psychology is very strange sometimes. My mother didn't want to worry me, but because I was completely indifferent, she now tried, with obstinate insistence, to make me see the seriousness of the situation.

Nonetheless, the real tragedy was that my father's condition had worsened terribly. I knew he missed me, and I felt an intense need to see him, too. In the heavy atmosphere that surrounded me, the thought that I might not ever see my father again was unbearable. But the Gestapo continued to keep our house under surveillance, blocking my way.

I studied the situation from every angle and decided to play all my cards. Besides, I had thought of a way to go home with minimal danger.

Our house, as I mentioned, was on September 3rd Street and was the second one from the corner of Trikorfon Street. Over time, the guards had somewhat relaxed their vigilance. There were usually only two, and they walked our pavement or the one across the street, from the one side street to the other, stopping now and then to chat. Often they would sit in the coffee shop across the street. From there they could keep an eye on the door, and thus their consciences were clear that they had the house covered.

A large part of this block was once my grandfather's. He had cut a street through his property and named it Trikorfon Street. The property was divided among his children and houses were built. Relatives lived in all of them. In the back, the houses' gardens were divided by fences or by railings.

I sent the necessary instructions, and one night late in June I set out, armed, and reached the back corner of Trikorfon Street from the back roads. My sister Popi appeared at the other end of September 3rd Street. She fixed her hair to signal that the Gestapo guards were far away and that the road was clear. I advanced to Trikorfon Street toward my uncle's house. All of the useful doors were waiting for me, half-opened. I pushed the front door and went in. From the back door, I went out into the

147

garden. I jumped the fence and crossed into our yard. Using the inside service stairs, I got up to the third floor. Overcome with emotion, I embraced my mother and advanced toward my father's room.

We approached the bed. Father was breathing from his mouth with difficulty. The cancer in his nasal cavity obstructed his breathing and his vision. His eyes were barely open, and I doubted he could see anything.

I truly adored my father and felt a sob building up in my throat. "I've come, Father," I said to him, "I've come to see you."

The beloved head turned slightly. His eyes opened more. He smiled. "I see you. I see both of you," he said with great effort.

I bent down next to him and held his hands. He squeezed my hands with unexpected strength. He was trying to speak, but I couldn't understand his words. I was only able to discern, "Have my blessing."

I could no longer hold back my tears. I pulled away and went into the bathroom to throw a little water on my face. My mother and sister, who had come up from the street by then, came near me. As I was bending over the faucet, some bullets fell out of my pockets and rolled on the tile floor.

"Isn't it more dangerous for you to be carrying a gun?" Mother asked.

"It is indispensable," I replied. "I must not fall into their hands under any circumstances."

I stayed in my father's room a long time. He no longer seemed to sense my presence, but the smile had left its trace on his face.

"It's strange," Mother said, "that he was able to see you. For many days now he hasn't been able to see at all…"

❋　❋　❋

In the beginning of July I was finally able to secure my escape abroad. I was to leave with an organization that specialized in escapes using caïques. They usually departed from a spot near the town of Kimi on the eastern coast of Evoia Island, about 150 kilometers from Athens. From there they sailed to Agrilia on the Turkish coast, just east of Chios Island. Plenty of well-known people had left the same way and were now in Egypt. After the liberation, I learned that the organization that helped me escape was the *Vyrones* led by John Ioannidis and Loukas Linaras. (The title *Vyrones* ["Byrons" in English] was inspired by the name of the English poet Lord Byron, a great supporter of the Hellenic Revolution against the Turks in 1821.)

I owe my contact with this organization to one of the cute little games that fate sometimes plays. There I was, the leader of an organization that counted among its members superior harbor people who had dealt with escapes. I had promises from high-ranking members of other organizations that had realized such escapes in the past. But I was still in Athens, waiting. Then suddenly, my innocent and uninvolved girlfriend declares one night, between two kisses, that she can secure for me, if I'd like, a way to easily leave for abroad. Without a doubt, the situation presented a very funny picture.

A group was to leave before the end of the month. Someone who was to go with them decided to postpone. I would take his place. We took care to make inquiries and were satisfied that everything was perfectly well-organized. My luck was smiling. As a matter of fact, it was grinning from ear to ear.

In this state of some new emotional euphoria, seeing that my departure was now certain and near, I made a mistake that almost cost me everything. I relaxed my strict seclusion and started to go out at different times of the day to meet some trusted people whom I considered well-informed in all matters of our national struggle. I wanted to find out as much as I could about the actions of national organizations and partisan units, as well as the manifestations of EAM's communists.

I wanted to be extremely well-informed in all aspects of our national situation so that I could give an accurate picture of our internal problems to foreign as well as our own authorities. I tried to be well-prepared to use my trip to Turkey in every way possible, since I expected to have the opportunity to meet with high-ranking British officers and the ambassadors of Greece and Great Britain.

Given the state of things in Greece, from my own observations and verified by those of others, two vital and interdependent claims had to be presented to the Allies forcefully.

(1) The systematic supplying of the communists was laying the groundwork for the destruction of our country. The only logical explanation for this strange tactic, we concluded, was that the British had made a huge mistake in their estimation of our internal reality. They believed that by supplying Greece's left wing they would gain two important benefits: (a) they would hit the enemy more effectively today, and (b) they would get the leftists on their side tomorrow, thereby securing their future influence in the Greek sphere.

They had to understand that this tactic was causing the exact opposite result for both of their goals. The communists in Greece were always a minimal minority. They continued to be just that today, despite the phenomenal blossoming of leftism. Therefore, the British were not developing a more effective resistance by supplying this minority. On the contrary, they were dividing our internal struggle, causing conflicts among Greeks themselves and lax operations against the common enemy.

It was also utopian for them to believe that they would win the leftists even in the future. On the contrary, they were creating a situation that would undoubtedly drive Greece toward the establishment of a communist regime, its subjugation to the interests of neighboring Pan-Slavism, and its ending up as one of a bloc of eastern communist countries.

British tactics in the matter of the Bulgarian conquerors and torturers of our people in Northern Greece were having the same effect as the previous mistake. We heard broadcasts from London and Cairo making friendly overtures to the hated Bulgarians, encouraging them to abandon their German allies and side with us and, naturally, alluding to future exchanges. The British policy was infuriating and unacceptable to the Greeks.

A deadly danger, worse and more permanent than the enemy occupation, was threatening our country: internal clashes between Greeks resulting in long, drawn-out bloodshed. Is danger as made more obvious by sorrowful events that forebode the Greek future as dark and distressed: (a) Recent clashes between the communist partisans of ELAS and General Zervas's national partisans of EDES, which had begun to annihilate each other up on the mountains. (b) The plan of extreme nationalists to create "Security Battalions" that would hit the communist groups in cities. This plan was incited by and to the great satisfaction of the Germans and Italians. (c) Recent movements of EAM that — following British recommendations — showed friendliness toward the Bulgarian oppressors of Greek Thrace by publishing pro-Bulgarian articles in its newspaper *O Apeleftherotis* (The Liberator) and proclamations for the autonomy of Macedonia. This evoked a general outcry, and EAM was soon forced to camouflage its intentions with anti-Bulgarian displays and slogans of liberation.

These events and many others marked the road of destruction that British policy was paving for Greece. We felt obliged to send an intense danger signal to our friends and allies and to influence them to re-examine their policy.

In short, this was the first claim. Of course, at that time we did not recognize the true intent of the side of British tactics that deliberately cultivated our internal division. The elements of this organized political conspiracy will be discussed in future chapters.

(2) The other claim, also vital, concerned the support of national organizations. The struggle of these organizations was, after many attempts, finally unified.

No politics or other ideological disposition divided this common effort. Only communism systematically torpedoed the general unification of those Greeks for whom liberation was the only goal. Organizations with noteworthy effectiveness in Greece such as *Ellinikon Aima* (Greek Blood), *Ethniki Drasi* (National Action), *Ethniko Komitato* (National Committee), *PEAN – Panellinios Enosis Agonizomenon Neon* (PanHellenic Union of Fighting Youth), *Iera Taxiarchia* (Sacred Brigade), and others that we did not know then, but which the Allies certainly would have known, struggled with the meager means they could scrape up to print secret newspapers and other publications, to man the partisan units or create their own fighting teams, to relieve the families of patriots, and to mobilize delegates all over Greece. They contributed in every way to maintaining the national morale of the enslaved people at high levels and to keeping the liberation effort invigorated.

On the other side of these national organizations was EAM. It displayed wealth and all kinds of resources from abroad, spreading thousands of proclamations at every chance and providing abundant financial support for its followers. As mentioned earlier, thousands of pure and enthusiastic Greeks were misled by the patriotic appearance and the obvious support that EAM had from the Allies. Thus they thickened its ranks, inadvertently strengthening the penetration of communism into our country.

So by what means could the national organizations lead the people toward the pure liberation struggle that they really desired? How could they deal with publications that were, of course, handed out free, even though with the inflation they must have cost a fortune, a fortune that did not exist. How could the people trust organizations that did not seem to be supported by the Allies?

Thus there was an immediate and imperative need for the support of national organizations with all kinds of material and financial resources. This constituted the second general claim.

✳   ✳   ✳

Whenever I left Admiral Hors's house to carry out my various meetings in the light of day, I always took as many precautions as I could. Before opening the door, I would examine the road thoroughly from the half-opened window. When I went out onto the usually deserted Kikladon Street, I would go in a different direction every time.

By now this sort of practice had become a way of life, something that stayed with me long after the liberation. Little by little, I trained myself to follow, from the corner of my eye, what was going on behind me as I walked without letting this concern be noticed by others. Going up and down pavements, the turns of the streets, some basement stair I had to circumvent, or some ground floor windowpane I had to avoid, a slight turn of my head at the moment that I made a much more obvious move was enough for me to review the situation around me. It was impossible for the anyone to be behind me for a distance greater than 100 meters without my realizing it. If that happened, I would change paths until we parted.

I always wore my panama hat and glasses, shaved my moustache, and avoided commonly frequented places.

I usually returned at night with the same meticulous precautions. I never went into the house if there was anyone else in the street, so I was sure that no one would discover my hideout.

Despite these measures, the Germans managed, it seems, to discover the street on which I lived, although they couldn't pinpoint the exact door. And then, too, my good fortune showed her presence once more in an improbable way.

Above the Admiral's apartment, on the third floor, lived Colonel Argirios Danellis with his family. I believed that they did not suspect anything about me, because I rarely appeared when they came down to the house, and then I would come in from the front door like a visitor. Events proved that they did understand that I was hiding, but they were discrete and didn't show it.

One night, it must have been after 11, we were eating in the dining room when the doorbell rang. We immediately got rid of the third dining set and I locked myself in my room. It was Colonel Danellis from the upstairs floor.

"The Germans have blockaded our street and are searching the houses," I heard him say. "I don't think it's possible for your guest to get away. But I considered it my duty to warn you to take precautions."

As soon as the door closed, I went out to the hall. The Admiral and Mrs. Hors looked at me, speechless. They knew I had heard.

We proceeded to the parlor. I turned off the light and we looked outside through the half-opened shutters. To our right, an armored car blocked the corner. From the left, armed soldiers were advancing. They had certainly come out of a car that blocked the other corner of the street. They were moving rather quietly, a strange demeanor for Germans. We saw some coming out of a house across from us and going into the next one. Soon, our turn would come. I had to make an immediate decision.

I turned and faced the sharp look of the Admiral and the questioning, worried look of his wife. They both had their eyes fixed on me.

A long moment of silence passed.

"What are you going to do?" the Admiral finally asked.

"I must go out onto the street right now, immediately, before they come to our house. You quickly bury the guns in the garden's soft soil. Unfortunately, there isn't a way out from back there. I'll go out as usual from the front door, but I'll try to make sure they don't see where I came from. I hope I can do it. If they ask me for an identification card, I will show it. Perhaps they aren't looking for me and will let me pass."

"But if they are looking for you?"

"Then they will arrest me. But they will never find out where I was hiding. If I stay here, they will arrest all three of us. And they will not hesitate, my Admiral, to execute you."

"Do you think this is the best that can be done?"

"Yes. I think this is what I must do…"

The Admiral raised his head a little and pinned his eyes on mine. With his rich white hair and beard and the regal look that illuminated his features at that moment, he had the appearance of an old lion. I will never forget his self-denying and heroic words that etched themselves indelibly into my memory. It was an exceptional moment, one of those that are sometimes born in the story of an individual person and come to characterize the story of an entire people.

"*I adjure you,*" he said, "*to answer me on your word of honor as a Greek and with the responsibility of your national mission: What would you do if we two did not exist and were not in danger?*"

Nothing remained for me but to be sincere. "I would remain hidden here and, if needed, I would strike. I would either save myself or they would pay dearly for my life."

"*And this is what you will do,*" the Admiral said. "*You have an obligation to this country, and only this is what your duty dictates you to do.*"

He added more calmly, "We two are old. We have both our children in the war. We have to fulfill our duty till the end."

His wife was standing beside him and her face was lit by a smile that was barely perceptible. She felt proud and was unbelievably brave in her sweet simplicity.

I quickly drew up a plan. Two doors separated us from the street, the outside door of the building and the door of the apartment. I would leave as soon as we heard the bell or banging on the outer door, descending from the veranda toward the garden. From a small door next to the veranda, I could squeeze into a tight, dark corridor that led to the street from the main entrance or from the little door of the half-basement. The layout was complicated enough to stall those doing the search, and there were some well-camouflaged places to hide. I would easily have the time to go down before they even knocked on the apartment door.

If in the end they did find me, I might still have a desperate chance in the narrow corridor. I might find myself facing just one German. I would have to shoot him and go out into the street, trying to make way toward the right where only one house separated us from the closest corner, and then turn and disappear into the dark alleys.

Meanwhile, I inspected my pistols. I will never forget the faces of my beloved friends as they calmly watched me clean the bullets of the automatic with a cloth and refill the magazines. They had made their great decision and the moral satisfaction filled them with unimaginable serenity.

The time passed. It was soon two o'clock in the morning and still no one had shown up at our door. The car had disappeared from the corner, but now and again we could still hear German voices in the distance. We didn't know if they were relevant to the blockade, but we didn't risk opening the outside door to see. We had begun to tire.

"I think that it would be best for us to get some sleep," I said to my friends. "We can't spend the whole night on our feet."

"That's exactly what I was going to recommend," said the Admiral. "As a matter of fact, we should save our strength for every possibility."

"If all goes well," I said, "you might not find me here in the morning. I must change hideouts. I'll leave as soon as I can."

Full of emotion, they embraced me and we kissed. "I don't know how to thank you," I whispered.

"Have a good night's sleep," the Admiral said. "Let's go, my Lily." He tenderly placed his arm around his wife's waist and they went to their room.

I lay down on my bed, dressed and with the pistols beside me. I was always a very light sleeper, so I didn't fear a surprise attack.

At six the next morning, I looked out the window. The street was deserted. I opened the outside door cautiously and made sure no one was about. I quickly turned the corner of Kikladon Street and distanced myself from the house, walking normally toward Kipseli market, where the morning's activity was getting underway. Among the working people I felt secure again.

So what had happened last night? Something very improbable in its simplicity. As I soon found out, the Germans had searched all of the houses across from and surrounding us, without finding the person they were looking for. They had, by accident, neglected only our house...

❋　❋　❋

Around 8:00, I met Stavros Vrachnos at the Technical University. In a few words I told him about the previous night's blockade. A short time later, he led me to my new hideout at 128 Solonos Street.

I found everything exactly as Stavros had described it to me a few days before. A young couple, Anthony Alexiou and his wife, accepted me with true enthusiasm. They had a comfortable apartment on the third floor of the building and had arranged a pleasant room for me in the back part of the house, with a window looking out onto the garden. It was exactly what I needed. However, they had hired a maid in the meantime. She was a good girl from a village, and she did not go out even to the grocer. But just in case, they told her that they would be entertaining their cousin for some days, a "Mr. George," who had come to Athens from the provinces for therapy. They said that my nerves had been affected and therefore I was not able to go out during the day because the light bothered me. I would only go out a bit at night to go to the doctor. Thus everything was arranged perfectly.

The good people took care to make my days as pleasant as possible. They gave me books and kept me company. Although Anthony Alexiou was totally deaf, we debated about a thousand things because he understood everything by reading lips. But something made an even bigger impression on me: it pleased him when I played songs of the time on the piano. He would sit next to me and hold his metal lighter in his hand, against the piano top. He sang without melody, saying the words in time with the rhythm of the vibrations he felt with his hand. When I changed songs, he would immediately change, too.

Only the maid avoided me as much as she could. She had become afraid of me with these stories about the light that bothered my nerves and my nighttime therapies. As a matter of fact, one early afternoon she was convinced that I should be locked up. They sent her to knock on my door with a cold glass of orange juice on a tray. It was an intensely hot day in mid July, and I had lain down naked. Hearing the knock, I wrapped myself in my sheet and half-opened the door. I took the orange juice and locked up again.

When I came out of my room a little while later, I found my new friends roaring with laughter. The girl, terrified, had put all reservations aside and told them clearly and plainly that she would not go to this nut's room again. "You should have seen him," she said, "wrapped in the sheet, pretending to be...an ancient Greek." At least the juice had not slipped from her hands...

❉   ❉   ❉

During that time, Alexander Kairis was trying to communicate with us from inside his cell, at least mentally. He wrote long letters without knowing if and when they would reach us. And – strange for his temperament – he wrote poems...

Some months earlier, on those unforgettable nights when we would meet at Popi Sakelaridis's, Alexander and I would often occupy ourselves with long discussions on literary topics. Alexander, who was a strong writer of prose, could not capture the manner in which a poem was written. He maintained that the care required to formulate one's thoughts within the restrictive mold of a verse could only be achieved at the expense of meaning. I countered by describing the exaltation of the poetic moment that gives spontaneous birth to words in organic conjunction with their internal music, just as the course of a speech gives birth to a speaker's master-crafted phrases woven with his personal style into a harmonic whole. As much as I maintained that the quest for meter or the search for rhyme often leads one to exceptional pictures or new meanings, Alexander insisted that even Aeschylus or Shakespeare would have written greater works if they hadn't subjected their words to the restrictions of meter.

Now in prison, Alexander Kairis, shaken daily by his doubtful fate and approaching death, crossed into the condition of sensitivity that leads to poetry. Among his wonderful letters, letters of a particularly philosophical person with a genuine literary vein, even among the three scientific treatises that he had the composure to write, Alexander also gave us some splendid poems drawn from life and the heroic psychology of the convicted. Here I give a sample of these lively verses which teach us many things, very many things indeed...

EXECUTION

Shaken was the blessed serenity of night,
Footsteps, unlockings, rustling, and buzz.
Daybreak; the moon bitterly smiles,
As if the same reflection reaches there:
— they take them...

With a frozen heart, and bated breath,
You stand before your door, you carefully count
Heads, that will fall and will soon be buried,
And from your lips, spontaneously rises a prayer
— for those they take...

The air is full of shivers,
You feel from all the cells, the heavy thumping pulse
(You see a mother, a sister with the black veil)
You hear, drowned and deep, a sigh
— of one of those they take...

Suddenly a lively voice — a voice that will be silenced...

Tears the dim light with a "Farewell, guys!"
Now you hear, drowned-out, a storm of foreign curses,
But the voice does not scare: "Soon liberation for you!"
— And now they go, they take them...

This same spiritual sensitivity also seems to have brought Alexander Kairis the message of my father's death. With absolutely no information turning him in this direction, out of pure intuition, the truth was revealed to him.

My father died on the July 17, 1943. We have a letter from Alexander dated July 21 which says:

> ... Since yesterday, I have had a very lively impression from a dream that has stayed with me very vividly. I saw Rigas's mother, very aged and with a pained expression, dressed in mourning. She was completely alone in a big house...
>
> ... I do not understand why this dream gave me such a strong feeling, but even though I don't believe in such things, I am starting to think that perhaps something is going on with Rigas's father who was so seriously ill. It also struck me that not only was Rigas not in the deserted house, but not a word was said about him, as if he did not exist...

How close my beloved friend was to me despite his personal misfortune. How indestructible were the bonds that always tied us together, eradicating the distance and bringing us into communication through unexplainable channels...

❋   ❋   ❋

A similarly astonishing phenomenon brought me close to my father at the moment of his last breath.

On the night of July 16, just before the curfew, I was hurriedly returning to my hideout on Solonos Street. I took out the key to open the outside door and I stopped...

An intense spiritual impulse dictated that I go home without delay. I turned as if I was hypnotized and reached September 3rd Street as fast as I could. I headed straight for our door without any precaution. I opened it with my key and ran up the stairs. Then I proceeded, silently, to my father's room. I heard him breathing hoarsely. My mother and sister got up as soon as they saw me and came near me, dazed.

"Your father is dying, my boy," said Mother. "The death rattle began a short time ago."

All three of us sat next to him. "How did you know to come just now?" my sister asked shortly thereafter.

"I don't know..."

I stayed there, next to him, until the early hours of the morning. Now and then he shook his hands as if he wanted something. However, I didn't give any sign of my presence. Mother had told us to not disturb his final moments.

I left at dawn because my family was worried about me. Father was still alive. "Take care of yourself, my child," Mother said. "Now we will only have you."

I told her that I would phone to learn the latest news. When I went out, the street was still deserted...

I called the house around ten. Mother answered. Thinking the phone might be tapped, I gave a name we had agreed upon. "Papageorgiou here. Pray tell, please, how is Mr. Rigopoulos?"

Mother did not remember the name. "Who are you, please? What Papageorgiou?" I insisted. "Tell me, please, how is Mr. Rigopoulos?"

"He died this morning," Mother said.

I hung up the phone and headed home. Nothing could have stopped me.

I found my entire family gathered in the parlor. My father was already in the coffin.

Shortly, my mother begged me again to leave. "I don't imagine you'll show up at the funeral," she said. "Take care that we don't have a new calamity. Leave by the back way…"

The next morning I stood at a corner a few blocks from my house and looked toward the door. I saw the coffin come out and I waited for it to pass in front of me. Then, I immediately turned and distanced myself from the funeral. My family told those who asked that I was ill. Most of them understood.

I spent the whole day closed in my room thinking of my father without shedding even one tear. Inside me burned a terrible anger against the Germans who, on top of everything else, had deprived me of the last sacred duty to a father I adored. It was a blow beyond my power to control. I lay awake almost the entire night. At dawn, the overwhelming need to honor the memory of my father before his fresh grave caused me to set aside all prudence.

I thought that if the Germans understood the psychology of the situation, they would definitely send their people to keep the cemetery under surveillance for a few days. However, I decided to clash with them if I had to and even die on my father's grave to gain the satisfaction that I had not abandoned him.

The safest plan was to go as early in the morning as I could. As soon as the gate was opened, I went into the deserted cemetery and stood before the grave. There, breathing in the aroma of the flowers that covered my father's grave, and feeling his blessing flood me, I was able to recapture my spiritual serenity.

I left as I had arrived: undisturbed. That night, in my bed, liberated, I was able to cry…

❈   ❈   ❈

On the night of July 27, I finally received the long-awaited message. We would leave in two days. There would be a general meeting on the July 29 at 12 noon at the Geka brothers' coffee shop on the corner of Agion Theodoron Square and Evripidou Street. There I was to ask for "Mr. Andronikos" and tell him that I was coming from "Pantelis." My appearance had to be that of a person going to buy foodstuffs from the surrounding villages. I had to have my regular identification on me.

The next night, I met my mother and spoke about my departure the next day. I told her that I would drop by the house the next morning around 11 to take a bag with a loaf of bread, some cheese, and a couple of gold pounds that were the basic means of trade back then. I would enter the house from the back yards with the same precautions I had taken previously, even though it seemed that as of late the surveillance had finally ceased, especially after the death of my father.

Mother listened to me without saying a word. Only now am I more aware of the shock she must have been going through in those moments and her admirable self-control.

That same night, I said farewell to Mitsos Rediadis, Stavros Vrachnos, and my girlfriend, to whom I owed the realization of this trip. Mitsos was to command Service 5-16-5 during my absence.

Weighing the dangers I would face, we had to consider what would happen if I failed to return. Mitsos would operate with unlimited jurisdiction, would maintain cohesion in our Service, and, if he found a way to transfer messages abroad, would put our organization back into full operation while taking every precaution.

Stavros was to keep his people in a state of immediate readiness, as were the other division leaders. I begged him further to say farewell to his cousin Admiral Hors and his wife on my behalf and express once more my gratitude and admiration...

For the last night I returned to sleep at Alexiou's house. The moment I was ready to lie down on the bed, I heard a sudden noise at the window, as if someone had thrown a clump of dirt which exploded on the shutters. I turned off the light and carefully opened the window. Just outside one corner of my window a dizzy sparrow was fluttering around. I took it inside and looked at it. It did not seem to be wounded. I set it down beside me on the floor, sprinkled some crumbs around it, and put out an ashtray with some water. I slept with the window wide open. In the morning, to my great pleasure, I saw that the bird had flown.

I am not superstitious and I never believed in mystical symbols. On the contrary, I flouted every superstition. I wouldn't hesitate to be the third to light my cigarette from a single match, or to set out for a dangerous mission on a Tuesday, just to prove the nonsense of superstition.

Deep and unlimited faith I have only in God. I believe that only fainthearted people without imagination can be atheist. Such people are unable to let the soul overcome the limited power of the mind and equate perfection — inconceivable for man but unquestionably existing — with the divine.

I also believe in the huge indeterminate possibilities of man that we cannot yet understand, like intuition, clairvoyance, and telepathy. These are purely natural phenomena that perhaps some day we will be able to analyze and control.

Thus, I contend that my beliefs are down to earth. But that bird, which slammed into my window yet spread its wings to the blue sky the next day, the same day that I was to risk the great leap toward freedom, filled me with indescribable joy and optimism.

In a little while, I stopped by my house, bolstered my mother and sister with a few words out of my true belief in the future, and slung the bag over my shoulder ready for departure. We did not embrace and we did not kiss. Maybe the warmth of farewell would have broken our morale. We only put up a hand in a heartfelt gesture that encompassed all of our love.

I admired, and will always admire, their bravery at that moment. A few days after Father was lost they were losing me as well, without knowing if they would ever see me again. They were left alone in the storm of the occupation. But they saw me to the back door with a smile, as if I was leaving for a small excursion.

Shortly thereafter, I was proceeding with great strides toward the coffee shop on Agion Theodoron Square.

PART TWO

CHAPTER D

THE CONSPIRACY

GREECE, TURKEY, SYRIA, LEBANON, EGYPT. ABUSE OF TRUST.

The atmosphere in the coffee shop was suffocating. My waiting drew on and on. At 12:00 noon, in accordance with the instructions, I had asked the shop owner for "Mr. Andronicos." It was now 3:00 and no one had approached me. Every once in a while, the shop owner nodded at me reassuringly.

All kinds of people were going in and out of the shop and others were sitting there chatting or looking around. I spent my time trying to figure out which ones might be fellow travelers. This diversion somewhat eased my anxiety.

Finally, around 3:30, someone stood next to me. "Follow me to the Marathon buses, Menandrou Street," he whispered. Soon I saw many of those I had suspected in the coffee shop boarding the bus with me.

Everything went well until we reached Stavros, where we met our first road block. An Italian non-commissioned officer got on and asked for identification cards. The fact that he was Italian calmed me down. I soon had my identification card back and we continued on our way. The second road block was just after Pikermi. We sailed through there with similar ease.

In the meantime, the locals going to Marathon struck up conversations with us. "You won't find much food," they told us. "A little corn perhaps, and maybe a cabbage, but don't expect any meat." We had led them to think that we were black marketeers.

Before Marathon, the bus stopped in a deserted location. "We'll get off here," the mission leader announced.

Then the villagers understood. They yelled "Farewell!" and "Good liberation!" and "Till we meet again!" as we withdrew toward the tall bushes that surrounded the area.

Soon we found ourselves near the sea at the Gulf of Evoia. The place was quite wooded and gave us good cover. It opened into a small bay. A boat waited, moored next to the low rocks. We got in and slowly set sail for Evoia on the opposite shore. If a naval patrol ship had stopped us, we would have said that we were going to the neighboring villages for food.

At dusk we stepped on land again and nestled ourselves under the trees. The vegetation was abundant, creating an ideal place to remain unseen. When night fell for good, we followed the leader and his two escorts up the paths. We had to keep up or we would lose them in the dark.

We walked in silence, stepping as quietly as we could. In some places the path went through Italian outposts, so we had to be particularly careful.

Now and then the guides halted us. We huddled against tree trunks so that we wouldn't stick out, and we waited. One of the guides would go on ahead and be away for some time. When he returned we continued our way.

I had the misfortune of almost completely tearing off the sole of my shoe. I cut the cord from my bag and tied my shoe together.

We reached the Aegean Sea before daybreak. In a short while we finally got to lie down in a cave formed by the rocky coast. We spent several hours there, waiting for the caïque that was to arrive that afternoon.

The caïque appeared on the horizon at about 3:00. It seems that some of the locals who showed up had seen it before we did. "They're good people," the leader reassured us. "They come every time the caïque arrives. When there's room, we take some of them with us. Those left behind don't talk. They simply wait for another chance."

Soon the caïque came alongside one of the rocks that formed a natural jetty. It was a beautiful, light red sailing boat. We embarked quickly. Some settled in the cargo area, but I preferred the deck. I wouldn't have liked to travel without being able to see where we're going. I lay down under the boom so that its gathered sail would protect me from the sun. Around 4:30 we were on the sea again, heading toward the island of Chios. The caïque followed a route similar to the one I knew our caïques had used. At night it would pass to the south of Chios and bring us to the Turkish coast by daybreak.

The weather, which had been good in the morning, started to worsen. However, the caïque was handling the waves easily and making good speed at about 8 knots. At this point, the trip was pleasant.

At night, the wind really intensified. A devilish north wind took hold, forcing the captain to turn north toward the island of Psara so that he would not have to take the wind broadside. Practically all of us got seasick. My light summer suit was useless against the cold, which pierced me to the bone. Each large wave filled the gathered sail on top of me with water, which then drained onto me through a hole. I felt terribly ill and was shaking unbelievably from the cold. I was certain I would pay dearly for this night.

In those moments, when life seemed to be draining out of me, I felt a hand rubbing me intensely. From the oilskin jacket I was able to discern in the dark, I realized that it was one of the crew, someone unknown who will always remain unknown to me. I felt blood circulate more warmly in my veins. And I felt the humanity of my unknown friend warming my heart.

The next morning's sun found us off the coast of Turkey.

We anchored in a small gulf not far from the shore and waited for the Turkish authorities. I took off my clothes, set them to dry on the deck, and dove into the diamond sea wearing nothing but my underwear. The morning swim and brief sunbathing completely revived me from the night's adventure.

Soon we proceeded, accompanied by Turkish gendarmes and two Greeks, from the Agrilia, where we disembarked, to Alatsata, which was not far away. They sat us on the ground in the yard of the police station. They took our personal information and ... our lighters! (They said they were forbidden in Turkey.) Then they took us to wash up at the baths while they disinfected our clothes in a kiln. The blue shantung suit I was wearing had turned blackish-green. When this ceremony was finished, they led us to the village square, sat us down again Turkish style, and treated us to some local sweets.

That night we reached Smirni (Turkish Ismir) by bus and took up lodging in a big caravanserai with a paved courtyard. We ate meat in a broth, which our bodies truly needed. We gave our personal information again. They didn't allow us to go outside the caravanserai into the city. However, the Greek consulate promised that we would soon be able to circulate freely.

Permission to leave the caravanserai finally came the next night, but only for those of us who were permanent or reserve officers. They also gave us vouchers that would allow us to stay in a decent hotel and a few Turkish lira for minor expenses. The following morning I bought a pair of linen shoes, as mine had abandoned me for good. I then went around Smirni freely.

One would imagine that sudden freedom after so many years of slavery and danger would have felt wonderful. Yet I didn't feel any real joy or relief breathing the free air of this beautiful city which had maintained its Greek character. Perhaps the dramatic events of late had exhausted me. Perhaps the seriousness of my mission and my desire to return to Greece as soon as possible occupied my thoughts. Or perhaps the tragedy that continued in our enslaved country squelched any personal feelings of happiness.

I remember sitting in one of the best clubs in Smirni on the second night. I had been invited by a Turk, a dear friend from my university years. I sat there listening to the orchestra and devouring an exceptional filet, but I didn't feel any comfort or satisfaction. On the contrary, the abundance and luxury constantly reminded me of the misfortune I had left behind. It brought me nothing but sorrow.

Once I could move about freely, my first step was to go to the British consulate.

The words of Nicos Menegatos from that night I first met him in the grove of Nea Smirni were still ringing in my ears: "...ask for a British Major with the pseud-onym 'Hatzis.' He's the head of our service. Don't trust anyone else, either Greek or British..."

As strange as Menegatos' advice seemed to me — to protect myself from friends and Allies who did not belong exclusively to our service — I decided to follow his instructions to the letter. I had nothing to lose if he was wrong, and his precautions might prove invaluable. With time I would form my own opinion on this matter.

I figured that the British consulate would be the most secure place for me to start pursuing my goals. I could not imagine then that that was the exact place where they would delude me in the worst way...

[As the reader will have noticed, in addition to the wonderful people he has come to know in detail from this book, I also mention persons whose deeds condemn them. I speak of some people who exploited misfortune, of Greek mechanics who manufactured anti-aircraft artillery for the Germans, and of individuals who came to administer the Bank of Greece, obsequiously serving the conqueror. In these cases, however, I do not mention their names. I do not want to write them next to names that are worthy of our memory. I do not want to degrade the level of this book by recording their names for posterity. The historian, if he so desires, will not find it difficult to match dates to situations and uncover the names of these unworthy Greeks.

He can do the same for the British I mention in this unpleasant matter of the Allies' betrayal. It is a matter that cannot diminish, even the slightest bit, the admirable contribution of the British to the Allied struggle. Likewise, it cannot change our feelings toward a people distinguished by the superior level of their culture and their enviable virtues.

It is possible that the British whose names I suppress in this matter were acting under orders. Thus, it could be that their personal culpability was extremely limited or even nonexistent. It is not out of the question that they had been deluded themselves. Perhaps when they someday read these lines they will appear in public to settle their positions themselves.]

At the British consulate I asked to see the Consul. A British Major soon appeared and introduced himself. As I later learned, he was well-known in Smirni at that time.

"The Consul will be away for a few days," he said, "but would you like to come into my office? I have jurisdiction over matters that involve Greece."

I told the Major that I was the leader of Service 5-16-5 and that I had made this trip specifically to meet Major "Hatzis" in Constantinople. The British officer was reticent. "Can you prove your identity?" he asked me.

"I can describe instances of our cooperation with your people. I can tell you details concerning Menegatos, Paliatseas, and Tratras. I can recite, word for word, telegrams that we exchanged with your secret services. I can relate details concerning our contacts with you that only the leadership of our organization could know."

"Very well," the Major said. "Please tell me these things."

I spoke to him for a long time. Here and there, he made some notes or asked for clarifications. He indicated that he knew Menegatos, but seemed to be learning of his execution for the first time. He didn't know about the executions of the other men, either. He asked me to tell him the names of other members of our organization.

"Permit me to omit mentioning the names of members who are still living and are still in Greece. This is a general and inviolable principle of ours."

The Major was understanding. With great interest, he asked for more general news from Greece. He asked about the movements of national organizations, the manifestations of EAM, and the Greeks' feelings toward the King. A friendly conversation on the general situation followed, giving me every reason to be optimistic.

"Come back tomorrow," he said when our conversation had ended. "I'll see that you're given every assistance and tell you what gets decided about these matters." He took me to the door and shook my hand warmly. "I congratulate you on your actions," he said. "I'm very glad to have met you."

The next day, the Major greeted me even more warmly. "We're giving you top priority to leave immediately for Cairo."

"For Cairo?" I questioned. "Why not for Constantinople as I asked?"

"Because the leader of the service you had contact with is in Cairo."

"But Menegatos told me explicitly that the leader of his service is Major 'Hatzis' in Constantinople."

"Major 'Hatzis' does not exist. No British service exists in Constantinople. Menegatos had orders to give false information in occupied Greece. Here, however, you are on free land and we can tell you the truth. The superior authority of the British secret services is in Cairo. Only there can your requests be considered."

I had no reason to doubt him. Besides, I didn't have a choice. I thanked him and asked when I could depart.

"Tomorrow a group of Greeks is leaving for Halepi, in Syria, where there is a camp for people who have escaped from your country. It'll take you two days to get there by train. From there some are allowed to go on to Egypt, but it is rare for anyone to leave the camp in less than a month, even if he is a superior officer or politician. For you, however, we've made special arrangements. As soon as you arrive, present yourself to the camp commandant. We'll telegram him an order to secure your departure without delay. You'll be in Cairo four days from today."

I thanked the Major once more and bade him farewell, totally satisfied. I did not yet suspect that, perhaps at that very moment, Major "Hatzis" in Constantinople was desperately trying in vain to learn something about the people in his service who had been executed, and why our organization had suddenly stopped showing any signs of life.

＊　＊　＊

The trip into the depths of Turkey was slow and monotonous. The train's straw seats were barely tolerable, but I could walk in the corridor when I felt cramped. We journeyed through vast, boundless plains, practically uncultivated. We only saw vegetable gardens near the riverbanks, where the water of God could reach them. People lazed about in the train and in the fields. Here and there we passed through villages, filthy and stinking. Some of their names reminded me of old stories from the unfortunate Greek campaign in Asia Minor in 1920: Afion Karahisar, Konia... In the mountains, my eyes beheld a wild beauty.

I spent the two days of the journey in absolute seclusion. My fellow Greek travelers were swapping tales of their adventures during the occupation and of their escapes. All they knew about me was that I was a reserve second lieutenant. Outside of a few words, I didn't want to take part in their conversations. So the others looked at me warily, probably with some skepticism. A colonel somehow seemed to be the leader of the group, and he didn't miss a single opportunity to treat me brusquely and rudely.

The Turkish travelers and train employees jabbered around us in their incomprehensible tongue. When they looked at us, their expressions were anything but friendly.

At the border, Syrian customs and railway officials boarded the train and the atmosphere changed immediately. They smiled as they approached us, spoke excellent French, and did their jobs with civility and courtesy.

Soon we arrived in Halepi. The British received us and led us to the camp. There we once again became a herd of animals. They made us strip, sprayed us with insecticide, made us bathe in communal showers, disinfected our clothes yet again — my suit was now a blackish red — lined us up to drink our tea, handed us two cans of food, and sent us to 20-bed makeshift tin barracks to rest.

I immediately asked to see the camp commandant. After a thousand ordeals, I finally managed to get in. I asked him about the telegram he must have received by now and he almost threw me out. "It does not exist," he thundered, "nor will such a thing exist. Go to your barracks!"

I'm stuck here, I thought.

The next morning, as our Colonel was trying to bar me from pouring myself a drink from the communal water pitcher, a British officer came into the barracks yelling my name. Speaking a flawless, formal, modern Greek in his British accent, he announced, "The camp commandant sends his regrets about your meeting yesterday, but he had not yet received the telegram you were expecting. As soon as you're ready, you can depart for Cairo. A British sergeant and a soldier will escort you to facilitate your journey." I thanked him, and said that my bags had been ready for some time and that I was at his disposal.

I shook the hands of all my fellow travelers to bid them farewell. The Colonel squeezed my hand with a sudden cordiality. "Till we meet again in Cairo," he said. "I hope to come in a few days myself. It would be a pleasure to see you there."

Soon I was on an express train traveling in a comfortable compartment along with some other Greeks. As we sailed across the Syrian desert, now and then I saw cavalrymen with their burnooses and carbines galloping off into the boundless expanse. I later met some of these Syrian Arabs, who have no relation to common Arabs. They are princes of the desert.

The sergeant assigned to me was a wonderful young man from London. He told me he was an Oxford student, and he spoke that exceptional English whose sound and phrasing embodies, one could say, the entire tradition of the British Empire.

We talked about a thousand things: science, art, music, the terrible problems of the war, and the unsettled lives of people and nations. We spoke about Greece and the supreme struggle of her enslaved people. We lost all sense of time and soon found ourselves in Bayrouth. There we interrupted our trip to spend the night in a hotel.

I learned that Greek war ships were anchored in Bayrouth harbor. I thought I might be able to learn something about my friends, the Hors brothers (the Admiral's sons), so I told the sergeant that I was going to run to the Greek base for a short while. "I'm sorry, sir," he replied, "but I have orders not to let you stray from our planned itinerary."

My surprise must have showed intensely, because the poor boy turned as red as a beet and began stammering incomprehensible phrases, begging my pardon. "I thought I was given an escort as an honor," I said. "Now I see that I am a detainee."

The sensitive, cultivated youth must have felt terrible. He must have developed a trust in me on the train, and perhaps I had even won his admiration. I could tell from his next action that his conscience had rebelled, because it was so contrary to British mentality and discipline. He stood at attention and said, "Sir, I have developed a personal opinion of you. I cannot follow this order. I feel that I must take this responsibility upon myself. I only ask that you return quickly."

"Thank you," I replied. "I will be back at the hotel within an hour."

With incredible emotion, I soon saw the Greek flag on our free ships and spoke with officers and sailors who gathered around me to hear news from the homeland. Marios Hors, the younger son of the Admiral and a sublieutenant on a submarine at the time, came ashore after having been summoned by a special signal. He heard news of his family for the first time in years. With great delight, I heard that in Cairo I might see my close friend Michael Hors, who was serving there as a reserve second lieutenant in a vehicle unit that arranged transports.

Early the next day we resumed our journey to Egypt.

※ ※ ※

The Cairo headquarters of the British secret services was housed in a large central building. This was the famous MO4.[1]

The sergeant left me in the hall and an elegant British captain came toward me. He introduced himself, speaking perfect Greek. He said he had lived most of his life in Greece and was in charge of Greek affairs for his service.

He took me to his office where I explained who I was and the goal of my trip. "My intention is to return to Greece as soon as possible," I concluded.

"We've been notified about you," the Captain said. "Our service needs a short time to decide what to do about this situation. In the meantime, you'll have to tell us every detail of your organization and all you know about Greek matters. We'll entertain you in a villa for a few days, where I hope you'll find every comfort. If you'd like, we can leave immediately. However, the villa's location is a military secret, so we have to transport you in a sealed car. We'll try to make your stay there as brief as possible."

By now I was sure that I was a detainee. Who knows what else I would have to face? The defense receptors I had acquired in occupied Greece sounded an alarm.

I was soon locked in the back of a car driven by the Captain. The windows had been covered with iron plates. As we set off I looked at my watch so that I could time the trip. From the car's acceleration and vibration as we left the city, I estimated that we couldn't be going more than 60 kilometers per hour. We reached our destination in half an hour, so at that point I figured we were about 30 kilometers outside of Cairo.

When the car door opened I was in a beautiful garden enclosed by a very high wall. A heavily barricaded iron door closed behind us. The villa was in the middle of the garden. Its architecture was complex, in the style of an old castle with outside stone staircases.

An Englishman in civilian clothes came out to receive us, accompanied by a young Greek in an air force uniform. An Arab, dressed in a fez and a caftan (*kelebéa*) with a red, silk belt, bowed to us as we went in.

"I hope you won't feel uneasy here," the Captain said. "Tomorrow morning you'll work with one of our people." Then he bade me farewell.

The Englishman led me to a comfortable room. He opened a drawer of well-ironed shirts and undergarments and said they were for me. A brand new pair of pants in my size was hanging in the closet. In the bathroom, there was everything for a gentleman's toilette: a shaving brush and razor, aromatic soaps, after-shave lotions, and Yardley cologne. "Dinner will be served in one hour," said the Englishman. "I'll leave you now to let you settle in."

I bathed, freshened up, dressed myself well, and felt like a civilized person again. I dined alone in the dining room, served by the Arab. He offered the platter with a bow, holding his palm to his chest. The food was worthy of the best hotel.

When I had finished, the Englishman brought me into the library for coffee. "These books are at your disposal," he said. "Perhaps you would like a game of backgammon. If you play ping-pong, there's a table in the garden. The young Greek is a wonderful player..."

---

[1] The British secret services were officially known as the SOE, the Special Operations Executive. MO4 was a cover name for the SOE in Cairo.

They did whatever they could to make my stay enjoyable. Such refined behavior is typical of the special culture of the British. It also represents the long-standing tradition in their policies. If I was the person I claimed to be, I was worthy of their high standard of hospitality. If I was someone attempting to trick them, they held my fate and my very life in their hands. My real identity would definitely come out in the methodical interrogation that was to follow.

The next morning I told the whole story of Service 5-16-5 in minute detail to another Englishman, who came specifically to see me. His questions were few, but always skillfully crafted to draw out deeper analyses of the events I described.

When the interrogation was over, this person knew almost everything the reader knows about Service 5-16-5. Everything, that is, except the names of my colleagues. On this point I continued to be adamant. I had seen many superficial events in occupied Greece cost people their lives, so I was not about to risk anything. Later, I would see if I could ask the British for their help with Alexander Kairis. I would have to be exceptionally careful. Aside from everything else, there was the real danger that German espionage in Cairo reached into the archives of the MO4, just as we reached into the confidential archives of the Germans in Athens. So I decided to maintain absolute secrecy about my colleagues' names for the time being, inviolably applying the security system we had adopted in Greece. I declared that I would not reveal the names of any of my collaborators who were still living. But I didn't find the understanding here that I had found in Smirni. The Englishman pursed his lips in a characteristic British manner and his friendly tone was replaced with a frigid, distant one.

Then my interrogator asked what I knew about the other organizations in Greece and about the opposition between the national organizations and EAM. This gave me the opportunity to speak about the need for support of the national resistance and the dangers created by supporting the leftists.

He asked what Greeks think about the return of King George and I told him that only the leftists concerned themselves with this question. All others were interested only in liberation.

The next morning I was subjected to one more lengthy questioning by a second visitor. This was a true interrogation, using all the dialectical methods designed to draw me into contradictions if I was lying. The new interrogator was truly well-qualified. He was intelligent and a master of psychology. He had studied my previous statements with great care and had examined their various points in minute detail. He used only a single sheet of notes, which he held in his hands. The entire interrogation was conducted with impeccable manners and without any hint of distrust. On the contrary, even when it was obvious that he was trying to confuse me and lead me into a contradiction, the Englishman maintained British tact and treated me with complete respect.

Only one point led to a lively conflict with him as well: he asked me to give an account of the funds our organization must have received from the British. "The financial matter wasn't touched upon in your statements yesterday," he said. "You must've taken regular remittances."

I answered that I had refused all financial help when Menegatos offered it. "Until now," I told him, "we didn't need to ask for funds."

He seemed to be surprised. "But all of the serious espionage units are financed," he said. "Yours must be some small organization."

That's when I became furious...

By now I was certain I was in the hands of people who didn't know us. The Allied service that had been in contact with us for so long, the service of Major "Hatzis," would surely know that we had never been sent money because we had refused it. They would also know our size from the type and importance of the information we transmitted.

These people didn't know us and were ignorant of our deeds. After making sure that I wasn't a German spy, they had tried to pry every useful piece of information out of me. Menegatos was right. There was some strange conflict going on between the different British secret services. Major "Hatzis" must surely exist in Constantinople. He was in charge of "our" service. I had fallen into the other services' hands.

All of this crossed my mind in a split second. My internal alarm, which had been somehow relaxed by my good treatment, sounded again. Of course, I didn't want to reveal anything about the suspicions and feelings that had flustered me. However, I gave outlet to my emotions by replying harshly.

"So, do you judge organizations by the money you appropriate to them or by their results? The information our organization transmitted to you resulted in the sinking of at least 55 enemy ships. In your hands you have plans for fortification projects and movements of enemy units. We have given you top secret information, even plans for *future* enemy operations. Aren't these criteria important to you?"

"Forgive me," the Englishman replied calmly. "My choice of words was unfortunate. You are absolutely correct."

That night I sat by myself in the garden trying to put my thoughts in order and foresee the future. Would I escape from their hands? Would I finally be able to carry out my mission?

I studied the mysterious villa. Its exterior size was too big to contain only the interior rooms I knew. Yet there was no visible communication between those rooms and the others that must be in there. What could be hiding in those other areas? A large, reinforced antenna extended into the starlit sky above the peculiar roof. So they must certainly have a wireless set in there. Lying back in my chair I looked up at the constellations in the clear night sky. The polestar was hanging on the tail of the Little Bear like a shining gem. Somewhere toward the north was my unfortunate homeland. Would I succeed in returning and find my comrades waiting for me? Would we be able to continue our work?

At that moment, somewhere off in the distance, a train whistled. Slowly, I discerned the sound of a steam engine intensifying as it approached. It was coming directly from the north and heading due south.

I jumped up and ran to my room. I had bought a map of Egypt as we passed through Bayrouth. I unfolded it and looked at the rail lines out of Cairo. Among them I found one that ran from north to south, from Cairo toward Upper Egypt. This must be the line on which the train I heard was traveling. Along this line I measured 30 kilometers from Cairo — the distance I had estimated as we were driving to the villa — and found myself at the Pyramids of Giza.

Now, at least, I knew where I was.

The next day the Captain showed up again. He had brought some of the Greeks I had traveled with from Halepi to the villa. "Your stay here is over," he said. "From now on you may circulate freely. All that's left is to return to our city offices in the same way we came."

I got into the sealed car again and we headed back. The anger that had been building from the previous day made this blind trip even more depressing. At some point the car stopped and the Captain opened the door so I could get out. "You can come sit up front with me now if you would like. I'll show you a bit of Cairo."

We crossed the verdant Gezira, the bridges of the Nile, and the beautiful streets of the center. A great throng dressed in caftans and fezzes and military uniforms circulated on the sidewalks. The Captain showed me mosques, kings' palaces, stores, and big hotels. The British policy of hospitality continues, I thought. He was presenting a civilized counter-balance to the obstacles they were about to interpose between me and my goal.

With a considerable dose of malevolence, I thought to demonstrate to the Captain just how trivial the measures they were taking to keep the villa's location secret really were. As he was pointing out the rich vegetation, I dropped it on him. "Really," I said, "it's something I noticed in the villa's wonderful garden as well." Then, with all the naïveté I could muster, I added, "It impressed me even more because I thought the area around the Pyramids of Giza was a desert…"

The Captain jolted at the wheel. "How do you know the villa is near the pyramids?" he exclaimed.

I completed my small revenge by leaving the mystery unsolved. "Two years of espionage in Greece makes these kinds of deductions rather easy," I answered him.

"I beg of you," the Captain said emphatically, "to give me your word of honor not to reveal the location of this villa to anyone until after the war has ended. It is a top secret!"

"You have my word," I replied. "But from the moment you verified that I really am the leader of a Greek organization and that you have trusted for such a long time, you could have allowed me to leave the villa in a regular car."

"I'm sorry," the Captain answered, "but this is the system in our service."

We were soon sitting in the office of a senior MO4 officer. "Unfortunately, the service did not grant your request for a new wireless set to return with to Greece," the officer told me. "We congratulate you on your accomplishments and commend your desire to continue. Your services will be recognized in writing, but one of our inviolable rules prohibits organizations that have been discovered by the enemy, even partially, from being allowed to continue. Other organizations exist in Greece that are continuing your work."

So here was the blow I had been waiting for. There was no danger to the Allies if Service 5-16-5 continued its mission, only benefits. Despite the fact that there were other worthy organizations providing information — some perhaps even more worthy than ours — some void would certainly be created by our absence. It was impossible for all organizations to have penetrated the same exact sectors and to be transmitting the same exact information. The explanations they gave me did not hold water. Something else must have been going on, and I was sure that I would some day find that out.

"Besides," the MO4 senior officer continued, "in Greece you would run a deadly personal risk with the Germans looking for you. Our denial is for your own protection."

"This is exclusively my business," I responded. "I understand the situation and I am determined to take the risk. The gains that will result are incomparably greater than any potential loss. If you choose to waste an organization that is entirely ready to continue operating and has already proven its usefulness to the Allied struggle, you must have very serious reasons that completely escape me."

"I'm sorry, but this is the system in our service," answered the officer, just as the Captain had a short while ago. It seems that "the system in their service" was to give this answer whenever they could not find anything else to say or whenever they had something to hide.

I saw that the best thing for me to do was to get myself away from the MO4 as soon as possible. They had someone escort me to the Greek Information Service which would take care of the necessities for my stay in Egypt. There I felt more comfortable among my own people. I completed a form and gave a brief statement. I also sent a prearranged radio message to my family using my father's name as if it was my surname: "Rigas Dionysiou notifies his mother and three sisters that he is well."

Soon my name was found in the list of reserve officers. Later I learned that they knew more about Service 5-16-5 than the British. They gave me some money, a voucher that allowed me to settle in a fairly good hotel, a note authorizing me to procure military clothing, and the address of a tailor who later made me an excellent uniform.

Dressed again in my unevenly faded suit and linen shoes, and with my unshorn head, I must have looked worse than I imagined. I realized this from a cute episode that very same evening on a central street of Cairo. Amidst the Arabic and British that I heard all around me, I heard two young girls walking near me speaking to each other in Greek.

"Look at him!" one said. "Doesn't he look like a gravedigger?"

"But I'm not a gravedigger," I replied, enjoying their embarrassment. "I'm a weary traveler from Greece. As soon as I put on my officer uniform I will be much better looking." The poor girls fell over each other trying to excuse themselves. Finally they made amends by having a beer with me and promising to meet me again when I was more presentable.

The first phase of my trip had ended. For some reason my attempts and hopes had hit a strange British barrier. I had verified that some important conflict was splitting the British secret services, but I could not guess its cause at that time. This had completely thwarted my plans. So far, my adventurous journey from Greece to the Middle East had been in vain.

But I was finally free, free to move as I pleased. And this was something that was critically important.

ONE MONTH NEAR THE PRIME MINISTER

The seat of the Greek government was housed in a beautiful villa in the efflores-cent Zamalek, right in the middle of the Nile. As soon as I was free, I presented myself there and requested that I be allowed to see the Greek Prime Minister. I thought this was the only road that might lead to some success. I would set out the situation and ask him for assistance. Hopefully, this would help me get to the bottom of the strange situation I had faced, learn the truth about the British attitude toward me, and continue my mission according to its original plan and my friends' anguished expectations in Greece.

Seeing the Prime Minister might also allow me to complete my mission's sec-ond goal: to report to responsible officials on the concerns of Greek patriots for the dangers being created by strengthening Communism in Greece and the need for support of the purely national organizations. Of course, I had reported all this to the MO4, but by now I no longer trusted that service. The head of the Greek government might be the only person who could demand that the British make a radical change in their policies dealing with Greece.

Prime Minister Emmanuel Tsouderos received me immediately. He knew my name and my family even though he didn't know me personally, and he was anx-ious to hear the latest news from Greece. He was very interested to learn that I commanded an espionage organization and to hear about the deeds of Service 5-16-5.

[The reader may well wonder how a man of my young age at that time could get to see the head of our government and be allowed to discuss matters of supreme political importance with him. These breaches of hierarchical formality were simply part of the spirit of that strange time. Our political leadership, far away from Greece, was intensely interested in learning what was going on back home. My position as the leader of a national resistance organization who could also report the views of other such organizations gave additional weight to everything I intended to tell the Prime Minister.]

I spoke to Tsouderos at length and in minute detail. I told him about the situation in Greece and what the resistance was doing. I explained the threat of communism and EAM and the repercussions that British policies toward Bulgaria were having on the victims of Bulgarian brutality. I recounted the actions of the national organi-zations and the prospects for the internal struggle.

Emmanuel Tsouderos listened to my reports on these vital matters with rapt attention. At every point he agreed with the views I presented. He then explained to me with all sincerity that the Prime Minister of Greece was completely powerless against the British.

"The hope that I could convince them to change their policies in Greece is mini-mal," he said. "I've discussed many of your points with them and repeatedly con-tested their policies. I'm just a voice crying in the wilderness. Our relations have reached critical points many times. I would like you, Mr. Rigopoulos, to write a memorandum to me putting all the details you've reported in writing. Your views present an important picture of reality as you've personally lived and perceived it. I'll raise these issues with them again, and I'll use your memorandum to bolster my arguments."

The head of the government kept me for over two hours. He promised that he

Note from Prime Minister Emmanuel Tsouderos

would also take a personal interest in the situation of Service 5-16-5. I left the Prime Minister's office with renewed hope.

While I was working on the memorandum he requested, I sent the Prime Minister a letter to stress in writing the need for me to return to Greece properly supplied so that we could continue the work of Service 5-16-5. Thinking that this was the memorandum I was to submit to him, the Prime Minister sent me a note written in his own hand:

> *Mr. Rigopoulos neglected to report on the existing organizations in detail, as he reported to me verbally. This would be useful for many reasons.*

Tsouderos has been accused of favoring the leftist climate the British were cultivating in Greece. This is not true. His note, which I saved and include an actual copy of here, is proof that he sincerely intended to ask the British to change their policies based on responsible testimonies such as the memorandum he had asked of me. This is why he wanted to learn about "the existing organizations in detail," and this is what he meant by his last phrase, "useful for many reasons."

Most of the text of my memorandum is included as an appendix at the end of this book. It reflects views that Tsouderos wished to support and documents vital matters of that time: the universal resistance of the Greek people; the actions and cohesion of the national organizations and their need for financial support; the synthesis, breadth, maneuvers, and achievements of EAM as well as its meager, purely communistic core; the congruence of British and communist policies on the Bulgarian matter; and the Greeks' need for their struggles to be fully honored after the final victory. My memorandum also points out that the Greek people themselves must decide after liberation on the matter of the King's return, and it characterizes as criminal all inopportune political actions that would cause division. Finally, it predicts the internal tumult that would follow if Greek rights were disregarded after the victory.

Two days later I was again received by the Prime Minister. I handed over my memorandum and he read it carefully. "It wouldn't have been possible to include everything you told me," he remarked, "but this will still be very useful. I'll have it translated into English immediately."

Tsouderos then spoke about my personal request. "The British secret services are unapproachable right now. So for the time being, you will not return to Greece. You'll serve here, which might prove even more useful. I would very much like for you to work closely with me. There are many serious matters that you could help me with." The proposition was interesting, especially since my service as a Second Lieutenant of Administration in the Greek army was of little importance.

Shortly, the Minister of War, Byron Karapanagiotis, came in. The Prime Minister introduced me. "He's too old to fight," he said to Karapanagiotis wittily. "I hope you won't object to him serving in my private office."

Thus I spent about a month near the Prime Minister, a month of inaction and no consequence whatsoever. I verified that the Prime Minister of Greece was well disposed, but actually a captive of the British. And even worse, he feared them.

A typical event will illustrate this situation. One day when I was in the Prime Minister's office they announced my friend, the British Captain from the MO4. Tsouderos opened a side door to an adjoining room and asked me to wait in there until the Captain left. "I prefer that he doesn't see you here," he said. Knowing my opposition to the MO4, the Prime Minister didn't want them to see that he had kept me beside him.

In the days that followed I had the opportunity to learn about Greek matters in the Middle East.

The British managed to give the impression that their general policy was to support the international communist organizations against the enemy because they had conspiratorial networks in place in all the occupied countries. This policy also justified British support for the communists in Greece. Our politicians watched like simple spectators as the communist front in our enslaved land grew stronger and corrupting propaganda was disseminated throughout our free army. Even worse, they became accessories to these unreasonable British policies and systematically gave way to the impudent demands of the communists, who used their well-known methods behind a democratic mask.

Leftist politicians, some of whom were also members of the government, contributed to this communist activity. At the same time, the question of the monarchy was coming to a head with frightful speed. The danger we had managed to avoid in occupied Greece was wreaking destructive havoc here. Greeks, among them patriotic, national-minded, courageous, but tragically brainless men, were misguidedly being led into a deadly internal conflict over the return or non-return of King George.

In the Middle East, our army was in the process of disbanding. On February 26, 1943, two Greek brigades rebelled, incited by communist agents. One was the heroic 1st Brigade that had written glorious history in the battle of El-Alamein. The Vice President and Minister of National Defense at that time was Panagiotis Kanellopoulos. Thanks to him, the 1st Brigade had seen action in the war and the Sacred Squadron of Commandos had been established. But now he had lost control of the situation. He was forced to resign and a new government had to be formed. The Prime Minister was now forced to include ministers acceptable to the rebels.

Outstanding officers were pushed aside and replaced by ones favorable to the leftists. Other heroic fighters were thrown into concentration camps. Those who had rebelled were granted amnesty.

Army discipline was shaken to the core. Soldiers did not salute officers on the street. Political instructors were essentially commanding the units. The microbe of dissent penetrated slowly yet surely into the navy, which until now had remained above the fray. The same disease infected our small air force. The single exception in this general decline was the Sacred Squadron. This unit had been created by Colonel Christodoulos Tsigantes, the brother of Major Yiannis Tsigantes who was killed on a mission in occupied Athens. Col. Tsigantes recruited volunteers personally. They came from everywhere and were mainly officers who would have to go through intensive commando training in Palestine and live the life of soldiers.

Amidst this hopeless disruption, the Prime Minister was trying to reconcile the irreconcilable. As I've said before, he had every intention to react to these events in some way, but he was neither imaginative enough to figure out effective plans, nor courageous enough to implement the plans he did devise.

The Prime Minister did me the honor of discussing with me, many times, the complex problems that his administration was facing. "My role," he would say, "has been limited to trying to dull the oppositions of my ministers. The government is in danger of collapsing at any moment, a development I am desperately struggling to avert." Or, "The military is systemically infected and there is no treatment for the disease. All of our orders face open hostility just because they come from us."

In one such moment, when disappointment had overtaken the Prime Minister, I suggested a plan that in some way grew out of my recent experience in Greece. "Communist propaganda is spread throughout the military using a 'conspiratorial' technique," I explained. "Why not spread national anti-propaganda the same way? Under the Communists' system, orders don't appear to come from the top. Everything is made to sound as if it comes from the people. Specialized 'instructors' influence others of equal rank. They relate 'from below' the decisions and actions ordered by the leadership. With such a system we could undermine politicking and cultivate a spirit of discipline and preparation for war. We could also use the same network to gather information. Many dangerous communist actions could then be thwarted before they could be carried out."

The Prime Minister endorsed these ideas immediately. "Suitable people exist. There are some high-ranking and many lower level officers whom I trust. These have their own people in their units. The material exists. If you undertake its organization, I'll place the appropriate personnel under your command immediately."

I said that I would be enthusiastic about organizing an invisible net of National Propaganda and Information within the military. "But how would I, a Second Lieutenant, be able to command my superiors?" I asked.

"Your rank will only be relevant for your payment. You will not circulate in uniform. I will give you a political appointment and you will command by my order."

"I was just about to bring that up, Mr. Prime Minister. Your order is of critical importance. The British secret services have eyes everywhere and employ an incredible network of agents. It is quite possible that they would learn of an organized conspiratorial movement within our military, find out who is leading it, and arrest me. Could I perhaps have a personal letter from you to serve as proof that I am acting on your order, which is intended to serve our national interests as well as those of the Allies? I wouldn't use such a letter except in the case of extreme need, and I'd only show it confidentially to the leader of the British secret services."

"You, who risked your life defying the Germans, now fears the Allies?!?"

"I don't fear anyone, Mr. Prime Minister, but I don't wish to find myself behind bars accused of conspiring against the Greek and Allied authorities when, on the contrary, I will actually be serving them. I would be proud to accept any conviction whatsoever if it resulted from my role in a national mission. It was in this spirit that I risked everything in Greece. However, I would never conceal the honorable truth and accept disgrace based on false accusations."

"I'm sure you understand, Mr. Rigopoulos, that the Prime Minister of Greece cannot appear to be hiding his actions from the Allies. You must use your experience to avoid being discovered. But if you *are* discovered, you must take full responsibility. I must not have any knowledge of your activities."

On this reef, the plan to counterattack communist propaganda using clandestine anti-propaganda methods analogous to their own was shipwrecked. From then on, a coldness developed in my relationship with the Prime Minister. It was a coldness from both sides, despite the fact that a level-headed, impartial observer would have concluded that neither of us was wrong. Each simply viewed the situation from his own perspective.

I finally asked to be released from the Prime Minister's service after an open clash over confronting the British about their policies in Greece.

One night, the Prime Minister told me that he had approached the British and used my memorandum to reopen discussions concerning the dangers created for Greece and for the Greek military by their strengthening of leftism. He said he had also addressed the need for them to support the purely national organizations. "I exhausted my arguments without getting anywhere," he said. "They simply refuse to understand that systematic reinforcement of the communists will cause them to lose control one day. The matter must be considered closed. Unfortunately, I have no more ammunition to throw at them."

"You have the ammunition of resignation," I answered.

"The government should resign? That would lead to chaos. No, Mr. Rigopoulos, our duty is to stay here on the rampart."

This last phrase set me ablaze. Forgetting the difference in position and age that separated us, I fired my last salvo.

"One 'stays on the rampart,' Mr. Prime Minister, to fight. You admit defeat. Oh no, sir. You have *not* been defeated. Submitting your resignation would secure only advantages for you. Either the British will hesitate to open a public breach with the Prime Minister of an allied nation and you will immediately win the battle, or, if they insist on maintaining their position and carry on with another government, as resigned Prime Minister you will have every right to appear at the ensuing Peace Assembly and demand restitution from those solely responsible for the damages to our country. As things are, you remain co-responsible. The government will be overthrown regardless of your decision, and then there will be true chaos."

The discussion had reached a terrible level of tension. The Prime Minister, who was now standing up, struck the table with his fist. "Mr. Rigopoulos, I have asked for your opinion on the special matters in which you have experience, not the manner in which I exercise my authority!"

"In that case," I answered, echoing his animosity, "please release me from your service. I can be of no further use here. I have told you everything I know in response to your questions and I have no other service to offer. As an officer, my duty is to fight. I ask you to please approve my placement in the Sacred Squadron." I bowed my head in a formal salute and went out the door.

Tsouderos was a mild-mannered man and an old, experienced politician. In addition, I believe that he liked me. In about an hour, he used some official pretext to call me to his office. Once he'd finished addressing the matter of duty, and despite my officious attitude, he smiled and said to me, "I know you're full of love for our land. We Greeks are hot-tempered, and we cannot discuss things calmly. Also, your age and the dangers you've lived through are not conducive to calmness. At any rate, I don't want you to leave my service. You'll be much more useful here than anywhere else."

"Mr. Prime Minister," I answered in the same conciliatory tone. "I am deeply sorry that I lost my temper and I ask your forgiveness. However, I also ask you not to insist on keeping me. I feel that I've done all I can here. In the Sacred Squadron I'll go through very interesting training in all types of weapons and commando techniques. I'll also become a parachutist and perhaps be among the first to participate in new operations. I feel that I belong there, and I would be grateful for your consent."

"Is it really necessary for you to confront danger yet again?" Tsouderos remarked spontaneously, forgetting for a moment about being Prime Minister and speaking with true fatherly tenderness. I smiled at him without answering. "Fine, my child," he conceded. "Go wherever God commands you."

I had two goals for my trip to the Middle East. I failed to achieve either of them. I would neither return to Greece to continue my work in Service 5-16-5, nor would there be any change in the misguided handling of Greek matters.

The reasons why I failed were now clear to me. The MO4 represented Great Britain's leftist-friendly policies in Greece. These policies did not result from true pro-communist leanings, but from poor estimation of the actual number of communists in Greece and complete ignorance of the psychology of the Greek masses. Service 5-16-5 was not one of their organizations, and it was even attempting to thwart their plans. Thus it had to be neutralized.

These were my thoughts at that time. Later, when I returned to Greece, I was given the opportunity to identify other, even more deep-seated reasons for the MO4's tactics which I could not suspect when I was in Egypt. I address these in another chapter.

In any case, one thing was certain: only events would convince the obstinate British that their policies were creating terrible dangers, even for themselves. Unfortunately, Greece did not have a strong political leader who could forestall the upcoming troubles and prevent them.

So I would stay in the Middle East. Service 5-16-5, which had been organized with so many sacrifices and waited, always ready, to continue its services, would remain unused. Fatalistically, I would observe all the deplorable events that followed. They were events that any logical person could have foreseen, and they followed with mathematical precision.

RAIDS FROM AIR AND SEA. THE GREATEST MOMENT OF ALEXANDER KAIRIS. CONSEQUENCES OF MISTAKES.

If you headed north from Haifa up the Asiatic coast, you would find the modern and beautifully green Jewish village of Nahariya. Somewhere near there, you would see the Sacred Squadron camped next to an endless beach.

Around 300 young men, most of them officers, spent their days and nights undergoing intensive training to perfect a strange military art. They trained to fall suddenly upon an enemy stronghold at night in teams of five, ten, or fifteen men, quickly execute their destructive plans, and disappear like ghosts into the darkness from which they came before the enemy even realized what was happening. They also trained to establish advanced bridgeheads by making lightning-fast attacks from land, sea, or air and hold such positions between enemy lines until the regular army came up to relieve them.

To succeed in such operations, one needed exacting preparation. He had to train his body until it became a combination of rubber and steel... To shoot a pistol by reflex, from the hip without aiming... To master the Tommy gun, machine gun, hand grenade, mortar, and bazooka... To set explosives and time bombs methodically... To drive motorcycles, jeeps, and ten-wheeled trucks with equal ease... To land rowboats and motor boats... To scale precipitous ravines and mountaintops... To ski over snow... To be invincible in Japanese jujitsu and knives... To jump from heights of many meters and from fast-moving vehicles, rolling to avoid injury... And to parachute into the void even at night, starting the battle before he even sets foot on solid ground.

This was commando training in the Middle East, the training of the Sacred Squadron.

Leaving the Prime Minister's office on September 16, 1943, I found myself blocked by the Army Staff of the Administration Service. I was, after all, an officer of Administration. The head Colonel did everything in his power to keep me in Cairo. He would have succeeded, too, had I not had the good fortune to run into Colonel Tsigantes himself, who had come to the Army General Headquarters on matters dealing with the Sacred Squadron.

When I told Tsigantes that I had been informed that the Sacred Squadron already had its full allotment of men, he grabbed me by the arm, totally beside himself, and went from office to office slamming doors. "They undermine me at every turn," he said, boiling with anger, "but they won't it have their way." He quickly got me marching orders for Palestine.

Michael Hors, son of the Admiral, joined the Sacred Squadron at the same time. He was my closest friend, the architect who had escaped from Greece in October 1941, and the one on whom we had placed our hopes to contact the Allied secret services. When, to my great joy, I met him again in Cairo where he was serving as a second lieutenant in a vehicle unit, he told me of his adventures in Nigdi, Turkey, where he was held in a concentration camp for almost a year. (The passage through Turkey had not yet been organized back then.) After he was finally able to make his way to Egypt, Michael needed to spend considerable time recovering in a hospital.

This explained why those of us back in Athens waited in vain for the communication we hoped he would arrange, and why we finally had to make contact with the Allies by other means.

Michael was disappointed and disillusioned by his hardships, the inaction in his current unit, and the general condition of the military in the Middle East. An ardent patriot by family tradition as well as spiritual disposition, he spoke to me about the Sacred Squadron. It was his idea for us to join this unit, and to him I owe the most intense experiences of my military life.

As soon as we found ourselves camped near Nahariya, we realized how different the mentality was there and how unique the training was. Everyone maintained his individuality without being flattened by the steamroller of military discipline.

Colonel Tsigantes was perhaps the only person who could have commanded such a unit during those turbulent times, one composed of daring young Greeks who volunteered without pompous shows of patriotism. They simply wanted to lend a hand in the liberation of their country and return to their homeland.

Tsigantes was an exceptionally gifted officer. His huge size, with a bit of a stoop, broad shoulders, and monocled eye gave him a commanding presence. His knowledge was encyclopedic, and he had a noble air.

Tsigantes was also reckless and loved revelry. When he drank or opened his filthy mouth, none of us could keep up with him. One night he parachuted with us onto Samos Island without ever having taken even a practice jump. Just like that, he dropped out the airplane's door and tumbled into the darkness. On the Island of Rhodes, he competed with his officers to see who could be the first to kick out a ceiling lamp. Heavy as he was, he fell and broke his leg.

In Nahariya, he would come out early in the morning and ask, "Who's in the mood for jujitsu today? Who's up for machine gun practice? Some of you team up and conquer the top of that hill over there. Go ahead, run! I want you back here by noon!"

And woe to the fellow who did something Tsigantes didn't like. Such thunder and lightning spewed out of that man that it would have been better for the ground to open up and swallow you than to have to stand there and face him.

This was the commander of the Sacred Squadron, the man who was needed.

We completed the intensive commando training without even realizing it. At Rama David Airport near Haifa, we had the fantastic experience of parachuting. This is, I believe, the most rugged but also the most thrilling of all sports.

I will not describe all the operations of the Sacred Squadron here in detail, despite their many fascinating aspects. Doing so would be beyond the scope of this book. However, I will sketch some of them briefly to give the reader an idea of what they encompassed.

One night, twenty Sacred Squadron commandos attacked the capital of Lesbos Island from the sea. They destroyed the Gestapo's local headquarters, killed as many German officers and soldiers as they could, burned their records, liberated the captives, and retreated without a single casualty. Only one of our men was injured, when a stray bullet of our own broke his collarbone.

On Simi Island, some of our commandos raided a big German base, again from the sea. They set fires, detonated explosives, and sprayed machine gun fire. Eight of the enemy were killed, 15 wounded, and about 125 taken prisoner and loaded onto the caïques. Nine of our men were wounded.

On Samos Island, 200 Sacred Squadron paratroopers dropped from ten airplanes into deep darkness. I was lucky, falling into a thick grove of holm oak. The wind carried our team toward the foot of a mountain, onto the rocks. We had casualties. But the Italians would not fight. They sent word to us that Italy was ready to give up, and it would therefore be foolish for them to risk their lives on the eve of capitulation. We held the island for a month, while the Germans pounded us mercilessly. Aside from four of us who were badly hurt on the rocks during the jump, and two or three who were hit by the Germans, again we didn't suffer heavy losses.

In general, the Sacred Squadron's losses were not in proportion to the extent of its operations. This was due to the special training of its men and their use of surprise attacks. In all of its operations in Northern Africa (1942) and on the islands of the Aegean Sea (1943-1945), the total losses amounted to 14 officers and 9 soldiers killed, 28 officers and 30 soldiers wounded (*Formal Report of the Sacred Squadron*, 1945). The enemy's losses, however, were incalculable.

It was exceptionally lucky for me to find myself in this elite unit. The antithesis between the magnificent uplifting of the secret struggle and the bitter disappointment of my failed efforts in the Middle East had created a grievous void inside me. I was now just a pawn in the Sacred Squadron. However, I was giving myself wholeheartedly to a common effort, and I was living in an environment where my comrades and I were bound by similar emotions and convictions. Immersed in the kinship of these pure and brave men, I was able to find myself again.

Indeed, on Samos, enraptured by the feeling of once again stepping on free Greek soil, I was able to write a long poem full of the images and pulsations created by that nocturnal jump.

At that time we believed that liberation of our land was at hand. During our stay on Samos in November 1943, Italy almost completely capitulated. At last, you could clearly see that Germany would lose the war. We already felt victorious.

However, after the month that we held the island, the British called off the entire landing operation and took us back to Syria. Disappointment replaced our enthusiasm. The Germans returned to Samos and the unfortunate Samiotes paid dearly for their premature celebrations of liberation. Clearly, things were not happening as fast as we thought. Many struggles and sacrifices still lay ahead of us.

Upon our return, the British gave each of us a 20-day leave to go wherever we wanted, rest, and have a good time. It was a consolation prize. Michael Hors and I headed to Alexandria. We ended up spending very little of our leave as intended, because we were given the opportunity to get familiar with a strange new type of nautical operation: war with armed caïques.

✻ ✻ ✻

As chance would have it, at that very time an old acquaintance of Michael's, Commander Andreas Lontos, was organizing a unique flotilla of motorized sailing vessels. Even without being schooled in International Law, one would classify these as pirate ships. As soon as the Germans discovered them, they declared them illegal. If their crews fell into German hands, they would be executed without trial.

Lontos suggested that we ask the Sacred Squadron for permission to train with him for three months so that we could learn to captain such vessels. In exchange, we would train the crews as commandos. This is exactly what happened, and once more our spirit was regenerated.

We wore the navy's blue uniform with a black beret, our army officer pips on our shoulders, and our Sacred Squadron and parachutist badges on our chests. Arbitrarily, we also added a gold anchor on the sleeve. Thus we made a uniform that didn't conform to any existing regulations. Once, when I presented myself to the leader of the General Staff, he looked at me in amazement and asked what I was and what uniform I was wearing.

"Second lieutenant," I replied, "captain of an armed caïque." As we had agreed, I added, "This uniform was given to us by ... the British."

The general shook his head. "They never tell us what's going on..."

Thus, our uniform was in the pirate spirit as well, but it was truly a thing of beauty.

Andreas Lontos was a handsome man. He had a neatly groomed black beard and an elegant appearance. He hadn't hesitated to take on the difficult task of organizing the flotilla, which he accomplished through frequent and persistent appeals to both the Greek and British authorities. He loved that flotilla with a passion.

Lontos was also trained as a commando. He had captained a caïque in the first flotilla he managed to get the British to create. He then found eight small sponge fishing boats from the Dodecanese and got permission to establish the "2nd Anglo-Hellenic Schooner Flotilla." This flotilla was manned by volunteer officers and sailors that Lontos recruited personally. Few people in the Middle East worked with such fervor and inspired creativity.

Lontos' idea was to unleash small, light (14- to 16-ton) caïques into the Aegean Sea, disguised as fishing boats or transport vessels but carrying powerful, camouflaged armament. Such caïques could travel in all kinds of seas and in all kinds of weather and pass over minefields to surprise the enemy. Their crews would land and wreak destruction on the Greek islands and coasts where nobody would ever expect them.

When Michael Hors and I received our caïques — simple sponge fishing boats — we took them out onto the slipways and supervised their transformation into military vessels. In the meantime we trained the crews, and we ourselves, along with the other captains, received navigation training from Lontos and the British.

As with the Sacred Squadron, detailed descriptions of the caïques' operations are beyond the scope of this book. Again I will just try to give the reader a basic idea of their scope

We would depart from Alexandria and pass across the foamy Mediterranean to Cyprus. From Cyprus we would set sail for the enemy-occupied Dodecanese, and from there deep into the islands of the Aegean Sea. We could also approach certain parts of the Turkish coast where we knew the Turks would not hit us.

The flotilla had its losses as well. A few miles from Alexandria, one of our caïques was hit by a German plane as it returned from a mission. Its captain, Ensign Vasilis Anastasiou, was killed by two shells in the forehead, and many of its crew were wounded.

On another mission, an armed enemy vessel riddled Michael Hors' caïque with shells. Michael himself was slightly injured while firing a machine gun, and so were many of his crew.

My caïque and its entire crew plus eight British commandos were lost in a clash with an enemy gunboat on the western coast of Rhodes. The caïque had sailed for a two-day mission under a substitute captain, the English sublieutenant Nichols, who was also lost. I had left my caïque for these two days in our base on the Turkish coast under orders of the sector's English commanding officer and had gone to Kastellorizo Island by torpedo boat to get a formal certificate of health which was missing from my personnel file.

Of course, no one knows if I could have saved my boat and crew had I been in command, or if I would have been lost along with them. But the fact remains that in the heat of the battle, my temporary English substitute — who didn't speak any Greek — could not command the inexperienced sponge divers I had trained in my own way. Sending them off under his command was a death sentence.

It is not difficult to imagine my emotional reaction to the loss of my ship and crew. Once again I had lost people I loved and who loved me. Fate seemed to constantly put me into conflict with the English, whom I truly like as individuals and admire as a people. As a result, I had a violent dispute with the English commander who, unbeknownst to me, had scheduled this mission during my absence. This conflict created an unpleasant atmosphere that finally forced me out of the Anglo-Hellenic flotilla.

Aside from this sad story, my wartime service with the caïques was unforgettable. From December 1943 through August 1944 I lived a sailor's life between Alexandria and the open sea. In the Flotilla, as in the Sacred Squadron, I was surrounded by people with whom I was well-matched, people who voluntarily threw themselves into dangerous situations wholeheartedly, serving a cause they saw tied to their very existence.

As a volunteer unit, the Flotilla was also a cadre of officers from all backgrounds: army, navy, and air force. These men required only brief training to assume command of armed caïques. However, common mentality ties people much more strongly than common background. We would sacrifice anything for each other. To this day, the shared experiences of that time still bind some of us together.

The fact that neither the Sacred Squadron nor the Flotilla took part in the mutinies and revolts that stained the Greeks' beautiful struggle for liberation was no accident. People whose hearts pined for their enslaved homeland and gave their all to the struggle had neither the desire nor the time to deal with politics. On the contrary, they were furious with those who made the combatants' missions and actions more difficult by their opportunistic politicking. As it happened in occupied Greece, it also happened in the Middle East: all true patriots who had any brains at all were finally united, without worrying about differences in their personal views.

For example, it is telling that Lontos was a fervent royalist while Tsigantes was a long-standing follower of Venizelos[1] who had even been dishonorably discharged from the army by the royalists in older times. Their struggle, however, was now common. In both units, royalists and democrats served together as brothers. The Sacred Squadron, in conjunction with the 2nd Schooner Flotilla, fought in the islands during the war's entire period of political anomaly in the Middle East. Some of the officers and sailors of the flotilla who happened to be in Alexandria during the mutinies took part in the counterattack to recapture the rebelling ships.

---

[1]Venizelos, Eleutheiros (1864-1936). Cretan politician who served several times as Prime Minister. His name is associated with democratic reforms.

Thus there was harmony and cooperation between all real patriots in the Middle East for the common good, just as there was in enslaved Greece. Such cooperation was independent of personal convictions and individual differences, and far from the conflicts between political parties and ideological movements. The reader may remember the analogous situation in the case of Perrikos and Vovolinis.

Despite all this, the incredibly absurd policies of the British, combined with the inaction of the Greek officials, soon led us to the brink of the abyss. Whether we wanted to or not, all of us who dreamed of fighting united for liberation and liberation only, would soon have to neutralize the internal danger that flared up right under our noses despite all our warnings and protests.

Between operations, we would rest in hospitable Alexandria. In the open sea we experienced gripping adventure that satisfied our spiritual impulses, and in Alexandria we experienced the warmth one searches for when he is far from his homeland and his family.

Greeks who were permanent residents of Egypt opened their homes and arms to us. They tried in every way to show us that they hadn't forgotten their homeland or those fighting for its freedom. Many of their Alexandrian homes were true mansions, and in the evenings they were filled with Greek and British uniforms. There we found our civilized selves again. There we encountered political and military figures, people of art and culture, and leading merchants and businessmen. There we listened to the most interesting conversations. There we could forget about the war for a while, listen to music performed by select soloists and exceptional ensembles, and dance the night away, carefree and merry…

At one of these soirees, and unhampered by formal protocol, I met Crown Prince Paul, a man of great heart and pure patriotism. At that time he was trying to overcome the Allies' objections and secretly cross into Greece to offer his assistance to struggling Greeks in any way he could. The Crown Prince has honored me many times since then through his friendship and later, when he was King, by frequently receiving me in official audiences and inviting me to receptions at the palace.

I remember him in Alexandria at that time, speaking with his distinctive honesty and simplicity about how the liberation struggle had to be coordinated and about the constant mistakes that were creating terrible dangers. I remember him speaking against the Greek leadership and heavily criticizing, one by one, almost all of our politicians. I remember him expressing his indignation with the British policies and actions that were undermining the Greek resistance and the future of our country. And I even remember him playing the piano. He made up for his small lack of dexterity with musicality and knowledge that revealed true spiritual wealth, cultivation, and sensitivity. Gina Bahauer, the famous Greek pianist, said of her "student," Crown Prince Paul, with her characteristically charming style: "If only I had his big hands that can span ten keys, you would really see what I could do!"

Gina was another of the select people I met during that time. She lived in Alexandria then and gave hundreds of concerts for soldiers, visiting all the Greek and British camps in the Middle East. Her music and gaiety gave us uplifting optimism every time we faced difficult moments. Her lively fingers overcame all technical difficulties, translating all the power and beauty that enveloped her into exquisite melodies.

❊　❊　❊

Around the end of May 1944, while I was still with the Flotilla, a piece of news from Greece snapped me back to the occupation with an incredible shock.

Michael Hors and I were in Cairo for a couple of days and were spending the night at a friend's house. Completely unexpectedly, I learned that Alexander Kairis had been executed. I was talking with Spiros Theotokis in a corner of the parlor. Theotokis had just arrived from Greece as a political representative and would soon become Minister of Provisions. He brought a lot of interesting news from home and asked many questions about the situation in the Middle East.

At one point, I casually asked if he had heard anything about Alexander Kairis, who was in the Averof Prisons accused of espionage.

"Are you talking about the Kairis who was recently executed?" he asked.

"Executed?" I managed to whisper. My heart fluttered unsteadily in my chest.

Amidst the wide-ranging flow of our conversation, Theotokis did not understand the depth of my shock. "Yes, he was executed a few months ago," he explained. "His execution, as well as his amazing composure in his final moments, caused a great stir in Athens. It seems that he spoke wonderful German and addressed the firing squad with such eloquence that he made the guns shake in the soldiers' hands. The Germans hit him and broke his glasses before shooting him."

I managed not to reveal the storm building inside me. Only Michael Hors, who knew the situation, was in a position to understand. All I said to Theotokis was, "Kairis was my friend, my close friend."

Later, Michael and I walked to a secluded area on the muddy banks of the Nile. His companionship was invaluable to me. Michael was the type of person who knew to remain silent and compassionate while listening to me talk about my great childhood friend, about the great Greek he knew only minimally, but for whom he had all the details needed to warrant unbounded admiration. His soul ached along with mine.

Morning found us in the dim, deserted bar of the Shepherd's Hotel, where we sat, an empty bottle of old cognac before us, still chatting about the rare, exceptional, and peerless patriot who was now gone...

Many days passed before I regained my normal rhythm. I was tortured by an irregular pulse and shortness of breath, maladies that had never afflicted me before then. It seems that the sequence of hardships had sapped my endurance.

It was not only my close friendship with Alexander Kairis that caused me this deep depression. It was also the thought of this strongly emotional person, with his sensitive psychic receivers and highly refined perception, suffering general scorn and contempt without protest while he proceeded on his great way with mighty strides, not revealing to anyone his secret mission or his deep pain. The thought that he would never see himself reinstated into the good graces of the national conscience was unbearable to me.

We others were exalted and uplifted by our work. We had the privilege, within the general subjugation, to feel free. We viewed the cruel conqueror with condescension and mockery. We only approached him as needed to undermine his foundations. Our honor and pride remained intact. Even our harbor people, who had the thankless job of working under the immediate supervision of the conquerors, went about their regular professional work. It did not appear that they were offering any special or exclusive services to the enemy.

But Alexander Kairis, this proud man, was forced to swallow his pride and play the role of a submissive servant. Everyone considered him a traitor, and a venal one at that. The virtuous and upstanding Alexander, whose honesty was mirrored in the way he looked you straight in the eye, was forced to flatter, to feign, and to lie. His moral conscience revolted along with his wounded ethics.

Only when Kairis was finally exposed and sentenced was he essentially liberated. Only then was he able to complete his satisfaction for the patriotic work he had done. At last he could throw the truth in the face of the conqueror and every arm-chair supporter of patriotic ideals.

All of the suppressed pride, all of the revolting sincerity, could at last find free expression. Alexander decided to unleash this outburst in a grand way, at the precise, frightful moment at which he would face death. He prepared for that moment consciously, with incredible composure and supreme wisdom. You might say that he waited impatiently for that moment from within the confines of his prison cell. His letters, which I hold in my hands today, are incontrovertible evidence of his internal uplifting.

On October 19, 1943, the day after he was sentenced to death, Alexander wrote:

... I am maintaining my composure and self-control as best I can,
and in a way that I think will allow me to face that moment with
the same calmness and spiritual serenity when it comes...

On October 27, five days before his execution and completely prepared for the great passage, he wrote:

... The moment is approaching for me to taste that something, the
great unknown of life, which for thousands of years has tortured
all the wise men of the earth with its mysterious essence. This mys-
terious unknown – I will meet it soon! ...

Thus I will acquire more knowledge and wisdom than the wis-
est man on Earth! Is it not worth the trouble?

With this resolve, and with this sublime vision, Alexander Kairis faced the firing squad on November 2, 1943, along with seven others. From eyewitnesses who had the painful duty of assisting the condemned in their final moments, we learned the stirring details which clearly confirmed Alexander's true character.

In his report to the Archdiocese of Athens, the Archimandrite Vasileios Libritis wrote:

... At 6:55 AM the first execution began. Alexander Kairis stepped
up to his calvary first with a haughty air. His sentence was read.
His answer to the question of his last request was to insult the
Germans in both the German and Greek. ... All the German sol-
diers and officers bowed their heads, troubled, gloomy, and stupe-
fied. Two German soldiers immediately tied him to the stake and
tried to blindfold him against his will. During this cruel struggle,
they broke his glasses...

Kairis spoke in both German and Greek. With his words he wanted to not only humiliate his enemies, but also to send one last message to his compatriots and friends, a message that would always bring his memory to life.

I transcribe here the words that the second Archimandrite in attendance, Kyrillos Softas, passed on to us. The words that shocked the German soldiers and officers. The final gift of his enlightened mind.

You are dishonest cowards, violators of human freedom. Soon
Greeks will avenge our deaths and hang the guilty in the main

squares of Germany. We die so that Greece can live. You die as
individuals and as a people, blindly following Hitler, an insane
criminal, on the road to destruction...[2]

At this point, an officer and two soldiers rushed to stop him. They struck him in the face, breaking his glasses. They tried to blindfold him, certainly not out of compassion to spare him from seeing the rifles of his despised executioners, but to shield them from seeing the Greek's fierce, condemning glare.

Watching this frightful scene, the other condemned men began to sing the National Anthem in loud, fearless voices. The German officer quickly saw that he was losing control of the prisoners and discipline in the firing squad. With one final, rough effort, he succeeded in tying his victim and immediately ordered his execution. The Greek song of valor and freedom accompanied the discharge of the German rifles...

Thus Alexander Kairis died as he wanted, proudly and beautifully.

He died as he had dreamed it in the last verses that spontaneously poured from his soul and his thoughts on October 28, 1943, when he awaited death in his cell at any moment:

> *Each of us awaits a moment;*
> *Which will it be — how will you know? ...*
> *But sometimes you know which moment it will be,*
> *For it is the only one that you await...*
> *You endeavor to stand great,*
> *As this is also great,*
> *To face it composed and confident*
> *Worthy of the moment, which is*
> *The only certain one,*
> *The final moment!*

❀   ❀   ❀

Events in the Middle East rapidly developed as any prudent person could have predicted. The fears I had expressed to the Greek Prime Minister a few months ago were very quickly justified, and in dramatic fashion.

When the communists felt strong enough, they openly revealed their true aspirations. This situation, born of British guilt and Greek tolerance, now had to be faced with serious and violent measures. With my thoughts constantly focused on enslaved Greece and her sufferings, which were increasing as we neared the end of the war, I followed all phases of the coup in the Middle East and experienced the anxiety it created. I will try to give an impression of those dramatic days in a few pages.

The news from Greece was disheartening. To the unbearable oppression of the conquerors was now added the terrorism of the partisans. They crushed every opposition to their plans, preparing to seize power after the liberation. EAM, thanks to the generous support of the British, had become frightfully powerful.

On March 16, 1944, EAM created the "Government of the Mountains." It sent word to the government in Cairo demanding reforms, including its own representatives for ministers.

---

[2]I firmly believe that these words are very close to Kairis's actual ones. They are extracted from those the priest told us, maintaining what we know of Kairi's mentality and his characteristic phrasing.

On March 25, taking advantage of the national holiday, EAM filled the walls of Cairo and Alexandria with revolutionary slogans and circulated propaganda via thousands of leaflets. Anarchy reigned in the Army Brigades, the Navy, and the Air Force. The climate turned revolutionary. They had long cultivated rebellion in the armed forces and it was now ripe. Their slogans called for the formation of a government with a "Pan-Hellenic character," that is, a government with the participation of EAM. They also demanded that the "fascist George" not return to Greece.

The responses of our politicians and military commanders were feeble. They believed they could cajole the stirring mob like a group of children. All the relevant proclamations and daily orders of those days show that they gave in to the rebels' demands. They attempted to assure the rebels that the authorities were working in their interests, and they pleaded with them to return to order by appealing to their patriotism. Such responses only served to reveal the authorities' naked weaknesses, thus intensifying the anarchy.

In his book *Report on the Action of the Royal Navy* (based on formal evidence), Vice Admiral D. Fokas wrote:

> *Whether from an unjustifiable feeling of security or simply from weakness, it seems that the government left the impending revolt to break out without the slightest repressive or preventive measure having been taken.*

Unavoidably, the situation worsened from day to day. On March 31, 1944, the Greek military garrison in Cairo revolted and seized control of several buildings. A revolutionary committee of 14 officers appeared and directed the revolt without anyone taking a single measure against them.

On April 3, under the leadership of sailors' and petty officers' committees in Alexandria, the Greek fleet and ground services revolted. The rebels managed to seize the naval garrison headquarters and the Cadet School. They also tried to seize control of the Naval Ministry buildings and the fleet's headquarters, but at these points the British stopped them.

Only then did our Allies begin to wake up and recognize the danger. Beginning April 4, they forbade the circulation of Greek military personnel without permission from the British Department of Security. They surrounded the various buildings of the naval services with strong guards and arrested several of the rebellion's instigators. This intervention caused even greater turmoil.

In the week that followed, the rebellion became generalized. Sailors held officers in confinement, chased them from their warships, or threw them into the sea. By now complete anarchy not only prevailed, it also clearly appeared anti-British. The British attempts to partner with the leftists had failed.

Having reached the edge of the abyss under these dramatic conditions, Tsouderos's government was obliged to resign. It was a delayed, forced resignation due to abject failure that could have been prevented by an earlier, voluntary resignation of political boldness.

On April 12, 1944, King George urgently hurried to Cairo from London and appointed Sophocles Venizelos as the new Prime Minister. Venizelos immediately formed a new government.

On April 14, the Soviet Union dropped its mask. With an announcement on its official radio station in Moscow, it openly adopted the communist movement in

Greece, which it had methodically cultivated with the full support of the British.

The British now became more decisive. Admiral Cunningham, the leader of the British Eastern Mediterranean fleet, threatened to sink Greek ships if the Greeks did not manage to reseize them and reinstate order by April 18.

After a short and final extension to this deadline was granted by the British and after Vice Admiral Petros Voulgaris was put in command of the fleet, the operation to reseize our rebelling warships was launched on April 23 at 2:30 in the morning. In only one hour, the battle was over. Three ships were captured, and the rest surrendered by 10:00 that night. The casualty report listed 4 officers and 3 sailors dead, with 40 wounded. By April 29, the rebelling warships of Port-Sahid had also surrendered, and the warships of Malta did the same a bit later. The rebels were thrown into prison camps.

However, this victory of the legitimate forces did not quell the general uprising. Just the opposite occurred.

The leftists circulated ultimatums to be presented to the government and the crews signed them right on our own warships. The British prepared to strike the rebelling 1st Brigade, but they hesitated, fearing that this great bloodshed would foster even greater fanaticism. Meanwhile, the camps of the captives became universities of communism. Systematic "enlightenment," methodical sermons, and sensational slogans infuriated the prisoners.

On April 26, Venizelos' government resigned, and the next day King George appointed George Papandreou as the new Prime Minister. Like his predecessors, Papandreou was a democratic man. His response to the King's mandate is one more example of how the democrats and royalists coordinated their opposition to EAM and communism. Papandreou's opinions can clearly be seen in a memorandum he wrote to the British ambassador even before he became Prime Minister:

EAM, whose head and spine are the Communist Party, today constitutes an organized armed minority which terrorizes the large, disarmed and unorganized majority of Greek people. The ELAS partisans are a class army, not a national one. The goal of EAM is to monopolize material power, which it then intends to use to usurp political power and impose an undisguised or veiled dictatorship under the pseudonym of a popular democracy.[3]

I had the opportunity to get to know George Papandreou quite well after the liberation. He had a charming, exuberant, and multi-faceted personality. He had many skills as well as many faults. In the Middle East, his skills proved their worth more than ever before in his political career.

As soon as Papandreou assumed his duties, he issued a proclamation addressed to the armed forces announcing his decision to carry out the "national unification" by accepting EAM representatives to participate in the government. This demand could not be circumvented any longer. At the same time, however, Papandreou stressed that "the military can belong neither to individuals nor to parties, neither to organizations nor to social classes. It can only belong to the nation." He heavily criticized those who had rebelled and declared that "they will be punished in proportion to their guilt."

[3]Excerpt from Papandreou, G, 1945. *The Liberation of Greece, Athens-Cairo-Lebanon-Cairo-Italy-Athens*. Editions "Alpha," I. Skaziki. Published in Greek with authentic documents of the period while George Papandreou was Prime Minister during the liberation, 1944-1945.

Forty days earlier, in March 1944, then Prime Minister Tsouderos had announced to his ministers that he had serious concerns that the Allies might recognize the "Revolutionary Government of the Mountains" that EAM had formed in Greece. After the rebellions in April, however, the British began to change their disposition, and after the "Congress of Lebanon" on May 17-20, 1944, they adopted a purely anti-EAM stance. This transformation can be attributed to the fact that Winston Churchill handled the matter personally. As we will see, Churchill later faced harsh criticism in the House of Commons for his actions.

In any event, given unwavering support of the British Prime Minister, Papandreou bet everything on this gambit and won. The communist organizations listened to the Prime Minister's caustic accusations against them at the Congress of Lebanon without protest and were forced to unreservedly condemn the rebellion they had incited and to consign themselves and the rebel ELAS forces to legitimate authority. Their participation in the government, after considerable reneging and delays, was finally restricted at a minimal level. As for the form of government, it was agreed that this would be decided by the Greek people in a free plebiscite for or against the King after liberation.

Under the new government, our military forces, which were in almost complete disarray, began to reorganize. In addition to the Sacred Squadron, which had stayed true to its charge, the 3rd Mountain Brigade was formed, staffed by disciplined officers and soldiers. They would shortly thereafter fight with peerless bravery in the Rimini region of northeast Italy.

At long last, all that remained was preparation for the return to Greece. However, when the Germans departed within a few months, EAM would dominate the country with its fighting units and attempt to play its last card by violating the written agreements. At that point we would once again need British help to avoid completion of the Greek tragedy and to protect common British and Greek interests at this critical confluence of Europe and the Mediterranean.

Once more, King George and the Greek Prime Minister would appeal to the British Prime Minister, and once more Winston Churchill would fight in the House of Commons to make the British proceed along the road dictated by current reality and historic need.

Return Home. An Agitated Liberation. The Final Loss of Service 5-16-5.

September 1944 arrived, and everything seemed to indicate that we would soon be able to return to Greece.

The war situation had completely reversed. The omnipotent German armies that had swept through France in a few days and worked their way into the heart of Russia, dominating continental Europe and plundering the African desert, were now turning their backs and abandoning the conquered regions one by one. They were retreating to a ruined Germany that was being bombed daily by thousands of British and American "flying fortresses."

The enemy's downfall had begun with the amazing Allied landing in Normandy on June 6. An enormous armada of 4,000 ships and thousands of smaller vessels crossed the Channel in the predawn darkness and created bridgeheads on the French coast. Simultaneously, 11,000 planes supported this tremendous operation by dropping strong airborne forces behind enemy lines. Within only a few days, the Allied advance had taken on fantastic dimensions.

Beloved Paris, for which we had shed tears when it became enslaved, was liberated on August 26, 1944. General de Gaulle led the parade of French fighters under the Arch of Triumph. On September 2, the Allies liberated Belgium, and the Germans pulled behind the Siegfried Line and onto German soil.

In Italy, the Germans retreated northward and abandoned the Gothic Line. The Allies re-seized Pisa. "Everything is now leaning our way," we liked to say, "even ... the tower of Pisa!" September 3, 1944 — the 5th anniversary of the outbreak of war in Europe — passed in an atmosphere of victory.

One by one Germany's allies capitulated and abandoned her. Then something still more telling happened: Italy and Bulgaria, who had been strong supporters of Germany and conquerors of Greece without having won even a single battle against it, declared war on their former ally. This was a prime example of the lack of integrity in those who acted as our conquerors for three and a half years, entrenched behind their powerful protector. Now they were rushing to betray him in his greatest hour of disaster.

The Russians broke through Romania on September 8, entered Bulgaria without any resistance, and soon reached the borders of Yugoslavia. Thus Greece now acquired a dangerous neighbor. Despite the general elation, our hearts grew heavy with worry that we might face an even harsher and more permanent occupation within the framework of tomorrow's free world.

On the northern front, the Russians entered Hungary, Czechoslovakia, Poland, and Finland, all within a few days. For these countries, the end of the war would mean the beginning of slavery under communism. Meanwhile, the British liberated Holland and broke through the Siegfried Line.

The Japanese suffered incredible casualties at the hands of the Americans. In one week they lost 501 planes and 173 ships. Now they, too, were paying for their treachery in Pearl Harbor.

That September, with mixed feelings of joy and anxiety, with our hearts and minds oriented to the impending liberation but also to the internal and external dangers that threatened us, Michael Hors and I left our naval careers in Alexandria and returned to the ground troops. The Ministry of the Navy, without thoroughly examining our records or specializations, gave us marching orders for the Training Center at Ismalia. "There they will arrange things for you properly," they said.

We knew, however, that such an assignment was a dead end, involving nothing more than training soldiers. The thought that we would be wasted in the narrow-minded confines of such a center was completely unacceptable.

I therefore risked court martial by illegally interrupting my trip in Cairo, leaving Hors to proceed to Ismalia on his own and cover my delay as best he could. I presented myself before the Army Staff General and asked for Hors and myself to be assigned to a unit on the Italian front, where the pounding of the Germans was accelerating with each passing day. There we would feel closer to Greece, and from there, something told me, we would sooner set foot on Greek soil.

In a few words, I told the General what I had done up till then, and it didn't take great effort to get him to approve my request. After all, people usually request transfer to the rear, while we were asking to be transferred into the eye of the storm.

Thus, on September 21, 1944, Michael and I found ourselves attached to a British unit in Italy that had asked for "liaison officers." This allowed us to leave very quickly. Within a few days we left Egypt for Italy with two other liaison officers and some British personnel.

I departed from the Middle East full of vivid and multifaceted emotions. Multicolored pictures and clashing experiences beat inside me, a restless and unsettled mixture. Egypt, Syria, Lebanon, Palestine, the inhumane desert, the Holy Lands, military camps, ancient and modern treasures, palaces and mud houses. British and Greeks, Arabs and Jews, politics and war. Attacks, successes, intrigues, and catastrophes.

I hold in my hands the essence of those diverse experiences: some of my articles and descriptions of my impressions that were published in military magazines, the handwritten text of a lecture on Greece I gave in Alexandria, and some verses jotted on various slips of paper. These verses are different from the ones I wrote in enslaved Athens. Though infused with the same personal credo, they now revealed some turmoil and bitterness.

We were leaving behind a life full of strong emotions. Beloved colleagues from the caïques, tied to us by so many vivid memories from land and sea. Colleagues from the Sacred Squadron, our bond forged in the incessant, vigorous training and indescribable operations. Friends from Alexandria and Cairo, Greeks of Egypt, and all types of foreigners who had given us their love and made our stay unforgettable.

However, we were taking our most serious worries and unanswered questions with us. How would the internal situation in Greece develop in the near future? Was the recent détente perhaps superficial? Would we celebrate the liberation of Greece in carefree brotherhood or would we face new, more deplorable complications?

In addition, what kind of conspiratorial game was the famous MO4 playing in Greece? What were the motives behind it, and what was the true goal of a particular block of British agents who were obviously undermining our unity? Would I ever discover the secrets of this situation?

Would I ever find the answers to why the British of Smirni and Cairo misled me, why they isolated me from the British service that knew us, and why they wasted the well-organized and still useful Service 5-16-5? I assured myself of one thing: that I would not rest until I one day found the answers to these torturing questions.

We flew over the vast sandy desert toward Algiers in a small transport plane, a crate that somehow still managed to fly. Everything in there creaked and shook. At one point, I noticed a liquid running like a brook from the left motor onto the wing. I went into the cockpit to tell the pilot.

"Yes, I know," said the Englishman indifferently. "We're losing fuel."

"Are we going to let it leak like that the whole trip?" I asked, trying to show the same indifference.

"We can probably manage to reach an auxiliary airfield 50 miles ahead," he answered. The word "probably" wasn't very encouraging, but I thought it best not to discuss it further. I turned to leave for my seat.

"Don't say anything to the others," the pilot called after me.

Ten hours later, after two intermediate stops, we finally reached Algiers. Just the thought that we were getting closer to Greece was enough to make us enjoy every moment of the trip and all its adventures.

In another couple of days, we flew over the foamy Mediterranean and found ourselves in Naples. As we looked around at this legendarily carefree city of song and joy, we felt nothing but grief. Everything was ruined and abandoned. Frightened people and women with fake smiles would approach British and American soldiers to get tins of food. We spoke with quite a few Italians and took some pictures with them. They cursed the Germans and proclaimed joy that we had liberated them. They were trying to fool themselves as well as us.

We walked around the city, always armed just in case, and thought about enslaved Athens just a short while ago, full of armed Italians with roosters' feathers on their helmets. We tried to laugh with justifiable malevolence. "What goes around, comes around," we would say. But we could not really enjoy ourselves. The humiliation and misery all around us was that great...

By the time we reached Italy, the battle for Rimini had ended. Everyone was talking about the action and the heroism of the Greek brigade that had led the Allied attack. We felt proud. Another of our units — once it extricated itself from the politicking and decided to help in the common struggle — worked miracles.

There was nothing more for us to do, but that didn't bother us very much. By now our only concern was to return to our homeland. We traversed Italy like tourists and reached Bari. There our impatience grew.

The Adriatic stretched out in front of us. We stood on the beach and looked toward the southeast. We felt that we could almost touch Greece. There, just a little jump, and we would reach her. Nowhere could we feel at ease, not even at the nice hotel where they had settled us along with other Greek and British officers.

The Germans were retreating from everywhere. We could get Athens on the radio, so we heard them. "The scoundrels are still there!" we exclaimed. "Why the devil are the British holding us here and not sending us to chase them? ..."

Our British colleagues tried to calm us down. "The end is near," they would say. "In a few days you'll definitely be in Greece. Maybe we'll all go together."

❄   ❄   ❄

Finally, the order came for us to get ready to depart. Our hearts fluttered. The

British opened their warehouses and clothed us generously and luxuriously from head to toe. They even supplied us with leather jackets and down sleeping bags.

Three British LCTs, a sort of medium-sized craft with bow doors for landing tanks, were waiting for us in the harbor. These were mainly loaded with boxes of supplies. It was still dark when we embarked, four Greek officers with a small unit of Scots. We doubted that we were sailing for Greece. We asked the captain, and he didn't know, either. He said he would unseal his orders in transit, after four hours at sea.

At last we left port and moved into the Adriatic Sea. Our anxiety had reached its zenith. Michael and I befriended the captain and the chief mate. We told them of our naval experience and they asked us to share the shifts on the bridge, alleviating half their work. These men were truly exhausted and really needed sleep. We scheduled our duty hours and, when the moment came, together we unsealed the orders.

The ship was destined for Patras. We Greeks were on our way to Athens! Finally! We were returning to Greece...

Although we had been expecting this, we choked with joy and emotion. With breaths cut short by knots in our throats, we two Greeks embraced each other and shouted in triumph. The British good-naturedly slapped us on the back and filled our glasses with gin, celebrating our return. We called the other Greek mates, too. For a long time, we accepted and gave blessings to all those who congratulated us as they heard the news. Everything slowly settled back down and we took our usual shifts.

That night I was alone on the bridge, sailing by crystal clear starlight. A light, fresh breeze rocked our ship. We were now sailing in the Ionian Sea. I kept the bow pointed toward Kephallinia Island, now and then correcting the helmsman under the bridge. I communicated with him through the speaking tube while I adjusted the engines to maintain our position relative to the other ships. My mind ran ahead...

We were not going to war, that was certain. The Germans had left. Our country was free. I could already taste the moment of joy when I would set foot on my homeland. I mused about the Greeks who, after having lived so many years in slavery, would come running toward us to see the Greek uniform in our land once again. I yearned to walk our beaches and embrace the unknown brothers I would encounter. By that time, nothing would be able to hold me back from rushing toward Athens to make sure all my loved ones were well. One by one I saw all of my family and friends and my close companions, with whom for so many years I had synchronized the beating of my heart and established indissoluble ties...

The next day, when I went up to take my shift again around noon, we were passing between Greek islands. I glanced at the map on which we plotted our course. We were south of Lefkada with our bow towards Ithaca. My heart leapt as I saw the green coasts and the deep blue Greek sky.

We were convoying single file with other ships and constantly changing our course. "We're following a channel through the minefields," the captain told me. He sat next to me and recommended that I trace the path of the ship ahead of us precisely. I had to guide the helmsman carefully, as he had no visibility whatsoever from his station under our feet.

I thought about how many German minefields like these Service 5-16-5 had sketched and sent to the Allies on our caïques. Now that we were safely passing between the mines, a couple of which we saw on the surface, I had living proof of the usefulness of our work.

We reached Patras just before nightfall. A crowd gathered on the beach and watched. As soon as the ship started to lower its bow door on the shore, we Greeks rushed to leap out. Spontaneously, we fell on our faces and kissed the ground with incredible emotion.

"Welcome home!" the people shouted from all around. We embraced those closest to us.

"Hello compatriots!" we answered. "It's wonderful to see you, too! Happy freedom to all of us!"

Some were wearing caps bearing the ELAS insignia. "Come, let us buy you a drink," they said to us.

They took us to a nearby coffee shop full of partisans who cheered the slogans shouted by their leaders:

"Hurrah for Liberation!"

"Hurrah for the Army of the East!"

"Hurrah for the Popular Army of Greece!"

We cheered, too, raising the glasses of wine they offered us.

"Everything is good, comrades," said one who seemed to be a superior of some sort. "But why do you want this crown on your cap? Why don't you just take it off?"

"It's part of the regulations for our uniform," we replied. "If the regulations change, our uniform insignia will change. But as long as the regulations exist, the insignia will remain as it is. There is no other choice in a regular army, compatriot."

"OK," they said, laughing among themselves. "We'll look at it that way." Then they treated us to another drink.

We returned to our ship, our enthusiasm supplanted by terrible anxiety. What did this strange reception mean, and how much breadth was there to this irresponsible authority that had received us?

It had grown dark when one of the mates called me to the bow. Three people had approached the ship and asked the British sentinel if they could speak to the Greek officers. We went outside and they introduced themselves. They were refined people. They said that some friends and fellow citizens had gathered at one of their homes and they wished to welcome us and talk about certain matters.

They seemed terrorized. It was obvious that they had taken measures to prevent their meeting with us from being noticed. They also seemed circumspect, even with us. Perhaps they had heard something about the anomalies of the Middle East and were not sure if they could trust us.

We agreed to meet them in the lobby of a hotel. From there we proceeded to a pleasant home before a set table. "Forgive us," they said, "but we can only offer you occupation-time foods."

The host raised his glass and welcomed us. He wished that we would find our families well, and that we would all soon see peace, happiness, and true freedom in our homeland once again.

Then they all began to bombard us with questions. Are more Greek troops coming? Will more British come? When will the Greek government return? These were things we did not know, but our ideologies became apparent from our answers.

Then the people took courage and spoke to us plainly. "The situation here is unbearable," they said. "As soon as the Germans left, a few days ago, the place filled with ELAS rebels. We are under their absolute control. They went out into the streets with megaphones and said that good democrats have nothing to fear. Their enemies are the enemy's collaborators, they said, and the monarchist-fascists. These will be punished by the Greek people.

"But who are the enemy's collaborators and who are the monarchist-fascists? Who will judge them and who will sentence them? And aren't all of these just pretexts to neutralize all of their opponents? Isn't it possible that they're going to start executions?

"The day before yesterday, Kanelopoulos, as the government representative, came by here with a couple of British officers. He seemed to be blocked by ELAS members. What course is the Papandreou government taking?

"Here in Patras," they concluded, "the people are patriotic and peaceful. Very few collaborated with the enemy, and we know each and every one of them. We are waiting for their punishment by the official government. The communists here are also few. All the others — democrats and royalists — are all friends. We are all loyalists who tremble at the thought that communism could prevail in Greece. What is our fate in the coming days?"

We didn't have even a single word of encouragement for these unhappy people. On the contrary, we shared their anxieties. We, too, hoped that the damage would not be as great or as general as it appeared. Could it be that instead of celebrating the liberation we would face a new form of slavery that would serve foreign interests behind the mask of popular rule? Would we perhaps have to prepare for a new and much more dramatic resistance, one which would fill us not with the pride of a Greek who fights a barbarous invader, but with the pain of a patriot who must neutralize the betrayal or even just the tragic delusion of his brothers?

The next day we ascertained for ourselves the omnipotence that ELAS, the armed section of EAM, had throughout the country.

ELAS members found caïques that would take us to Loutraki and gave us permits to proceed by land past the demolished Isthmus, toward Athens. Wherever we passed we got the exact same reception, which was an ostentatious display of military hardware and propaganda about the people's republic. Spit-polished armament, the same slogans, and the same songs were all part of the standard showcase. They would add new signatures to our documents and send us to the next station. We had no choice but to accept this arbitrary, high-handed supervision, as it was the only way we could get to Athens.

The nearer we got to the capital, the more dense the partisan units became, and the more stations and welcomes we had to endure. Only the faces of the natives we saw from afar, looking at us somberly, spoke of the real situation. However, they preferred to leave before we could approach them. The atmosphere was infused with fear.

This was the first impression of our return, the first picture of the liberation we had fought to secure with so many sacrifices and had waited for with such longing. With my heart turned upside down, I finally reached the door of my family home on October 14, 1944, two days after the German withdrawal and fifteen and a half months after my departure from Greece. Michael Hors and I were among the first Greek army officers to set foot in liberated Athens.

✳   ✳   ✳

Our house was closed. The outside door was dusty. No one answered the door to my older sister's apartment on the second floor either. Something was definitely wrong. I knocked on the third door, the one to the basement apartment, and was informed that my family no longer lived in the house. The Germans had come many times, turning everything upside down and taking things. I couldn't learn anything else. I tried to call my third sister, but the phone didn't work.

"Let's go to your house," I said to Michael.

"No," my good friend replied. "My family was not persecuted. Let's first find out something definite about your family."

At my third sister's house on Kaningos Square, the first person I saw was the doorkeeper. "Your whole family is upstairs," he said. "Your mother is there, too, with Mrs. Popi. Everyone is well." My heart fluttered. Only then did I realize how much I had worried.

I asked Michael to go up first. Moments of great joy need preparation just like moments of great sorrow, especially for people who have endured so many hardships.

One minute later, my sister Popi was running down the stairs and throwing herself into my arms. "I knew you were downstairs!" she said as she covered me with kisses. She was laughing, but her cheerful eyes were running like faucets. The tears she had held when I was leaving were now released.

We soon went upstairs, where I saw my mother, my other two sisters, my brothers-in-law, and their children, still embracing Michael and asking him when I would arrive. "Well, I think he's standing at the door," Michael said…

After not having seen my family for so many months, we were finally together. And we were all healthy. There was great happiness.

However, Michael had been away from home for three whole years. We had to leave for the Hors's house as soon as possible, so that I could prepare their reunion as he had done for us. In addition, we had news for them about their second son, who had also been away since the beginning.

"Go," Mother said, overcoming the desire to keep me close to her. "Go quickly so that they, too, can rest about their children. We owe them so much. We will return home. At last, we will now all have plenty of time to talk."

In a short while, in the Admiral's familiar home and in the joyful atmosphere of the reunion, I relived the endless days and nights of pursuit and danger, our dreadful anxiety for the prisoners, and our grief for those we had lost. I was filled with affection as I saw once again my great friends who had, without hesitation, put their lives in danger for my salvation. The three months we lived together and the great moments we shared made me consider them my second family. And they did not distinguish me from their own children.

There is nothing stronger than the joy of return. For a few days, I forgot all my concerns and anxieties.

I was once again in the house where I was born, now disheveled and ruined, but still full of love and memories. My father's gaze followed me from inside his picture. We always felt him near us, and we even talked to him. We could not believe he was gone.

My mother and sister went through difficult times while I was away. The Germans had entered the house several times, looking more for loot than information. They had kept my "file" open, and every now and then some bully would decide to come and terrorize the two lone women.

194

Then the requisitions began. Strangers came in and out of the house at will. They slept in the bedrooms and sat in the parlors. Supposedly they were bomb victims, but a motley crowd was ushered in without scrutiny. The situation became so unbearable that my family abandoned the house and moved in with a family of friends in Kifisia.

At one point, the German S.S. decided to settle my case. They sent a paper to my mother, ordering her to appear at their office on Merlin Street: the torture den.

If I had been in Athens, I would never have let her go there. But she decided to go, thinking that her children were in danger. She thought that if she didn't go, the Germans would probably arrest the whole family.

When my mother got to Merlin Street, she found everything in disarray. Two officers and an interpreter were in the interrogation office eating oranges. At first, they told her to wait. Later, they changed their minds. "You'll have to come back," they told her. "The officer who will examine you isn't here." They gave her a new day and time.

She presented herself again on the appointed day. My sisters and brothers-in-law watched from the home of a friend across the street.

Looking in from the entrance, Mother saw the Germans in fantastic disorder and distress. Some were gathering things, others were burning papers. No one noticed her. She turned and left as fast as she could.

My mother was very lucky. That same morning, September 8, 1944, the S.S. executed 72 people on a sudden order. Among those executed was the harbor pilot of Service 5-16-5, Petros Drakopoulos...

I saw the first of my companions as soon as I reached Athens: Mitsos Rediadis, Stavros Vrachnos, and Popi Sakelaridis. In the days that followed I saw many others from our organization. I told my friends all that had happened since my departure and the obstacles that had prevented my return. They told me what had been happening in Greece and explained the developments in Service 5-16-5 that had occurred during my absence.

I was truly fortunate that I had left Greece just as the resistance was beginning to lose its luster. The communists had intensified their attacks against the purely national resistance organizations to such a degree that the struggle against the Germans was overshadowed by the one between Greeks.

Full-scale battles had broken out in the mountains between ELAS and General Zerva's EDES partisans. ELAS launched a surprise attack on Colonel Psarros's Partisan Regiment 5-42 and butchered them all. This was particularly incomprehensible since Psarros, like Zervas, was a pure democrat. Indeed, Psarros was one of the officers dishonorably discharged for participating in the antiroyalist Venizelian movement of 1935.

In the streets of Athens, EAM members clashed with the combat units of national resistance organizations. The Germans took advantage of this situation by using the Security Battalions — Greek militias armed by the Germans to fight the leftists — against the communists. Stool pigeons wearing hoods to hide their identities testified as prosecution witnesses against their compatriots. Enemy collaborators grew bold and took on celebrity status.

By now the public consensus was that the British were basically responsible for this deplorable situation. They had generously financed the communists while undermining the national resistance in every way, finally waking up when they realized that the fuse they lit was out of control. But by then it was too late. All of these things were well known in Greece. For this reason, no one from Service 5-16-5 seemed surprised when I gave my account of the frame-up I had faced in the Middle East.

The origin of these leftist-friendly British tactics was a mystery to everyone. The explanation circulated by British themselves — that they supported the communist networks because they already existed and were ready to strike the enemy — did not explain continued support of them while actually undermining the purely national resistance organizations.

Equally unsound was the claim that Great Britain was trying to win over international communism and have it work to their advantage after the war. Every logical argument concluded that the strengthening of communism would serve only the Soviet Union.

There were also Greeks, as well as British, who maintained that some of our politicians had deluded the British Secret Services with misleading reports and actions. Others rekindled old stories suggesting that the British might be separating us into "British-friendly" and "German-friendly" groups as had been done with "Democrats" and "Royalists" after the first World War. But all of these interpretations were unsatisfactory. The British, and certainly the astute intelligence officers, would have had to be quite naïve to be misled by such folly. Something else must have been going on.

Arming everyone, without discrimination, for the struggle against the Germans was understandable to a certain point. But who really stood to gain from specifically strengthening communism in Greece? After putting down the Middle East movement, why hadn't the British used the disciplined and war-hardened Greek army, navy, and air force to seize the regions evacuated by the Germans rather than letting ELAS seize them uncontested? And why was the British Staff abandoning us now without any real military capability to avert the threatening anarchy? No one could yet answer any of these questions.

As for the undermining of Service 5-16-5 by MO4, the claim that they abolished every organization that had been discovered even partially by the enemy was a joke. If this claim had been true, EAM would have been abolished long ago, since so many of their members were in German hands.

Within our organization, things changed dramatically during my absence. After a reasonable waiting period, my companions realized that I must have been prevented from returning for some reason. Setting out again from the beginning, they tried collectively and individually to find a way to continue their struggle. But the Germans' pincers were becoming ever tighter, and their suspicions about some of our people were approaching certainty.

At that point, the Piraeus Harbor Master, Antonis Bachas, and his second-in-command, Dimitris Samantzopoulos, abandoned their posts. The Port Authority was paralyzed. Infuriated, the Germans turned Piraeus and Athens upside down trying to find them, but it was too late. Samantzopoulos stayed well hidden, and Bachas escaped abroad.

Mitsos Rediadis became a staff member of *Ethniko Komitato* (National Committee), whose leaders were our friends George Vichos and John Zacharakis. We had been connected with this organization for a long time, so Mitsos channeled all of his administrative energy there.

The leader of the Harbor Division, Manolis Koutsoudakis, tried with some others to continue surveillance of the harbor, passing information to Mitsos. However, someone betrayed Koutsoudakis to the Germans. The Gestapo blockaded his house and arrested his wife and his little six-year-old girl. They tortured the mother, and then tortured the child in front of her mother, persistently asking about Koutsoudakis and Bachas. They were unable to learn anything, but the little girl has since remained spiritually crippled. Koutsoudakis managed to hide, and a month later, in early January 1944, he managed to escape to the Middle East.

With this development, our harbor pilots were left without a leader and were completely cut off from the leadership of our Service. However, they did not give up. Exercising the permission we had given them made much earlier, they maintained contact with *Aliki*, an organization that initially arranged escapes but later formed an information division as well. Its leaders were Royal Navy captains E. Valasakis and K. Hasiotis. Thus our people were able to continue their efforts using this outlet. At the same time, they also contacted *Apollo*, an organization that specialized in sabotage but that could also transmit information. By that time my friend Alkis Delmouzos had become the leader of *Apollo*. Those of our harbor people who remained were thus able to continue their work a little while longer.[1]

Then the Germans found their tracks, too. They had been watching *Apollo* from all sides for quite some time. They had already executed the leader of *Apollo*'s Sabotage Division, Nicos Adam, along with five of his companions, in October 1943. At that point *Apollo* was in danger of disbanding. Alkis Delmouzos took on the leadership, helped those in danger to escape, recruited new members, and kept the organization on track.

On March 26, 1944, our harbor pilot, Petros Drakopoulos, sent a note about the departures of German ships to the leader of *Apollo*'s Naval Information Division, Alekos Ioannidis, at his home on Aharnon Street. The message was carried by *Apollo*'s liaison, Manolis Katsogeorgiou, a frail youth with a hunched back who nonetheless offered whatever he could to the struggle.

The youth went into Ioannidis's home and found Germans there. He tried to drop the paper surreptitiously into a vase, but the Germans saw him and grabbed the note. They took Ioannidis and Katsogeorgiou and threw them into the torture chambers. From them they learned the names of some of *Apollo*'s collaborators, the existence of our pilots' network, and the name of Petros Drakopoulos. "We went for certain people and got to others," the Germans said.

A few days before, the Italian hospital ship *Galileo*, which the Germans used for military transports, had been sunk by the Allies. The ship was lost with a full load of troops and military supplies. It was obvious that information about the military use and course of the hospital ship had been transmitted from the harbor. The Germans were furious. However, the informants had fallen into their hands completely by

---

[1]Koutsoudakis and Bachas were then dismissed by the Ministry of Merchant Marines on May 16 and May 30, 1944, respectively. The Ministry's authorities this decision as long as possible. The same happened to all the others, but all discharges were nullified after liberation. I verified the actions and persecution of our harbor people during my absence by cross-checking their accounts and reports with the MInistry's formal reports and with accounts by the family of Petros Drakopoulos, who was survived by his wife and five children.

chance. They had to arrest the pilots immediately.

The German police rushed out and turned the harbor upside down. On March 28, 1944, they caught Petros Drakopoulos on his way to the Port Authority. Damoulakis learned of the raid from passing sailors out at sea. He hurriedly moored his pilot boat and disappeared. Moros was informed by our head boatman, old man Savvatakis, as he was heading to the Port Authority. They both escaped down narrow paths. Since they had nowhere to hide, they slept a few nights in the cemetery. A few weeks later Moros escaped to the Middle East, too. This is how the last echelon of our harbor division was dispersed.

Of those working with *Apollo*, thirty-five were caught and thrown into the Averof Prisons, Petros Drakopoulos among them.

Months passed. Great efforts were made on behalf of *Apollo* members by the occupation-time government, the Archdiocese, and even foreign ambassadors of neutral nations. Alkis Delmouzos worked every angle for the salvation of his people until he, too, fell into enemy hands on the May 25. It was a miracle his life was spared. Meanwhile, Germany began to collapse.

September came and the Germans were preparing to leave. They finally declared that they would free the prisoners. They no longer had any reason to execute patriots. On the contrary, they had every interest in smoothing their retreat by not infuriating the Greeks and Allies any longer. The day the prisoners would be released was announced.

On the morning of September 8, Petros Drakopoulos's wife cheerfully took her children and went to meet their father outside the prison. Many others were also waiting there to take their loved ones home. A notice listing the names of prisoners to be released was posted on the prison door. The crowd was in a festive mood.

An alarming rumor was verified a short time later: the prisoners were no longer there. The S.S. had picked them up in trucks at daybreak. What could they have wanted with them? Where had they moved them? Out of breath, the prisoners' relatives reached the S.S. office on Merlin Street.

There they found some baskets full of clothes. Everyone ran to examine the baskets, agonizing over what they would find. One of Drakopoulos's daughters found a little basket containing her father's clothes.

"These are the personal effects of the executed," the guards said.

The day of joy turned into a day of tragic lamentation.

The vengeful mania of the defeated oppressor had been revealed with incredible sadism. Which of the ghastly monsters, honed from the Germans' harsh nature by the spirit of Hitlerism, had given the order to execute 72 people who were expecting to be freed that morning?

This was the last mass execution, the symbolic apex of a four-year long tragedy that the conqueror wanted to leave in the Greek memory. It was the final wrathful gesture of a bloodthirsty tyrant, who was despised, undermined, and humiliated by indomitable slaves.

The 72 prisoners had been led to the firing squad at dawn, believing that they were being led to freedom. Only when they reached a ravine in the Dafni area and found themselves surrounded by machine guns, only then did they realize the ter-

Petros Drakopoulos

rible truth.

At that point, a tragic chorus of 72 condemned people began to sing our national anthem. Among them was our indomitable pilot Petros Drakopoulos. Among them were Alekos Ioannidis of *Apollo* and the frail youth Manolis Katsogeorgiou. Also among them was Lela Karagiannis, the heroic woman who led a clandestine struggle that became legend. It was the final display of patriotic grandeur that had been established on the day the unforgettable Kostas Perrikos had first set the example: faith in Greece and courageous confrontation of an honorable death.

A young saboteur, Yiannis Houpis, pounced on a machine gun and turned it on his executioners, but he didn't know how to operate it. The Germans fired their first shots into him. Then the ravine roared with the howling machine guns, drowning out the proud Greek song.

This is how Petros Drakopoulos fell, the final loss of Service 5-16-5. He had not wanted to accept that we had been defeated after our persecution, and he continued his struggle until the last moment. His spirit remained youthful and indomitable, even in his sixtieth year.

The Horrible December. The Secret of the British Conspiracy.

Those of us who returned from the Middle East in October 1944 had the good fortune to see Athens for a few days without partisans.

On September 26, the Caserta Agreement had been signed in Italy, in which the EDES and ELAS leaders agreed to put their partisan groups, along with all Greek forces, under the command of the British General Ronald Scobie and to stay out of the capital.

General P. Spiliotopoulos had been appointed military commander of Athens. With the help of the gendarmerie, city police, and some of the national organizations, he even managed to keep order for a time. In the meantime, our first warships reached Piraeus. The historic battleship *Averof*, which transported the Prime Minister and members of the government, was guided to its mooring by our pilot, Kostas Moros. The first small echelons of Greek and British troops reached Athens. Special British and American services forwarded supplies and provisions to the country's interior.

These events let people feel and celebrate the liberation. We, too, experienced some of the greatest moments of our lives. We enjoyed the first great burst of enthusiasm in the streets and a storm of affection that nearly drowned us. We were objects of worship.

As soon as they saw the Greek insignia on our elegant British uniforms, acquaintances and strangers alike embraced us, kissed us, laughed, and cried. They asked us about their children and their husbands, and they took pride in us. We were not individuals, we were symbols. We represented Greek valor and all of the expatriates. Our friends and relatives became our shadows. We couldn't keep up with the joyous outbursts and never-ending requests to tell and retell stories of our military exploits and adventures. In those splendid, unrepeatable moments it felt like the whole world pulsated inside us.

Then, slowly, as the commotion of those first emotional moments died down, worry began to take over again, growing more intense with each passing day. Spontaneous, euphoric displays gave way to organized demonstrations. Impulsive, emotional expressions were neutralized by dry, rehearsed slogans. Outbursts of individual souls were lost in the herd stampede.

Fanatic mobs went around Athens waving flags: Greek, British, and Russian ones with hammers and sickles. They screamed "EAM, EAM!", "Kappa Kappa Epsilon!" (KKE, the initials of the Greek Communist Party), "Down with Glücksburg!" (a Prussian dynasty among the ancestors of Greek king), "Hooray for Government by the People!", and "Elections-Elections!" The flags and slogans provided a ceremonial air. The prime objective was elections as soon as possible, while all of Greece was still under the threat of armed ELAS partisans. In other words, they wanted to deliver the unarmed and terrorized Greek population to communism while it was still defenseless.

EAM had an impressive organization. Discipline and obedience to the leadership's orders were absolute. Transmission and execution of orders were accomplished with lightning speed. It was also obvious that there was wealth behind the sensational demonstrations. The innumerable printed proclamations, the luminous signs, the abundance of banners and placards, and the transport of thousands of demonstrators cannot be done without plentiful funds. These funds had, in a strange and thoughtless way, been granted to the Left by the British and were now being turned against them. This financial power gave EAM the ability to propagate its attractive slogans about a "government by the people" in a myriad of ways and to lure the masses into its disruptive program. From there it would be easy to arm its followers with the magnificent weapons provided by the British and ultimately to attempt a violent seizure of power.

In his book *The Greek Trilogy* (page 121), British Colonel and Information Staff officer W. Byford-Jones describes the impressions and thoughts of many British in responsible positions who saw the situation clearly but ignored the breadth of the British role in its creation. The excerpt below refers to the parade and reception of the Greek Mountain Brigade in Athens on the November 10, 1944, which was returning from Italy after its bloody but victorious battle in Rimini.

> *It was a stirring sight marked by pathetic scenes of reunion, as tearful wives and mothers, who had not known whether their soldier sons and husbands were alive or dead in the long silence which had followed their departure from Greece, rushed through the barriers to embrace their menfolk.*
>
> *The difference between the welcomes given to the British troops on their entry, and to the Greek Mountain Brigade, was most marked. While E.A.M. and K.K.E. had spent money lavishly on street decorations and flags and slogans to greet the British, thus giving rise to speculations, as did their own party political demonstration later, as to from where they had obtained the necessary money in this ruined and poverty-stricken land, these parties ignored the arrival of the Greek formations. ... The six E.A.M. ministers also absented themselves from the saluting base.*

The communists' hatred of all those who contended for a purely Greek struggle, without belonging to their party, was obvious. The disciplined Greek army was, for them, a serious obstacle to their subversive plans.

Seeing EAM's wasteful ostentatiousness, the well-meaning British officer Byford-Jones wondered, "... from where they had obtained the necessary money." In this matter, we Greeks were better informed. Dropped from British planes and sent by ship, submarine, or special envoy, a veritable treasure in gold sovereigns was conveyed to the Communist Party along with arms and abundant ammunition.

My friends in other information organizations and the secret press I reconnected with on my return informed me that not only had all British support to them been discontinued, but that loyal Greeks quite often faced real persecution. A characteristic example was revealed when the Germans once arrested an agent of the British "Force 133," a service that had succeeded MO4 and various other British secret services. In the agent's hands they found a list of Greeks earmarked for assistance in escaping to the Middle East by any possible means. All of the loyalists had been crossed off the list. Only the leftists had been assisted in escaping.

From Alkis Delmouzos, the leader of *Apollo*, I heard of his amazing adventure when he crossed over, in absolute secrecy, from Agia Marina to southern Evoia in December 1943. He crossed the island of Evoia at night to get to the Aegean coast, where he was to pick up wireless sets and explosive materials which Force 133 was sending him by caïque. ELAS partisans surprised him there and placed him under arrest.

This area was not controlled by the partisans. They had gone there specifically to intercept Delmouzos and get hold of the Allied supplies. They took him on a 12-hour march to their hideout in the mountains of northern Evoia. He understood that his life was in danger. However, he found an acquaintance of his there, a political commissar who happened to be dissatisfied with EAM and wanted to escape abroad. Delmouzos promised to arrange his escape if he saved him from the partisans and facilitated his mission. The commissar still maintained his influence over the partisans. Thus, Delmouzos not only escaped, but he also managed to salvage the supplies that would have fallen into ELAS's hands.

Alkis Delmouzos's opinion, which I publish with his approval, was that ELAS could not have known the time and place that Force 133's supplies would arrive *unless the British themselves had told them of it.* By playing this double game, Delmouzos told me, the British would achieve three goals. First, they would deny the supplies to the national side, giving them instead to the leftists whom they supported. Second, they would neutralize the *Apollo* leader, creating a serious crisis in a large, purely national organization. Third, they would succeed in placing the responsibility on ELAS, and no one would ever hold Force 133 liable for the loss.

Attempting to examine the social problems of that time objectively, I am convinced that the majority of fanatic EAM followers and ELAS partisans were neither communists nor scoundrels. They were simply naïve or uneducated patriots looking for a means to strike the conqueror. Once in the leftist organizations, however, they became absorbed and assimilated by the systematic practices of the communist leadership. Their initiation usually began with democratic sermons. Slowly their minds were saturated, making them forget their initial intention, hate their brothers, and become accomplices in the crime against their land and compatriots. But they did not believe they were fighting to oppress the majority of the Greek people or to serve foreign interests at the expense of Greek ones. On the contrary, they believed they were fighting for popular freedom, for democracy, and for neutralization of the remnants of fascism.

Certainly, many of them would never have taken up arms if they had not been persecuted by some of the extreme right-wing organizations. Such organizations were created out of the fear of communism, but they misused their power against individuals who simply had democratic convictions. It is quite natural for one who gets slapped around by an organized gunman simply because he does not share his beliefs to get his own gun and counterattack. Thus this abuse of power resulted in counterattacks justified by the widely-used slogan of "self-defense," but that justification soon overran its lawful boundaries and became an instrument of criminal activity against innocent people.

Two and a half years later, when I was serving as governor of the Yiannena prefecture while ELAS continued to wage guerilla war throughout the entire region, I had the opportunity to talk with many wounded ELAS fighters in the hospitals. Their reactions to me as a state representative were almost always the same. At first they viewed me with fanatic hatred and revulsion. Slowly they calmed down, and eventually some of them remarked, "What you're telling us sounds good, but what the others told us also sounded good, and we believed them."

Unfortunately, some of the educated elite of our land were abettors to this criminal "enlightenment" of our people. Some were inspired by misguided feelings of passion for freedom and empathy for the populace, while others simply didn't want to fall behind the spirit of the times. Some cooperated due to fear or opportunism, others out of ignoble interest. But all stood frightfully responsible for the deception that conned our masses and the bloodshed that soiled our land.

Thus, people deceived by the special "instructors" of international communism, who constituted the largest number of draftees, were joined with others who were truly unhappy and persecuted. The ranks were filled out with underworld scoundrels who saw the opportunity for looting and perverted criminals who thirsted for blood. This is how the stage was set for the tragedy that developed in Athens in December 1944. Following their German predecessors, these people carried out unimaginable torture and horrid mass executions of hostages they dragged with them to the mountains. They caused ruin and destruction to continue in the Greek countryside for five more years.

In some regions, those deplorable and abhorrent years were worse than the years under enemy occupation. The struggle of enslaved Greeks against a barbarous invader was filled with patriotic enthusiasm and national pride. These feelings served to balance all the calamity and pain. But now patriotic fighters were consumed by the thought that their enemy had been born in their own land and spoke their own language. Thus, while this struggle had examples of heroism and self-sacrifice, it lacked and could not possibly have spawned uplifting exaltation. It was born out of defensive expedience and national duty, but in its depths it harbored so much bitterness...

December 1, 1944, was the crucial day when the ELAS militia was scheduled to withdraw and be replaced by tactical army units. The order had been given by the government in accordance with the terms of the Caserta Agreement and had been approved by the six EAM ministers.

However, the ELAS partisans remained at their posts. The EAM central committee had decided to hold out against the state authority. The six EAM ministers withdrew and the government carried on its work without them.

On Saturday, December 2, the Cabinet put the Greek-British agreement into effect and ordered the demobilization and disassembly of all ELAS and EDES partisan units. EAM reacted in the usual way: demonstrations, banners, and slogans blared from street megaphones. The new target was Papandreou. Enraged mobs roamed the streets looking for trouble. Without light, without telephones, without transportation, and without food, Athens was a city of despair and fear.

At noon on Sunday, December 3, a great, noisy demonstration formed at Sintagma Square and moved toward the Parliament building.

The first shots were exchanged between the demonstrators and police near the Grande Bretagne Hotel and City Police Headquarters. These shots found their marks. There were casualties on both sides.

Two opposing views on the origin of the initial shots were reported by EAM and the government. The arguments lacked substantial credibility, because the December uprising was not touched off by someone who pulled a trigger by chance. It was a planned operation at the forefront of a rebellion designed to seize power.

I was on leave that Sunday and spent the night at my house. On Monday morning, as I was getting ready to leave to join the British unit in which I was serving, I heard shots outside and, immediately thereafter, the chirping of a submachine gun.

I looked out the window and saw partisans holding the street corners and roofs of houses, trading fire with the police. I had to try to reach my unit as soon as possible.

"I'll find out what's going on and send word back to you," I said to my family. "Don't leave the house for any reason."

I stood in the half-opened outside door. I saw an armored vehicle coming and rushed outside to stop it. The driver quickly opened the door and took me with him.

My unit was headquartered in a building on Panepistimiou Boulevard. I found the British preparing for battle. My commander said, "You can stay here if you want. I need a liaison officer in the office."

He was an exceptionally noble and exuberant person, with a big red moustache and sideburns. We had fought together in the islands. He was a Lieutenant Colonel in the British Special Boat Service (SBS), the commandos who had fought alongside the Greek Sacred Squadron in numerous daring raids. My commander had also lived in the colonies and viewed the war somewhat as a wild animal hunt, that is, a noble yet risky sport. He had many Greek friends, had learned some Greek, and had been fascinated by Greece ever since our fighting in the islands. When he found me under his command in Athens, we celebrated with glasses of whiskey at the British officers' mess. I am truly sorry that I cannot recall his name.

Now this man was setting out to come to blows with Greeks. It was out of character for him. Even though he said nothing about it, I felt that he found some satisfaction in keeping at least one of his Greek comrades-in-arms far from this graceless conflict.

As for myself, I took these things in stride. If the British had wanted me to go with them, I would have gone and done my duty. They didn't, and it was the first time I saw others leaving on operations without me and stayed back without protest.

I sent word to my family to come to the free zone as soon as possible, but my mother preferred to stay home for the time being. As things were, it would have been difficult for them to find another shelter, and the thought of being a refugee frightened her.

In the days that followed, I strolled Athens's central triangle formed by Omonia, Sintagma, and Kolonaki Squares, which was the operational center for Greek and Allied forces. Bloody conflicts raged outside in the suburbs. At the Theseion and Makrigiannis, and in Kaisariani, Greek and British troops, gendarmerie, and city police tried to drive back the partisans who had staged surprise attacks on the barracks, police stations, and administrations, mercilessly butchering any rivals who fell into their hands.

There were even clashes in the center. Most of the partisans had nothing distinguishing about their appearance, so they could move among us and congregate wherever they wanted. One day I saw a British tank fire a few shots and then ram the rolling iron shutter that blocked the arcade on Korai Street in the very center of

Athens, where the university buildings are today. Shortly thereafter, some people came out with their hands up. I later learned that they were part of the partisan staff and directed operations from there.

Another day, I was walking down the narrow Omirou Street, along the side fence of the Catholic church, ready to come out onto Panepistimiou Boulevard. All of a sudden I heard the characteristic sound of a mortar shell tearing the sky. The people on the boulevard had no experience with this light, gurgling sound and went carefree on their way. "Incoming missiles! Everybody drop!" I yelled and huddled at the foot of the fence.

Two mortar shells exploded in the middle of Panepistimiou Boulevard, right in front of the Bank of Greece. About ten people were hit and fell onto the street and sidewalks. Two British lay side-by-side, face down on the tramlines. Their brains were scattered all around. I tried to lift a woman dressed in black. She did not appear to be wounded, but she was moaning slowly. She turned her head and died in my arms. From her open purse, a pension book fell out with pictures of her and two small children. People all around me were helping the wounded.

A young girl, dragging herself across the asphalt with her hands, was crying loudly and calling me by name. It was an acquaintance of mine from Mytelene Island. "I can't stand up!" she was screaming. "I can't breathe! I'm going to die…" Her back was full of blood. Helped by two other men, I carried her to the municipal hospital. She had a shell fragment in her spinal cord, but she did not die immediately. She lived for quite some time, paralyzed and in horrible pain.

British tanks roamed Athens and shelled houses occupied by partisans. Machine guns chirped from the windows and street corners. Snipers fired from behind shutters. Most of the houses' facades were embroidered by shells. Every so often you heard explosions: ELAS was blowing up houses, collapsing them to block the streets.

The Germans and Italians had never hit Athens. They had respected the city and its historic monuments that shed light on humanity. Now we were seeing her destroyed in a battle we were fighting among ourselves. All of us who cared for Greece had tried to avoid that at any cost, but it was finally imposed upon us by the situation shaped by foreign hands despite our warnings, objections, and protestations.

I soon realized that inaction was not the right choice for me. I felt terrible seeing British fight alongside my fellow Greeks to secure internal peace in our land. Although a good deal of responsibility for the situation that had been created in Greece rested squarely on the political or military leadership of the Allies, what fault did the British soldier have? Had he fought the common enemy for so many years and managed to survive until the end of the war just to come and get killed in a secondary, local conflict that did not concern him? The average British soldier didn't understand this and wasn't expected to. What's more, he certainly was ignorant of the responsibility of his leadership.

These thoughts intensified the terrible emotional tension I felt as I watched the war all around me against people who, if they prevailed, would destroy our land. Once again I felt compelled to get off the depressing sidelines and actively contribute to the general struggle. By then, however, I had been cut off from my unit, which was defending the Averof Prisons and the Evelpidon School of Army Cadets.

In a moment when emotional need dispels all hesitation even if the goal seems unattainable, I decided one morning to try to get to my unit at the Evelpidon School more than a mile away. To do this I would have to bypass the roadblock defending the partisan-controlled area, Exarhion Square, and a good number of streets. If there was even the slightest reason to think that this plan might actually succeed, it had to come from my commando training. Those experiences had given everyone in the unit not only specific physical and technical skills, but also the confidence that a trained person can take on any mission no matter how many untrained opponents might stand in his way.

In spite of my determination, I did not succeed in reaching my unit. Bullets whizzed around me as I approached Exarhion Square. I advanced with my hand on my holstered revolver, carefully scanning the street corners and windows. By chance, I ran into one of my sister's friends, Efi Nomidou-Markezini. "Have you gone mad?" she scowled at me in a coarse whisper. "What are you doing around here in uniform?" Passing by me without stopping, she added, "Be careful that guy in the gabardine coat over there doesn't shoot you!"

I immediately turned down a side street and crossed over to the next parallel street. Strangers surrounded me. The sympathy they showed for an unknown Sacred Squadron officer was truly touching. "They're looking for you everywhere," they warned, "and they'll catch you! Quick! Hide and save yourself!"

They pushed me through an iron door into an enclosed yard behind a house. From my hiding place I heard partisans running in the street and shouting orders. Jumping the walls that separated one yard from the next, I came out on the other side of the block. I was, at last, very close to the Evelpidon School.

The road was practically deserted. All I saw were a few women. They looked around with curiosity to see who was being chased.

Our family doctor's wife, Despoina Zaverdinos, happened to be passing by. She looked at me, confused. "Your folks haven't heard from you," she said, "and they're worried sick. What're you doing here?"

The next moment, another girl I knew quite well, Eva Firiou, grabbed my hand. She had seen what was happening and, defying the danger, had run to save me. "To my house!" she said. "Quickly!" We ran a few strides together and went in through the half-opened door.

ELAS was doing a house-to-house search. As they approached my hiding place I jumped from a back window into the yard. They failed to find me, and after they left I went back into the house.

I was told that the searchers had been university students wearing crossed cartridge belts. Someone must have recognized me on the street, because they had asked for me by name. This made me think that my family must now be in danger as well. I abandoned my plan to join my unit, put on a civilian jacket to camouflage my uniform, and set out for my house at full speed to save my mother and sister...

The three of us spent the night at a friend's house. The next morning we went into the unoccupied area of Athens's central triangle. ELAS let people go wherever they wanted in the mornings to find food and provisions. This was also a way for them to move about freely in the mornings without anyone realizing it. "Hello, comrade..." we would hear from them. "Good morning, comrade," we would reply as we proceeded toward the roadblock separating the rival factions.

Two days later we learned that ELAS partisans had forced open our door, entered our house, and looted it clean. They grabbed anything that had been left by the Germans: clothing, blankets, watches, and even books from my library. Later, when we went back home, I found my bed and the wall above it riddled with bullets. The shutters had been smashed to smithereens.

With my back against the bullet holes in the wall, I peered through the holes in the remaining shutters. They had fired from a neighboring terrace. It seems that before they entered the house, they prepared the attack with ... an "artillery barrage." They'd had fun making a party of it.

✻   ✻   ✻

Forced back into inactivity, my nerves were tried again as I sat in the center of Athens observing its destruction. One night in mid-December I heard the amazing story of a political plot I had never suspected, but which must have created the whole situation. It was the logical explanation that Greek patriots had tried in vain to find. It explained such paradoxical events as the systematic British support of leftism during the occupation and the liberation of our country without the use of Greek and British forces that would guarantee law and order, except at the last minute and only after the personal intervention of the British Prime Minister.

It was also the answer to the questions that had tortured me since Cairo, when my return to Greece was thwarted by the MO4. It was the explanation I had sought for so long, given to me by chance at the British officers' mess.

I was sitting at the bar, glass in hand, next to a British captain. He was a tall and slender man of about my age. The British had a knack for establishing such pleasant oases amidst the fire of war. A small orchestra was playing popular Greek songs of the times. One particular instrument stood out, the violin of the soloist in our State orchestra, Frederick Voloninis. During those difficult times, he made a living playing wherever he could, mainly for the Allies' recreation.

The captain dealt with his boredom by mumbling along as the orchestra played little songs that most of the British had learned. "*Ta ma-tia, ta glika sou ta ma-tia...* (Your eyes, your sweet eyes...)." He seemed proud of his Greek.

"We learned many Greek songs in Constantinople," he said to me.

"You were stationed in Constantinople?" I asked.

"Yes, I served there for quite some time dealing specifically with Greece. I worked in the Intelligence Service."

I felt a buzzing in my temples. "Under Major 'Hatzis?' " I asked.

The Englishman looked at me in wonderment. "Yes, under Major Hatzis. How do you know him?"

"Have you perhaps heard of a Greek espionage organization called Service 5-16-5? Did you happen to know Nicos Paliatseas or Nicos Menegatos who were executed by the Germans?"

The captain suddenly showed interest. "Yes, I met Menegatos. We used him as a liaison. I've also heard of Paliatseas, the wireless set operator. The organization you mentioned must be the one we suddenly lost contact with. Who are you?"

I became terribly excited. I felt that the moment had finally come for me to find my way out of the labyrinth I had been wandering in for so long.

"If you'd like," I said, "let's find a quiet table. We have a lot to talk about." We moved far from the music and sat in a corner.

I told him our story and he purposefully filled in details that made me certain he knew everything about our communication with the British from Greece. He reminded me of things I had practically forgotten, unimportant little details of our collaboration that I had never mentioned to my interrogators in Smirni or in Cairo. It was certain that I had one of "our" people in front of me, an actual member of the British service that had received our messages and transmitted them to the Allied staff.

"Please tell me," he said, "what happened to make you suddenly cease communication? What happened after your wireless set was silenced? How did the two caïques get lost?"

I told him about how the Germans discovered our wireless set and about our persecution. I told him about the arrests and the executions, and about my escape. I also related the story of my attempt to meet Major Hatzis, which was undermined at the British Consulate in Smirni.

The captain listened intently. For an instant, an infuriated spark flashed across his face. I waited for his reaction. All he said was that this was not the first time his service in Constantinople had faced this sort of thing.

When I got to my deception by the MO4 in Cairo and the wasting of our service, however, the captain could no longer maintain his British composure. Boiling with rage, he burst out, "Ah, the bastards! They sabotage us from all sides! They are treacherous, they are ruthless…"

"But what's the reason behind these tactics?" I asked. "They're definitely not communists…"

"No, sir, they are not communists, they are worse! They get into bed with communism to achieve their own goals, ignoring the destruction it causes. They would sacrifice anything to overthrow Winston Churchill."

For a moment, I thought I had misunderstood. "Churchill?" I repeated.

"That's right, sir, Churchill, and all the Tories. The conservative party currently in power. It's a well-established plot to turn British public opinion against the Tories. The opposition Labour party wants to overthrow the government if they can, or at least win the postwar elections."

"But what does this British political dispute have to do with Greek matters?"

"If you followed the arguments in the House of Commons these days, you'd see the relation. Churchill is facing an unprecedented attack from the opposition parties for Britain's 'intervention in the internal matters of foreign nations,' and sharp criticism for 'violation of the principles of democracy.'

"This attack is the end game of lengthy maneuvering. Ever since the war began, the opposition Labour party has taken advantage of the Prime Minister's general approval to support anyone willing to resist the Germans by exclusively arming leftists in all the occupied countries. Greece is not the only country they've undermined with this conspiracy. They've created subversive movements in Belgium and most recently in Italy as well, now that she is on our side. Now they're trying to launch a similar movement in Holland.

"The Tory government certainly cannot sit back and watch countries be destroyed by British culpability. Thus Britain is forced to intervene and disarm those whom its own opposition party has converted into new oppressors.

"This plays right into the undermining hands of the Labour party, who are now unleashing serious accusations against Churchill. Such accusations find immediate support among the British people and servicemen who are fed up with the idea that money and British blood are being wasted on rectifying foreign anomalies.

"Churchill certainly is not failing in Parliament. His power and influence in the voting that follows each discussion remain undiminished. However, public opinion is being affected by the demagogic ballyhoo. The perception that Churchill is antidemocratic and oppressive is being carefully cultivated. The table is being set to defeat the father of victory in the next elections."

I listened to this amazing description of a fiendish, long-term political plot in rapt silence. I hesitated to accept it, but it was the only logical explanation for the excessive British support of EAM and its followers while simultaneously undermining all the purely national organizations and the anonymous, unorganized masses who remained loyal to our country. This explanation also gave logical continuity to all the events I had experienced, verifying the conspiracy without my being able to identify its motives or ultimate goal. Something else was also particularly important for me: at last I had the first direct confirmation that Major "Hatzis" and his service really existed in Constantinople. I would soon verify that this was completely true.

After parting with the intelligence service captain, I tried to put my thoughts and personal experiences into some kind of order. The words of an officer met by chance were certainly not proof. However, their accordance with events gave them considerable weight. The events I had experienced were irrefutable and now clearly intertwined...

As early as 1942, the liaison Menegatos had warned Service 5-16-5 to distrust the British secret services because they were undermining each other. If the need arose, he cautioned, we were only to meet with Major "Hatzis," the leader of the service we were in touch with in Constantinople.

In the British consulate in Smirni, I was deceived and sent to Cairo, after being told that "Hatzis" did not exist and that there was no British service in Constantinople.

In the mysterious villa near the pyramids, the MO4 claimed that they were the ones our organization had communicated with from Greece. As they interrogated me and tried to extract every bit of information they could about our contacts, our network, and internal Greek affairs, it became obvious that these people had no prior knowledge of us at all.

Back at the MO4 offices in Cairo, I was compelled to accept the wasting of Service 5-16-5, which, despite the blows it had received, still had valuable information networks in place and was still indisputably useful.

At the seat of our displaced government in Cairo, I saw the Greek Prime Minister scramble to hide his national resistance contact from a captain of the MO4. I also heard him express his intense anxiety over the support of communism in Greece and the Middle East, but saw him unable to do anything about it.

Eyewitnesses told me about all the obstacles faced by the purely national, non-communist organizations. I followed all the sad historical events that ensued both internally and abroad, and for which we paid with so many catastrophes and so much blood. To my great surprise, I saw my country liberated without the support of Greek and British troops that would immediately secure regions abandoned by the enemy. On the contrary, those areas were systematically left to the mercy of anarchy. And finally, I heard that one day Churchill had personally intervened in MO4, replacing everyone and causing a veritable earthquake in that organization.

The sum of all these indisputable events was enough to convince me that an obvious conspiracy did indeed exist. Whatever its goal, it followed a steady, long-term program resulting in serious damage to Greece.

The notion that support of the leftists was a secret political plan condoned by the British government could not survive any logical scrutiny. Such a plan must surely have benefited the Soviet Union at the expense of Great Britain. Thus, the support of leftism in Greece must certainly have been the work of a party unrelated

Rodney Bond – "Major Hatzis"
The intelligence officer who
really existed in Constantinople.

or opposed to Churchill's ruling government, and it must have been done without the knowledge of the very busy British Prime Minister.

This opposition party may even have had leftist sentiments. However, I believe that no British citizen would endanger British interests in a time of war out of ideological sympathy for the communist parties of other nations. The only explanation that could hold up was the infighting between the rival British political parties. Even if this rivalry originated from elements with leftist sentiments, it manifested itself in the form of an undermining political conspiracy.

A second consequence of this conspiracy was the creation of an elite Greek cadre of leftist and left-leaning politicians trusted by the British secret services. They tried to support this cadre even after the liberation so they could maintain control of the Greek sector.

None of us ever learned how many people participated in this conspiracy, or how many British services had a hand in this filthy situation and to what degree. We also do not know if these British services acted of their own volition or if other groups or blocks of powerful individuals played games in the chains of command and directed them from behind the scenes.

However, now that many mysteries of that time have ceased to be wrapped in secrecy, we know that the British service to which we had sent our information — the service that the Smirni Consulate assured us was "nonexistent" and from which we were isolated and blocked by the MO4 — was the *Intelligence Service of the Middle East*, whose seat was indeed in *Constantinople*. A commanding officer of this service was *Colonel Gibson*. We also know that the officer in charge of communication with Greece, the one who used the codename "Hatzis," was *Major Rodney Bond*. A *Captain Bolby* also served in a high position in the same unit and may have been the intelligence officer I met in Athens.

Another purely national organization that had exclusive contact with this Constantinople intelligence service was *Kodros*. Their leader, Takis Likourezos, met personally the staff officers of this service and with "Hatzis" in Constantinople.

Kodros had helped George Papandreou (the future Greek Prime Minister) escape from Greece in April 1944. Shortly after the liberation, Likourezos wrote a book entitled *Kodros – National Organization of Internal Resistance* that was printed in Athens by D. Tomeratos. This book describes Papandreou's escape in minute detail and provides the following information.

Papandreou was received by Major Rodney Bond ("Hatzis") in Agrilia, a seaside village near Smirni. The major had traveled from Constantinople specifically to arrange Papandreou's immediate passage to Cairo. Indeed, he had arranged for Papandreou to fly by special plane to Cairo within two days. Before departing from Smirni, Papandreou sent the following message to *Kodros* on April 14 via the Intelligence Service of Constantinople: "We arrived well. I am pleased to have met 'Hatzis.'"

Thus Major "Hatzis" of the Constantinople service not only existed, but was well known and very active in British secret service circles. However, it seems that his service did not belong to the conspiracy network, and therefore had to be undermined by all means.

A particularly reliable picture of the events that turned Greece upside down at that time due to the tactics of the rival British services is given in a speech by Winston Churchill delivered in the House of Commons on December 8, 1944. The speech was made in response to an opposition call for his censure over "British intervention in the internal affairs of Greece and other parts of liberated Europe."

Churchill gave an inspired analysis of the essence of a true democracy, explained the events and reactions of the time, and faced his rivals' combined attack and their constant interruptions with a clear and precise counterattack, putting the "the matter of trust" onto the floor. (Excerpts from this wonderful speech are presented in an Appendix.) In the vote that followed, Winston Churchill won the day with 279 votes to his opponents' 30.

Yet flashy slogans influence people more than logical arguments. The accusations of oligarchy and antidemocratic policies against the father of victory swayed the British masses. Within the British army, we heard over and over, like a refrain, "Churchill was good for the war, but now we need a democratic government for peace."

Winston Churchill lost the next elections. The destruction of Greece from the battle with communism seems to have been a small, necessary detail in this great affair.

As revolution took hold in Athens that December, a parallel but no less dramatic battle was going on outside. The outcome of that struggle would determine the country's fate decisively.

An intense propaganda campaign had been launched in the British military, circulating the notion that British soldiers were being killed in Greece and that this struggle had to end. Even the British Minister Harold Macmillan telegraphed his government from Athens that overpowering the rebels would require the commitment of very large forces, and he recommended that the British negotiate some sort of compromise with them.

Meanwhile, Churchill had attained a very important concession from Stalin. According to their secret agreement, Greece was to be considered within the British sphere of influence, not the Russian. Until then, Churchill had done whatever he could to repair the damage caused us by the British secret services. However, the continued public reaction, combined with the fears expressed even by his close advisors, started to seriously wear down his intentions.

During those crucial moments, King George hurried to meet the British Prime Minister and spoke to him bluntly. "... If British troops suffer casualties, the fault lies not with Greece, but with the notorious British Headquarters of the Middle East which, despite my protests, gave arms and money to organizations they should not have supported. ... It will be impossible for the British public, and indeed all mankind, to forgive anyone for the disgraceful deed of abandoning a small, but honorable ally" (Admiral P. Koustas, *Hellas in the Decade 1940-1950*, p. 364). In response, Churchill immediately ordered that the required supplementary forces be sent from Italy and he himself arrived in Athens on Christmas Day.

Churchill's arrival essentially marked the end of the December revolt. With the huge prestige that confirmed the measure of his amazing political personality, he immediately brought the representatives of all political parties together under the chairmanship of Archbishop Damaskinos. In the conference that followed in the Ministry of Foreign Affairs with representatives of the partisan armies taking part, he concluded his introductory speech by stating: "We have intervened in this dispute to do that which we believe to be our duty. We will carry out this duty rigidly and faithfully until the end."

Then he withdrew, leaving the various Greek factions to settle matters among themselves.

The outcome of this conference was that everyone accepted Archbishop Damaskinos as Regent. Within a few days, a new government was formed that won common acceptance. Our land had finally begun to move toward normalcy.

THE FINAL RECKONING

THE END OF THE WAR. HONOR TO OUR DEAD.

The war in Europe ended in May 1945. The German *Wehrmacht*, the steel war machine that had set out five years earlier with unstoppable catalytic force and leveled everything in its path, surrendered unconditionally. Allied flags flew in Berlin. In the underground bunkers of the Chancellery, ashes were all that remained of the frightful Adolf Hitler.

Three months later, the Japanese surrendered as well. The treaty was signed on September 2, 1945, in the bay of Tokyo aboard the armor-plated American warship *Missouri*. Two atomic bombs had more than paid back the surprise attack on Pearl Harbor and imposed the conclusive end.

These five years of the war were marked by incredible endurance and persistence. Within a very short time, virtually all of Europe had been stepped on by the enemy. England had been bombed incessantly, night and day. The Soviet Union had lost vast stretches of land and her dead numbered in the millions. Before an all-powerful enemy who had been planning the war for many years, the great European nations had proven themselves woefully uninformed and unprepared.

It would be pointless to try to place blame. Those responsible paid at least as dearly as those who were not. Their mistakes became lessons for the future.

Perhaps only little Greece was ready to face the onslaught right from the outset. She gave the Allies their first unexpected victory. She stalled the incessant enemy advance for six months, providing the great Allies with some breathing room for their delayed preparation.

If, however, no mistakes had been made, if the defenders had been able to stand toe to toe with the invader, if the waves of invasion had crashed upon rocks of resistance, the historic pages of unconquerable perseverance and sacrifice which led to final victory would never have been written. These five years would have been like any other time of war. They would not have framed a grand epoch.

We would not have seen enslaved peoples rise above the evils of war despite the pressure and privation of the enslaving yoke. They would not have set out, without means and without experience, to slowly but surely gnaw through their chains and hollow out the ground from under their oppressor's feet.

We would not have seen the Russian soldier, hemorrhaging incessantly, defend his land inch by inch. He would not have withstood being pushed back into the depths of his vast country without losing his courage and faith in victory. He would not have risen with unexpected strength, like another Antaeus, to throw the enemy out of his homeland and chase him into the bowels of his own land until he finally surrendered.

We would not have seen the British maintain their composure before the cosmic wrath of God and endure the war with their minimal means. They would not have worked calmly yet methodically, under the constant bombing of their very capital, to organize the ferocious counterattack that gave us victory. The inexhaustible resources of the Americans, combined with their realism, decisiveness, and the atomic bomb, certainly had a crucial effect on the outcome of the war. But if British perseverance had not been superhuman, or if British obstinacy had not been resolute, this war would have been lost in the first months.

Thus, over these five years we saw the fully armed invader crumble from day to day, while we saw the unarmed defender grow large and strike back destructively at the weakened monster. British and American planes filled the German sky by the thousands, burning everything from above, while armies of millions from the three great Allied nations fell upon the German capital from all sides.

The miracle of persistence and sacrifice had been completed. The powerless defenders had won. The horrible tornado had vanished, leaving a valuable conviction in the souls of those who survived: *faith in the limitless power of man to resist coercion and violence in defending his sacred and ancestral institutions.*

Athens now had a festive appearance. We were few when we started fighting for our country five years ago, and we were much fewer now. However, above the sorrowful gloom of the ruins and graves, one could discern a sense of supreme satisfaction on the skinny faces.

Slowly, the people found their laughter. We heard music and saw couples dancing. Life and youth reclaimed their rights. Joy was returning.

People took courage and began building amid the ruins. They rebuilt structures demolished by foreigners as well as by our own people. They worked with gusto and optimism. We saw houses getting whitewashed, streets being repaired, and smoke rising from chimneys. Fear and disappointment gave way to throbbing activity.

Only those of us serving in the armed forces remained practically idle. Our mission had ended.

I spent my free time writing articles for the newspapers even though I was still an officer and regulations forbade public statements by military personnel. I used easily understandable reviews of social theories and systems with vivid, practical examples to uncover reality as best I could, especially for those whose ignorance or naiveté had led them to adopt anti-national beliefs.

"What fascism is and why we fight it." "What communism is and why it is unacceptable for Greece." "Similarities between fascism and communism." "Activities that prevent us from claiming our rights and the economic and social development of our country." These were some of the topics that I attempted to clarify.

I believed that this effort was worthwhile even though it was addressed to a small audience. The vast majority of the Greek populace did not need such enlightenment. They had been so terrorized and had suffered so much from the rampaging "democrats" — who tried to exert their dominance even before we were liberated from the Germans — that they would have given anything not to relive this nightmare. This is why, in the elections of 1946, they overwhelmingly supported the royalist-friendly "People's Party" (*Laiko Komma*) and, in the plebiscite that followed, brought King George back to Greece as a guaranty for domestic security.

It has been claimed that these outcomes were a consequence of the terrorism of extreme right-wing organizations. Such organizations did indeed exist and they must have had a certain degree of influence. However, from personal experience during a campaign in the provinces, I can state that while I observed undeniable extremists on both the right and the left, I also observed the huge current in favor of King George's return. This current was genuine and widespread. It represented the Greek people's reply to those who did all they could to seize power violently, not hesitating to bring carnage to our land and tarnish our wonderful struggle for liberation.

❊ ❊ ❊

In this atmosphere of regeneration, many members of Service 5-16-5 gathered one night at my house. It was an assembly of people with deep common ties, many of whom were meeting for the first time. It was a gathering full of warmth and emotion. My old house filled with memories.

Mitsos Rediadis, Stavros Vrachnos, Antonis Bachas, Manolis Koutsoudakis, Popi Sakelaridis — each with his own team of collaborators — our technicians and our harbor people, all became acquainted and talked among themselves. They remembered common goals, common events, and common dangers. They relived moments when they had crossed paths without even suspecting each other's involvement.

This was also when I met many of my collaborators for the first time and when they first met me. I felt like we were brothers who had been separated as children, whose facial features we could no longer recall, but whose bond was forged by their history and common blood.

Toward the end of the evening, standing behind my father's desk, I tried to summarize the history of our service in a few words. I wanted each person to have a complete picture of the work to which he had dedicated himself so selflessly. In addition, I wanted each member's contribution to the general effort to be recognized as it should.

Reviewing our intentions and our gradual achievements, I sought to show how an idea that begins as nothing but a dream can become a reality. I spoke about our first movements which, after various failed attempts, gradually brought us into position to form our basic core. I spoke about our lack of experience and the means we tried to gain in spite of so many difficulties.

I told the story of the wireless set, how we acquired it and how we transmitted information. I noted the actions of each of our closest collaborators and those of the divisions. I described, in general terms, the way we insured accuracy and the security procedures we followed and gradually improved.

I recounted what we knew about the results of our efforts, the destruction and sinking of enemy ships and the harbor sabotages. I reported the events of Holy Thursday 1943 and all that followed: arrests and executions. I also spoke about my attempt to get us a new wireless set and caïques, and the undermining of my efforts by the British service in Cairo.

Finally, I admitted my mistake in refusing financial support for our service from the British, something that might have secured the continuation of our work. I remarked that it would have been difficult for them to waste an organization which had cost money. Ours had only cost human lives!

When I had finished this general account, and while the warmth invoked by its memories was drawing us all together from many angles, we discussed the present and together made some decisions about the future.

All members of Service 5-16-5, without exception, had offered themselves without expecting anything in return other than the satisfaction of participating in the struggle. This was simply something that each felt had to be done, and so it was. That was all.

We didn't expect anything in return now, either. Our mission had ended. Our only desires were to honor our dead and to have the State award them distinctions worthy of their actions and their sacrifices. These points found us all in agreement that night.

We felt that we could bestow proper honor on them with a civil memorial service in a public hall, attended by State officials and the Athenian public. Mitsos Rediadis and I undertook the organization of this commemoration. I also resolved to undertake the appropriate steps to have honorary distinctions awarded to our dead and proper pensions granted to their unprotected families.

Before the contributions of our six fallen comrades could be formally recognized, the State first had to recognize our organization. The steps needed to accomplish this goal followed the tedious road of application, multi-page reports, depositions, questions, and certifications by us and the different Greek and British services.

The result was that the Greek Military Liaison Office returned all of our correspondence after they received an answer from the Headquarters of the British Forces in Greece addressed to the Greek General Staff. In this answer, the responsible British office skillfully concealed everything about the rivalry between their secret services while certifying that they were indeed well aware of our organization and its leader. They wrote:

Subject: H.I.S. 5165[1]

We have been informed that Rigas Rigopoulos's Group was an *independent organization and did not operate for the I.S.L.O.*[2]

With this statement, the British services in Athens found a way to avoid the stumbling blocks without bending the truth.

At the same time, I received proof that my services were appreciated by the British authorities more than I had expected. They sent me a very prestigious "Certificate of Service" signed by the General Commander-in-Chief of the Middle East Forces, Sir Bernard C. T. Paget. The certificate stated that during the period of 1942-1943, Rigas Rigopoulos had "faithfully and loyally served the Allied cause and thereby contributed to the liberation of EUROPE."

As for the Greek authorities, current law provided no way for them to concern themselves with — much less officially recognize — a Greek organization that had worked for the homeland, whose existence and activities were known to Greeks and British alike, but which had operated as an "independent organization." The law required a "commission by the British authorities." Thus the responsible parties had clear consciences. The matter was closed.

Later, the State awarded the families of our executed members pensions equiva-

---

[1]H.I.S. 5165 refers to "Hellenic Information Service 5-15-5."

[2]I.S.L.O. refers to "Inter-Service Liaison Office."

lent to those given to non-combatants. These heroic men were grouped with the victims of random bombings.[3]

We of Service 5-16-5 then closed the matter ourselves, repaying the debt to our dead with all the formality we could muster. We organized a tribute to their memory that would render them the honor they were due.

On November 3, 1945, exactly two years after the execution of Alexander Kairis, Parnassus Hall filled to capacity with a dense crowd. They had come to join us in showing gratitude to those who had given their lives for us all. A boy scout honor guard manned the entrances and kept order. The podium was covered with a large Greek flag that draped all the way to the floor. Six small laurel wreaths had been placed on top of the unfurled flag at the base of the podium.

On the right, next to the speaker, sat the families of those we had lost. The family of Alexander Kairis sat in a position of particular honor. In the first three rows of the audience sat a bishop representing the regent Archbishop, a minister representing the government, the mayor, political leaders, high-ranking military officers, and other officials. Our intelligentsia was represented by a great number of its select members, among whom our great poet, Angelos Sikelianos, stood out. The members of our service were spread throughout the hall.

At exactly 6:00 PM, an old friend and distinguished speaker, the former government minister Leon Makkas, took the podium. Makkas had been part of significant national actions himself. He had also been imprisoned by the Italians and later escaped to the Middle East. With a few lively words, Makkas spoke about the resistance in general and Service 5-16-5 in particular. His brief introduction gave the audience a perspective on the memorial ceremony that was to follow. I stepped to the podium truly moved.

It is not easy to provide a complete picture of how we honored our dead that day, or to relate the emotional response of our public in just a few lines. But I will try to sketch the spirit of the homily I delivered, which began with a "roll call" of the dead.

On the day of freedom, when the roll was called for all those who fought, who struggled, who gave their bodies and souls for Greece, among many others six of our men did not answer...

Our fallen friends, in the special roll call today we will all hear your answers, sent from the streams of the secret bond that joins us. Let us know your presence, good friends, as I call each of you by name.

Alexander Kairis
Nicos Paliatseas
Petros Drakopoulos
Nicos Menegatos
Stamatis Tratras
Socratis Tselentis

---

[3]Just after 1967, under Prime MInister George Papadopoulos (who imposed a revolutionary and oppressive nationalistic regime on Greece until 1974), the State dealt systemically and extensively with the "National Resistance." A new law empowered a multi-faceted committee of high-ranking officers to investigate the substantial contributions of organizations and individuals to the liberation struggle. After a detailed examination and testimony, our organization, "HellenicPatriotic Society or Service 5-16-5 under the leadership of Rigas Rigopoulos," was recognized on August 8, 1971 by Royal Decree 549. Recognition had been delayed 26 years.

I recited each name slowly, one after the other, before an audience that held its breath. In the absolute silence that surrounded me, I felt the strong presence of the companions I was calling.

With my voice catching from emotions revived by their memories, I began to speak of each man individually. I told simple stories that came directly from my heart.

> *... Alexander, we had been friends since childhood. I remember the carefree years we spent together as teenagers, the years of intellectual and spiritual preparation. I always believed you to be a complete person, with a positive mind and good judgment. In each of your thoughts, I always saw the promise of a creative future.*

I continued by describing how Alexander Kairis had lived up to his youthful promise by demonstrating ethical creativity, spiritual creativity, and heroic creativity. I tried to give a true picture of his life and work. I even spoke about his philosophy and his poetry, which flourished in prison. I also spoke about his glorious end.

I spoke of the others in similar tones. I spoke of Nicos Paliatseas, a "kid" of 23 years with an indomitable soul. Hovering over the Morse key of his secret transmitter, Paliatseas had no regard either for the joys of life or the net of death the enemy was steadily tightening around him.

I spoke of Petros Drakopoulos, whose 60 years invigorated rather than weakened the beatings of his heart. He was the ghost of the harbor who went from boat to boat, from pier to pier, from coast to coast, gathering every type of information that might prove valuable. He worked without fear of persecution, until, in the final days of the war, he paid for his courage with his life.

I also spoke of Menegatos, Tratras and Tselentis, who served in the Allied intelligence. However, these men were no more strangers to us than our own people, because they fought for the same goal and died bravely for the same reason.

Throughout the hall I saw faces deeply moved. Acquaintances and strangers alike participated fully in the admiration and lamentation. Here and there handkerchiefs came out to wipe tearful eyes.

I finished by asking the State to also fulfill its duty, awarding these pioneers of freedom the honorary distinctions we rightfully claim as theirs...

> *... because these fallen heroes represent our people's emotional and spiritual grandeur which clearly exists, whether foreigners or native Greeks admit it or not, and which will one day come to be recognized...*

The teary-eyed audience broke into frenzied applause, endorsing the request and expressing all their respect and gratitude for those who had given everything so that we could live today in the freedom they had granted us.

Mitsos Rediadis ended the ceremony by talking about Greeks' and foreigners' obligations to our ruined country. He spoke of a national journey imposed by the duty to see that our heroic and painful sacrifices had not been made in vain.

At end of Mitsos's homily, while the applause continued, I took the six laurel wreaths from the flag and handed them to the families of those we lost. At least we had the satisfaction of honoring ourselves those whom our State had failed to honor. Backed by general approval, we bestowed on them the highest distinctions that our ancestors had reserved for victors and heroes.

In this emotion-charged atmosphere, in return for the laurel that I offered to

Alexander Kairis's family, I accepted the greatest gift of honor and love that I could ever have wished for. Alexander's brother handed me a sheet of paper on which my lost friend had written a poem for me. It had been found among his prison papers. Through tear-filled eyes I could only discern the title, "Rigas, Farewell!," and the familiar signature, "Alexander, Athens, Averof Prisons, June 1943." I put the paper in my pocket and we silently gripped each others' hands.

Alone in my office, in the room that had seen the simple story born from the pulsations of a few young people's hearts, I listened to Alexander talking to me through his bold, harmonious verses which unlocked so much human warmth and substance.

Rigas, Farewell!

To Rigas, my brother, the selected one, a few words:
The eternal separation was destined to come.
Yet the path we walked together
Raised me from the trivial to heights.
Around me is dazzling light,
Oh such a great road for a wayfarer, how joyful!
Even the taste of death feels worthy.
But think, deep within you:
The journey is not yet completed.
Ahead await a few — oh, what a thought! — miles.
Alone, from now on, get fast to the end.
And now, brother, tears, kisses, and whines.
Far from you
A heartfelt handshake is only right.
Farewell!

> *Alexander*
> *Athens, Averof Prisons*
> *June 1943*

The metric system, rhymes, and combinations of word sounds in these verses form a unique personal style that reflects Alexander Kairis's culture and his mental and spiritual refinement.

I read these verses many times, absorbing every word. I wanted to make them part of my soul, to insure that this great message from beyond the grave would remain unaltered.

Words, when one is staring death in the eye, are never inane. They are chosen to express meanings that convey the true essence of life.

As he was dying, Alexander wanted me to know that he had not spent his final moments thinking about the beauty of life, which his sensitive nature deeply appreciated. Nor had he spent them thinking of his youth or the joys he would leave with his departure.

He had overcome all material desires. He was above all ordinary and everyday things. He was on a much higher plane, and he found that the road that had let him to these heights was completely "worthy" of the "taste of death."

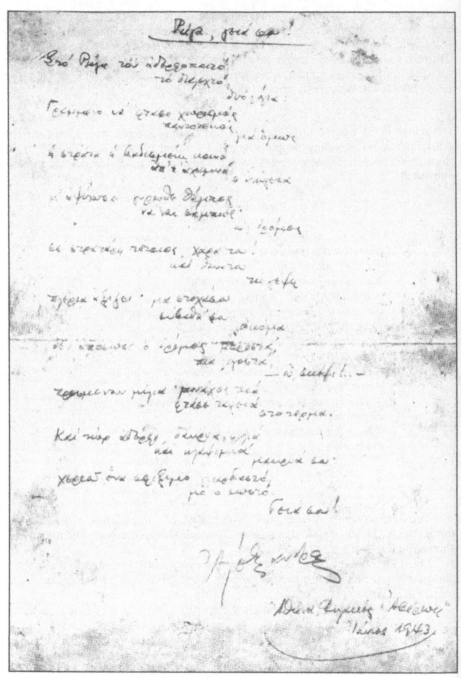

Ρηγα, γεια σου – Rigas, Farewell!
The metric system, rhymes, and combinations of word sounds
in these verses form a unique personal style that reflects
Alexander Kairis's culture and his mental and spiritual refinement.

One and only one worry still remained inside him:

The journey is not yet completed.

And this worry dictated his one last desire and order:

Alone, from now on, get fast to the end.

Alexander Kairis lived his final hours worrying about our struggle. We had to stay focused on a single goal: completion of the work we had undertaken. His loss should not deter us. He wanted our parting to be brave, without "tears, kisses, and whines." He wanted only a strong, manly handshake...

I saw this last command of my executed friend as the ultimate expression of his greatness. Even death was incapable of altering his course. He pursued the ideal achievement of his goals to the very end.

Reviewing now the complete picture revealed by the wisdom of time, I see the struggle of slavery as a general, wonderful whole. I hear the words of Alexander Kairis expressing not only the spirit of Greeks, but also that of all peoples caught in the terrible storm of that time, who never stopped marching toward the apex of their dreams, where great, fiery letters spelled out the word *Freedom*.

Since then, more than 50 years have passed. Many things have changed in Athens, in Greece, and in the whole world.

Technology has made huge leaps possible, and people, science, art, and even emotions stand ready to be folded into the general mechanization. Mankind gasps, struggling to keep up with its own progress without having first overcome the dangers that threaten it.

Man has set out to conquer the universe, even though he has not yet succeeded in deeply exploring himself. Old mistakes are repeated, and new roads do not seem to lead to security and serenity.

Let us wish that no one ever has to experience a tragedy similar to the one we endured. However, difficult moments show life in its true form and people in their true perspective. In such moments, it is certain that those who stand out from the crowd will be the ones who make life worth living and history worth perpetuating.

Let us further wish that someday the great miracle will happen: that one day Man will get to know Man, and that the age-old era of opposition and violence will give way to centuries of creation and collaboration. Heroism is not revealed only in war. The road to universal happiness requires struggle and sacrifice. The torch for this heroic effort is passed to new generations.

One should not believe that beautiful ideals have disappeared in our technocratic age. They always nestle in people's souls and reemerge at the right time.

Just like the squares and struggling gardens in modern, densely-packed Athens, awaken each April to exude the aroma of the bitter orange blossoms.

APPENDIX A

EXCERPTS FROM THE REPORT OF RIGAS RIGOPOULOS TO THE PRESIDENT OF THE GREEK GOVERNMENT IN CAIRO, EMMANUEL TSOUDEROS

Cairo, August 18, 1943

Mister President:

I escaped from Greece on July 29. As soon as I arrived in Cairo, I considered it my duty to present you a summary of certain events that have immediate implications for our country.

As you know, Mr. President, the Greek people have not abandoned their struggle. From the first moment of occupation, every patriot has tried to cause damage to the conqueror's materiel or morale and to transfer the spirit of resistance to those who have remained inert. Day by day, the popular resistance took on an organized form. Thus we can assert today that the greater part of the Greek people struggles in a deliberate and organized fashion for a single goal: national liberation.

In the beginning, some differences, mainly political ones, emerged between the major national organizations. With a few exceptions, I can happily report that these differences have vanished. For example, there is now close collaboration between *Ethniki Drasis* (National Action), *Stratia Sklavomenon Nikiton* (Army of Enslaved Victors), *Ethniko Komitato* (National Revolutionary Committee), *Iera Taxiarchia* (Sacred Brigade), and other such organizations. These organizations have even issued joint proclamations that all of them have signed.

The main goals of the Greek national organizations are: (a) To bolster morale so that the Greek people maintain their fighting spirit and remain vigilant. (b) To keep our people informed about various national matters and encourage unification and cooperation. (c) To provide information on the activities of the partisans and the internal front of popular resistance. (d) To report damage to the conqueror and the actions of the Allied forces. In general, they prompt and guide our people to follow the paths of their former epic feats. Thus, despite the weight of the yoke and harsh persecution by the conqueror, our people continue to be pioneers in the struggle of enslaved nations.

These organizations have also launched an intense campaign to convince people that the only thought that should occupy their minds today is the liberation of our land. Every other thought or discussion about the King or democracy or other political matters constitutes a crime against the homeland. Once liberated, the Greek people alone will have the right to settle matters concerning the political system, but only after more general problems are solved and the Greek people resume the position that will rightfully belong to them after the Victory. Every inopportune act leads to division, and we unfortunately know too well how much that has harmed us in the past.

Ethniki Drasis (National Action) publishes the bi-weekly newspaper *Machi* (Combat) and tends to be considered the most serious of the Greek organizations. *Stratia Sklavomenon Nikiton* (Army of Enslaved Victors), one of the oldest organizations, publishes *Megali Ellas* (Great Greece). About a year ago, a group of Kanellopoulos supporters broke away from *Stratia Sklavomenon Nikiton* and formed a separate organization called PEAN (*Panellinios Enosis Agonizomenon Neon*, PanHellenic Association of Fighting Youths). Despite its initial focus on the ideology of a single individual, this new organization did not neglect to move on to broader national issues, a fact that now makes it considered part of the national network of independent organizations.

Ethniko Komitato (National Revolutionary Committee) publishes *Eleftheri Skepsi* (Free Thought).[1] *Ellinikon Aima* (Greek Blood), another publication with the same ideological bent, is perhaps the most complete journalistically of these underground newspapers. It is published by a group that also frequently issues 20-30 page booklets on Greek unification, the Bulgarian matter, the harmful actions of organizations like EAM,[2] etc. The content of these booklets is precise and well documented.

All of these organizations, as well as smaller but no less patriotic ones, are in need of immediate and significant financial support. I have personal experience with the financial hardships one faces when working for the nation without a significant and steady source of income.

Let me now turn to the single significant exception to the general national spirit of understanding and cooperation. That exception is EAM.

EAM, with its purely communist leadership, organization, and principles, managed to attract a significant number of Greeks right from the beginning by camouflaging itself with a title that sounds like a national liberation effort. As I have mentioned before, everyone hungered to participate in organized national liberation movements, and the leaders of EAM did not deny participation to anyone. Greeks of all classes, views, and political or social ideologies swelled its ranks, believing they were fighting only for the liberation of their homeland.

Those who knew the true nature and ulterior motives of EAM could not oppose or expose it, due to the special conditions under which the resistance was organized. Doing so would risk harming the general Greek opposition to the conqueror. Thus, EAM gained a stronger foothold day by day.

This situation persisted until one day EAM made a big mistake: in an effort to take the pulse of the Greek people, they uncovered part of their future plans. They published an article in their newspaper *O Apeleftherotis* (The Liberator) in which they roughly characterized the Bulgarian people as martyrs, on the same cross of martyrdom as the Greeks. They declared that Greece would not have claims against these good neighbors after the final victory. Furthermore, they distributed leaflets in Thessaloniki advocating the autonomy of Macedonia.[3]

Not even a bomb could not have had the devastating effect of these statements. They caused a huge rift within EAM, and the organization began to lose members rapidly. Greek feelings and national conscience reacted emphatically.

---

[1] *Ethniki Drasis* and *Ethniko Komitato* subsequently circulated many other publications

[2] EAM stands for Ethniko Apeleftherotiko Metopo, "National Liberation Front."

[3] After the demolition of the Ottoman Empire, the territory of the ancient Greek Macedonian Kingdom has been shared between the established countriews of the Balkans. 51.5% remained Greek and the rest has been included in Yugoslavia, Bulgaria, and Albania. This arrangement created long-lasting problems in all of these countries.

The very existence of EAM was in danger. A cover-up would have been impossible, so EAM resorted to the only intelligent move it had left: it temporarily changed its name to EPON (*Elliniki Panelladiki Organosi Neolaias*, Unified Panhellenic Youth Organization).[4] Under this title, and using the national holiday of March 25 as an opportunity, EAM posted proclamations and published articles with a purely national character...

This tactic managed to stem the tide of dropouts. While winning back part of its membership, EAM took the time to revise what it had said and began to reveal the sameness of EAM and EPON. Since then they have wisely followed the direction forced upon them by the unshakable ideology of our people.

Thus we have proof that the Greek people are united in their ideologies. As soon as EAM tries to uncover its secret agenda again, it will risk losing the last of its members. Of course, we can only view the national unity as absolute if we disregard the existence of a thousand traitors, of which there are more in other countries, and thirty thousand agitators who have always been outside the law and had tried to destabilize the country even before the war. These are enough to create trouble in the mountains even now, but they are far from representing the people as a whole. On the contrary, the people overwhelmingly condemn them.[5]

The Greeks, Mr. President, are ready and willing to prove their unity and patriotism to anyone whenever they are called to do so.

As far as the Bulgarian matter is concerned, please allow me to comment on some broadcasts from London that are very painful to the ears of enslaved Greeks.

The Greek people have suffered and fought against the conqueror to their dying breaths. They did not hesitate to stand by Great Britain at the most critical moments. They contributed, perhaps as no other, to the turnaround of the war when their victories in Albania delayed the German attacks on Russia, and Africa. Despite the torment of slavery and starvation, the Greek people have continued the war against three tyrants, the Germans, Italians, and Bulgarians, with indomitable spirit as their only weapon. These people demand, that London radio not speak of the Bulgarians as a people whose current ruler, Boris III, led them to destruction and that it is now the right time for them to show their true feelings and rebel against him...

These London broadcasts, Mr. President, destroy our people's zeal for national resistance. I have heard good fighters on our internal front so disappointed by such broadcasts that they proclaimed, "We have spilled enough blood. It is time to stop the struggle if we are to see the Bulgarians as our masters after the war." These men were not cowards, nor were they indifferent to our country's fate. They were my comrades in our sacred struggle, some of whom have already fallen, shouting "Hurrah for Freedom!" as they faced German firing squads. I realize the need for propaganda addressed to the Bulgarians. But let it be heard in the Bulgarian broadcasts. There is no reason for us to have to hear it in Greek.

---

[4]This was the title of EAM's youth movement.

[5]The difference between the actual and perceived numbers of true EAM members has, until today, been unclear. The fact is that the number of armed EAM members who brought carnage to Greece after the liberation was minimal in comparison to the great unarmed majority of Greek people.

I fear that if, after victory, justice is not granted to the Greek people in every respect, our land might face internal turmoil with devastating repercussions that no one will be able to control. But the moment of victory is near. The Greek people await their freedom with each passing moment, striking the tyrants night and day in any and every way they can.

We are blessed, Mr. President, to be allied with the great peoples who see dispensing justice as one of the basic tenets of their existence. And the day to dispense justice will come. The Greek people, worthy trustees of international rights centrally located at a critical point in the Mediterranean where Divine Providence and history have positioned them, will continue to fight beside their great Allies for peace and civilization.

With deepest respect,
Rigas D. Rigopoulos

APPENDIX B

EXCERPTS FROM A SPEECH BY BRITISH PRIME MINISTER WINSTON CHURCHILL BEFORE THE HOUSE OF COMMONS

December 8, 1944
A Speech to the House of Commons in a Debate on an Amendment
regretting British intervention in Greece and other parts of liberated Europe.
The Amendment was defeated by 279 to 30.

from

The Dawn of Liberation: War Speeches by the Right Hon. Winston S. Churchill,
compiled by Charles Eade, Cassell and Co. Ltd., 1944

commentary in italics by R.R.

boldface added by R.R. to emphasize particularly important passages

The value of the speech which has just ended was, I thought, that it showed how extremely complex these Greek politics are. ...

I address myself to the Amendment as a whole, and I must point out that it does not deal only with Greece, but with other parts of Europe. ... **Before I come to particular countries and places, let me present to the House the charge which is made against us. It is that we are using His Majesty's Forces to disarm the friends of democracy in Greece and in other parts of Europe, and to suppress those popular movements which have valorously assisted in the defeat of the enemy.** Here is a pretty direct issue, and one on which the House will have to pronounce before we separate this evening. Certainly, His Majesty's Government would be unworthy of confidence if His Majesty's Forces were being used by them to disarm friends of democracy.

The question however arises, and one may be permitted to dwell on it for a moment, who are the friends of democracy, and also how is the word "democracy" to be interpreted?

* * * * *

In the remarks I have made about democracy and the attitude I have taken throughout the time I have been burdened with these high responsibilities, and broadly I believe throughout my life — in the remarks I have made, and in my statements representing the policy of His Majesty's present Government, I stand upon the foundation of free elections based on universal suffrage, and that is what we consider the foundation of democracy.

But I feel quite differently about a swindle democracy, a democracy which calls itself a democracy because it is Left Wing. It takes all sorts to make democracy, not only Left Wing, or even Communist. I do not allow a party or a body to call themselves democrats because they are stretching farther and farther into the most extreme forms of revolution. I do not accept a party as necessarily representing democracy because it becomes more violent as it becomes less numerous. One must have some respect for democracy, and not use the word too lightly. The last thing which resembles democracy is mob law, with bands of gangsters, armed with deadly weapons, forcing their way into great cities, seizing the police stations and key points of Government, endeavoring to introduce a totalitarian régime with an iron hand.

* * * * *

Do not let us rate democracy so low, do not let us rate democracy as if it were merely grabbing power and shooting those who do not agree with you. That is the antithesis of democracy.

* * * * *

During the war, of course, we have had to arm anyone who could shoot a Hun. Apart for their character, political convictions, past records and so forth, if they were out to shoot a Hun, we accepted them as friends and tried to enable them to fulfill their healthy instincts.

We are paying for it in having this Debate today, which personally I have found rather enjoyable, so far. We are paying for it also with our treasure and our blood. We are not paying for it with our honor or by defeat. But when countries are liberated, it does not follow that those who have received our weapons should use them in order to engross to themselves by violence and murder and bloodshed all those powers and traditions and continuity which many countries have slowly developed and to which quite a large proportion of their people, I believe the great majority, are firmly attached. If what is called in this Amendment the action of "the friends of democracy" is to be interpreted as carefully-planned *coups d'état* by murder gangs and as the iron rule of ruffians seeking to climb into the seats of power without a vote ever having been cast in their favor — if that is to masquerade as democracy, I think the house will unite in condemning it as mockery.

* * * * *

The Amendment on the Paper has particular reference to Greece, but it is a general attack on the whole policy of His Majesty's Government, which is represented as supporting reactionary forces everywhere, trying to install by force dictatorial government contrary to the wishes of the people. ... It is not only in Greece that we appear to some eyes, to the eyes of those who support this Amendment, to be disarming the friends of democracy and those popular movements which have assisted the defeat of the enemy. There is Italy, there is Belgium. ...

Here Winston Churchill provides an extensive review of the conditions that forced the British government to intervene in Belgium and Italy and to disarm the "friends of democracy" in favor of the "Constitutional Administration." He admits that the same could have occurred in Holland. However, he also points out Britain's continuous support of Marshal Tito, the leftist Yugoslavian leader, and his Partisans. He then comes to a detailed exposition of the Greek matter, which, as he says: "... forms the mainspring of the Vote of Censure we have to meet today."

About the Greek government, he states:
... the Greek Government ... is the constitutional Government ... which can only be displaced by a free vote of the people.

Concerning the dispatch of British forces to Greece, he explains:
At an hotel in Lebanon in May, 1944, a long meeting was held between the Papandreou Government and the leaders of all parties in Greece, including E.A.M., who we brought out by air. An agreement was reached to establish a joint Government which could take over power in Athens when, with or without the help of the Allies, it was freed from the Germans. ... **Mr. Papandreou repeatedly appealed to us in the name of his Government of all parties, including the Communists and E.A.M., to come to the rescue with armed forces, and was much disappointed when I was unable to give him any definite reply.**

The British troops were welcomed enthusiastically as they entered Athens, and so also was the Greek Brigade, which had mutinied earlier in the year, but had now been freed from the mutinous element. I took great trouble about this Brigade, to give it a chance to redeem its reputation. It not only redeemed its reputation, but won renown for the Greek army by entering Rimini at the head of the Allied Forces and wresting it from the Germans.

Concerning EAM and ELAS, Churchill says:
... during the years of Greek captivity I must say that E.L.A.S. devoted far more attention to beating-up and destroying the representatives of the E.D.E.S., commanded by Colonel Zervas — a man of the Left by our standards, less extreme than E.A.M. ... I say, devoted themselves more to attacking Zervas and his followers on the West side of Greece than they did to attacking the Germans themselves. For the past two years E.L.A.S. have devoted themselves principally to preparations for seizing power.
...

He continues by recognizing the negligence of his government, which allowed the fostering of this convenient preparation:
... We may, some of us, **have underrated the extremes to which those preparations have been carried or the many privations and cruelties which have been inflicted on the village populations in the areas over which they prevail.** I have taken every pains to collect information, and everything I say on fact in these matters has been most carefully examined beforehand **by the officials who are thoroughly acquainted with the details.**

At this point, an uproar interrupted the orator. The simple and verified truths threatened to destroy the popular opinion that had taken so many years of arduous work to prepare. The situation in the hall of the British Parliament forced the Prime Minister to say:
I really must be allowed to continue my argument. Of course, in this House we are Conservative, Labour, Liberal and so forth; we are not E.L.A.S. and E.D.E.S. as

some gentlemen seem to imagine.

* * * * *

I have stated our action in detail. I must admit that not everyone agreed with the course we have taken, for which I accept the fullest responsibility. There were those who said, "Why worry about Greece?" ... but His Majesty's Government felt that having regard to the sacrifices that they made at the time of the German invasion of Greece, and to the long affection which has grown between the Greek and British people since their liberation in the last century, and having regard also to the decisions and agreements of our principal Allies, we should see what we could do to give these unfortunate people a fair chance of extricating themselves from their misery and starting on a clear road again. That is the only wish and ambition which we had, or anyone in the British Government had, for our entry into Greece and for the action forced upon us there. That is our only wish, and, personally, I am not ashamed of it.

* * * * *

... Moreover, we did not feel it compatible with our honour, or with the obligations into which we have entered with many people in Greece in the course of our presence there, to wash our hands of the whole business, make our way to the sea, as we easily could, and leave Athens to anarchy and misery, followed by tyranny established on murder.

* * * * *

If I am blamed for this action I will gladly accept my dismissal at the hands of the House; but if I am not so dismissed — make no mistake about it — we shall persist in this policy of clearing Athens and the Athens region of all who are rebels against the authority of the constitutional Government of Greece — of mutineers against the orders of the supreme Commander in the Mediterranean under whom all the guerrillas have undertaken to serve.

* * * * *

I have no fear at all that the most searching inquiries **into the policy we have pursued in Europe — in Belgium, in Holland, in Italy, and in Greece —** the most searching examination will entitle any man into whose breast fairness and fair play enter, **to accuse us of pursuing reactionary policies, of hampering the free expression of the national will,** or of not endeavouring to enable the countries that have suffered the curse of German occupation to resume again **the normal, free, democratic life which they desire, and which, as far as this House can act, we shall endeavor to secure for them.**

APPENDIX C

PHOTOGRAPHS

THE CENTRAL MEMBERS OF SERVICE 5-16-5

Photographs and activity summaries of the group's members who were directly associated with the administration.

A. ADMINISTRATION DIVISION

Rigas Rigopoulos
Sociologist
Leader

Mitsos Rediadis
Lawyer
Second in Command

A. Administration Division (*CONTINUED*)

(No Photo Available)

(No Photo Available)

George Zentelis
Law Student
Administration Liasion
with Sections

Nicos Paliatseas
*First Sergeant in the
Greek Air Force*
Wireless Set Operator
Executed by the Germans

An Anonymous Boy
never gave his name
Averof Prison Liasion

Railways Department
Activities: Reporting on German rail transports.

Popi Sakelaridis
Member of the Board
Department Leader

Francis Petrits

George Leousis
*Employee of the
Bank of Greece*

B. Harbor Division

Activities: Reporting on ships, convoys, material loaded, minefields in the sea, etc.

Information provided by this division resulted in the sinking of 55 Axis ships by the Allies.

Merchant Marine Captain
Manolis Koutsoudakis
Chief Pilot, Pireaus Anchoring Office
Division Leader

Commander
Antonis Bachas
Piraeus Harbor Master

Lt. Commander
Dimitris Samantzopoulos
Harbor's 2nd in Command

Captain
Kostas Moros
Piraeus Harbor Pilot

Kostas Damoulakis
Piraeus Harbor Pilot

Captain
Petros Drakopoulos
Piraeus Harbor Pilot
Executed by the Germans

(No Photo Available)

Savatakis
Chief Boatman

C. German Headquarters Division

Activities: Penetrating the Confidential Archives Room and providing the Allies with the most valuable of information.

Only one member.

Alexander Kairis
Lawyer
Employee of the German Engineering Command
working with the Commander of Southern Greece
Executed by the Germans

D. GENERAL INFORMATION DIVISION

Activities: Drawing enemy installations, storage facilities, mine fields, and every kind of construction and fortification on the coast and inland.

Stavros Vrachnos
Chemical Engineer and Lecturer
National Technical University of Athens
Division Leader

Nicos Kriezis
Chemical Engineer

George Eleftheriou
Chemical Engineer

Dimitris Thanopoulos
Chemical Engineer

Thanos Savas
Chemical Engineer and
Executive, Hambakis &
Savas ship repair factory

Antonis Embirikos
Executive, Atlas
cement factory

George Kambanis
Merchant Marine
Captain

E. Division of Independent, Collaborating Individuals

(No Photo Available)

(No Photo Available)

George Hadjigeorgiou
Commander, Royal Navy
Provided connections with valuable
Navy informants.

Aristeidis Papadopoulos
City Police Officer
Supervisor of the Confidential
Archives Department in the
Subdivision of General Security

(No Photo Available)

(No Photo Available)

Nicos Menegatos
Liasion with the
Allied Intelligence Service
Traveled to and from Turkey
to transport written
information and drawings.
Executed by the Germans

Socratis Tselentis
Agent of the
Allied Intelligence Service
Executed by the Germans

**Rigas with Mother,
a volunteer head nurse**
leaving for war
Athens, October 28, 1940

Admiral George Hors
*who hid Rigas in his house when
he was being persecuted by the
Germans*
1940's

Rigas with Adjutant Takis Papadopoulos
At the Sacred Squadron Camp, El Basa, Palstine
Fall 1943

Rigas and Michael Hors
captains of armed caiques
Port of Pafos, Cyprus

**A group of the Sacred Squadron's officers
aboard the Mother Ship**
*in a "hide out" somewhere on the Turkish coast,
east of the Greek Island of Cos
Rigas is directly behind Lt. Colonel E. Calinskis
(with white beard), Michael Hors is on Caliski's right*
Easter 1944

**Steering his armed caique
in the Aegean Sea**
*in enemy-occupied waters
followed by Michael Hors*
Spring 1944

Waiting to embark for "my Greece"
Bari, Italy
October 11, 1944

Taking a shift on LCT 396
Ionian Sea during return to Greece
October 16, 1944

Rigas in Smirni (Ismir)
after escaping from Greece
August 1943

Rigas in Palestine
Parachute training
Fall 1943

Rigas with sister Popi
Athens
Fall 1944

Rigas with Popi Sakelaridis
Athens
Fall 1944

Lily Hors, Popi Rigopoulos, Marika Rigopoulos, Admiral Hors, Rigas Rigopoulos
The Admiral's Wife, Riga's Sister and Mother, the Admiral, and Rigas
Early 1950's

Rigas steering his small sailboat
Summer 1998

Rigas with Jesse Heines
Athens, November 25, 1999

ABOUT THE AUTHORS

Rigas Rigopoulos is a sociologist, social psychologist, and writer. He graduated from the Athens University of Economics and continued his study of the social sciences in Paris and London. He writes and speaks Greek, French, English and German.

Rigas began his career at the Bank of Greece and worked there almost until the end of the German occupation. After the liberation he became Governor of the Ioannina County, consultant to the Prime Minister, and a special consultant in several ministries and enterprises. He established and directed a company for the study of social relations. Rigas has written sociological and historical books, literary essays, a theatrical play, three collections of poems, and many pieces for radio.

During the war, Rigas created and led a resistance organization known as Service 5-16-5. Six of his collaborators were shot by the Germans for espionage. Rigas escaped to Egypt and volunteered for active duty. He served as a commando, captained a motorized sailing vessel, and raided occupied Greek islands. Two of his books concern the struggle in occupied Greece and the war in the Middle East and the Aegean Sea.

Rigas is still very active today at the age of 89. He lives in Athens with his wife Anny and writes for many hours a day. Their only child, Dionysis, is his best friend and closest collaborator.

Rigas and Dionysis now see Jesse Heines as another member of the family. Their three-year collaboration to bring *Secret War* into English has brought them very close. In addition to developing a fond fatherly love for him, Rigas has very much admired Jesse's courage, sensitivity, and perceptiveness while struggling with the Greek language and dealing with the many delicate details in editing and polishing the English text. Rigas believes that the result succeeds in preserving not only the meaning, but also the style of his original Greek text.

Jesse M. Heines is an Associate Professor of Computer Science at the University of Massachusetts Lowell. He met Rigas Rigopoulos through a professional association with Rigas's son, Dionysis, through the Fulbright Foundation and the National Technical University of Athens.

Jesse was instantly fascinated by Rigas's story and intrigued when he learned that *Secret War* had already been published in Athens. Although he speaks no Greek, Jesse asked Rigas to allow him to create an English edition of the book. Rigas was taken by Jesse's enthusiasm and cautiously agreed to let him to give it a try.

Jesse approached one of his Greek students to help him find a translator and was soon talking to that student's cousin, Eleni Dedoglou. Eleni completed the initial translation while she was an undergraduate student at UMass Amherst. Jesse then worked with Rigas and Dionysis over the next three years to produce the text we have today.

Jesse is grateful for the support and encouragement he has received in this project from André Gerolymatos, Nicholas Gage, members of the Lowell area Greek-American community, and of course the entire Rigopoulos family, as well as from his wife Bonnie, who has now developed a refined taste for feta cheese and Greek olives!

Printed in the USA
CPSIA information can be obtained
at www.ICGtesting.com
JSHW022321140824
68134JS00019B/1226